NONVIOLENCE IN
POLITICAL THEORY

Iain Atack

EDINBURGH
University Press

© Iain Atack, 2012

Edinburgh University Press Ltd
22 George Square, Edinburgh EH8 9LF
www.euppublishing.com

Typeset in 11/13pt Palatino by
Servis Filmsetting Ltd, Stockport, Cheshire, and
printed and bound in Great Britain by
CPI Group (UK) Ltd, Croydon CR0 4YY

A CIP record for this book is available from the British
Library

ISBN 978 0 7486 3871 0 (hardback)
ISBN 978 0 7486 3378 4 (paperback)
ISBN 978 0 7486 3379 1 (webready PDF)
ISBN 978 0 7486 4967 9 (epub)
ISBN 978 0 7486 3377 7 (Amazon ebook)

The right of Iain Atack to be identified as author of
this work has been asserted in accordance with the
Copyright, Designs and Patents Act 1988.

CONTENTS

FIGURES

PREFACE

Nonviolence has been a central feature of my research and teaching in Peace Studies for more than ten years and for even longer as a basis for my practical involvement in campaigns for peace and human rights. It is through campaigning, teaching and research that I became interested in exploring the deeper connections between nonviolence as a form of political action and some of the central issues of political theory, concerning the role of power and violence in human affairs.

Much of the writing about nonviolence has focused on chronicling and documenting its uses in specific campaigns or political events, sometimes as a core element of significant social and political change; in other cases, to be supplanted by various forms of political violence; and, in some instances, to be defeated or crushed by more powerful political opponents. Efforts to assess the reasons for these successes and failures, and to provide a more strategic and systematic approach to using the methods of nonviolence effectively, have also been prominent in the literature on nonviolence. These discussions have been shaped, to some extent, by the distinction between so-called principled and pragmatic proponents of nonviolence – the former, basing their commitment to nonviolence on ethical or, perhaps, religious principles; and the latter, on evaluations of its political effectiveness.

My aim in this book is to take these discussions and debates to another level. Nonviolence as a form of political action necessarily connects to some of the core themes in political theory, concerning forms of political organisation, the relationship between the individual and the state and the role of violence and coercion in political institutions and processes of social change. In other words, it encompasses issues and concerns that go beyond a specific focus on documenting historical examples of nonviolence, or its distinctive characteristics as a form of strategic political action, to connect to broader themes within political theory. This book is an attempt to evaluate some of the core concepts and assumptions associated with nonviolence, in the context of these broader themes and debates within political theory.

The purpose of this evaluation is both to critically examine some of the theoretical presuppositions of nonviolence and to argue that such an exploration of nonviolent political action can contribute to, and expand, the scope of political theory. In other words, instances of nonviolent political action are not simply spontaneous eruptions of popular sentiment (although this can be one of their apparent features) that are somehow marginal to the essential issues of political theory. Rather than being mere political epiphenomena that somehow distract us from the real business of politics, such examples of nonviolence in action raise crucial and profound questions for central themes within political theory. Thus, it is hoped that such an exploration of the place of nonviolence within political theory will strengthen our understanding of nonviolent political action and help bring it in from the margins of political debate and discussion, through demonstrating its relevance and contribution to some of the central themes of political theory.

My colleagues in the Nonviolence Commission of the International Peace Research Association have provided an open and congenial environment in which to subject some of the ideas and arguments in this book to critical scrutiny, in the form of papers presented at successive IPRA conferences. Some of Chapter 5 appeared as an article on 'Nonviolent political action and the limits of consent' in *Theoria: A Journal of Social and Political Theory* 111 (December 2006). Similarly, much of Chapter 6 is reprinted with permission from 'Pacifism in international relations', in *The Ashgate Research Companion to Ethics and International Relations*, ed. Patrick Hayden (Aldershot: Ashgate, 2009).

I would like to thank the Irish School of Ecumenics and Trinity College Dublin for providing me with the research leave that allowed me to complete the manuscript for this book. My colleagues – Etain Tannam and Gillian Wylie, in particular – bore the brunt of my absence from the International Peace Studies programme during this time, for which I am very grateful. The postgraduate students in the International Peace Studies programme also provided a helpful forum for testing, developing and scrutinising many of the theories of, and ideas about, nonviolent political action that appear in this book. I would also like to thank Nicola Ramsey of Edinburgh University Press for encouraging my book proposal on such a speculative topic and for her continued patience while awaiting delivery of the typescript.

Finally, I would like to thank my family for accepting my need for time and space for research, thinking and writing. Their interest in the values and actions that underpin my own involvement in, and questions about, nonviolent political action provided necessary support and encouragement at crucial stages in the writing of this book.

Iain Atack,
Dublin,
December 2011

INTRODUCTION

Nonviolent political action has played a significant role in achieving social and political change in the last century and continues to be a vital feature of many campaigns for democracy, human rights and social justice. Mahatma Gandhi and Martin Luther King were prominent proponents of nonviolence in the twentieth century, but nonviolent political action, or civil resistance, has also been central to toppling communist regimes in Eastern Europe, for example, and, more recently, in pro-democracy popular movements in Serbia, Georgia and Ukraine. The so-called 'Arab Spring' (especially in Tunisia and Egypt) and popular responses to the current global financial crisis, in the form of the 'Occupy Wall Street' movement, for example, demonstrate, once again, the widespread appeal and continuing relevance of this type of political action.

This book connects some of the central characteristics of nonviolent political action to fundamental themes within Western political theory. It examines some of the philosophical and theoretical assumptions of proponents of nonviolent political action, concerning the role of the state and the rule of law or the nature of social and political power, for example. The purpose of this critical scrutiny, however, is both to identify the contribution nonviolence can make to our understanding of some of the core concerns of political theory and, also, to move beyond discursive accounts of nonviolent political action to a deeper understanding of this distinctive form of political activity.

Thus, this book augments historical accounts of particular instances of the use of nonviolence for political purposes and, also, the efforts to develop a systematic understanding of the conditions for its effectiveness, with a critical examination of nonviolence in the context of political theory. Nonviolent action raises crucial issues for our understanding

1

of political power and the role of violence and force, or coercion, in human affairs, in particular. Nonviolent action provides an innovative and, at times, hugely influential approach to social conflict and political change and, yet, it remains somewhat marginalised, misunderstood or dismissed as, perhaps, an aberration or diversion from core political concerns. Similarly, proponents of nonviolence have focused on chronicling its successes, explaining its effectiveness and promoting its use, without necessarily assessing it against deeper issues and debates in political theory. Nonviolence can make an important contribution to political theory, but can also benefit from it, in terms of improving and developing its own theoretical sophistication. Exploring key themes of nonviolent political action, in conjunction with some of the central concerns of conventional political theory, will strengthen and deepen our understanding of both.

APPROACH TO THE TOPIC

There are three dimensions to the approach of this book – to the place of nonviolence in political theory. The first involves identifying key themes in some of the central proponents of nonviolence, especially Leo Tolstoy, Mahatma Gandhi, Martin Luther King and Gene Sharp. The second focuses on seminal texts in Western political theory, particularly those associated with social contract theory (Hobbes, Locke, Rousseau), because these help identify central issues that are relevant to a theoretical analysis of nonviolent political action. The third involves applying these central themes that have emerged from the examination of nonviolence and political theory to a discussion of shared issues or concerns.

Two shared themes emerge, in particular, from the examination of the conjunction of nonviolence with political theory, that are most useful for analysing nonviolent political action: power and violence. Such themes also reflect the two central components (sometimes implicit, rather than explicit) of nonviolence as a form of political activity. These are: a commitment to peaceful forms of political action and an understanding of the power of popular mass-based political movements. A full understanding of nonviolent political action requires an equal analysis of both its peaceful and its popular power components. These two components are interdependent, because the methods of peaceful political action (identified by Gene Sharp under the categories of protest, non-cooperation and intervention[1]) are effective, precisely because they are equally available to all and do not depend upon access to weapons or restrictive, hierarchical or secretive forms of military or political organisation. Peaceful or nonviolent forms of political mobilisation can be successful, precisely because they unleash the full potential of popular power.

According to its proponents, nonviolent political action is effective because it utilises a particular understanding of the nature of political power, known as the consent (or, sometimes, pluralistic) theory of power. In simple terms, this theory claims that the capacity of any regime to govern depends ultimately on the consent, compliance and obedience of the population it rules. When this consent or compliance is withdrawn by sufficient numbers of people (or social groups), no regime – no matter how oppressive or undemocratic – can survive. Nonviolent political action is effective precisely because it can organise the withdrawal of such consent on a mass basis, using the methods of protest, non-cooperation and intervention. This is the basis of the popular power associated with nonviolent political action.

Proponents of nonviolence – from Tolstoy through to Gene Sharp as prominent, prolific and representative examples – incorporate the full spectrum of what is sometimes identified as principled (ethical/ violence) versus pragmatic (political/power) approaches to nonviolence. Principled proponents of nonviolence tend to focus on ethical or, perhaps, religious objections to the use of violence. Pragmatic proponents, on the other hand, emphasise the political significance and effectiveness of nonviolent action and, hence, perhaps, its power dimension. Nonetheless, the book tries to build upon, and go beyond, these sometimes limiting and possibly artificial divisions between principled and pragmatic approaches to nonviolence, to examine such issues in the wider context of politicial theory. Thus, these themes of power and violence coincide with, and help identify, specific issues that emerge as core concerns at the intersection of nonviolence with political theory, such as state sovereignty and forms of political organisation and tensions between pacifism as an ethical position and nonviolence as a form of political action.

OUTLINE OF THE BOOK

Chapter 1 begins with the categories of principled and pragmatic approaches to nonviolence, to identify characteristics of nonviolent political action that are relevant to broader themes in political theory. Gandhi's pioneering use of *satyagraha* ('truth-force'), as a form of mass, nonviolent civil resistance,[2] provides a useful link between a philosophical or principled commitment to nonviolence and its effectiveness in achieving social and political change.

The second chapter focuses on social contract theory and justifications for the state as a form of political organisation that ostensibly limits and contains violence, while retaining violence as its ultimate sanction for preserving and maintaining the social order, both internally and internationally. Hobbes and Locke are examined as philosophers of peace, for instance, but tensions between individual autonomy, popular sovereignty and the centralised, hierarchical state are also explored.

The next chapter (Chapter 3) begins to apply some of these themes at the intersection of nonviolent political action and political theory. It opens with an examination of Tolstoy's three-part critique of the state, based on its use of violence, its reinforcement of social and economic inequality and its restrictions on individual autonomy or freedom.[3] It then examines Gandhi's more ambivalent attitude towards the state and civil disobedience as a form of nonviolent direct action that directly challenges the state. The chapter concludes by distinguishing between two forms of nonviolent action – civil resistance and transformative nonviolence – differentiated, at least partly, by their attitude towards the state as a form of political organisation.

Chapter 4 examines the nature of power from the perspective of nonviolent political action and, especially, the so-called consent (or pluralistic) theory of power, which forms the basis of explanations of its effectiveness. This view of power is especially significant for Gene Sharp, as a proponent of the pragmatic (and strategic) use of nonviolent political action.

The following chapter (Chapter 5) continues with this theme, by discussing some of the criticisms of the consent theory of power and embedding it in broader concerns around structure and human agency. In particular, Gramsci's concept of hegemony[4] and Foucault's views on micro-power[5] are used to expand our understanding of the consent, compliance and obedience that form the basis of this theory of power.

The final chapter (Chapter 6) moves from the focus on internal processes of political or social change, directed at an oppressive and unrepresentative state, for example, to examine the relevance of non-violent political action to international relations and the problems of war and armed conflict. It also shifts from the discussion of the role of power in nonviolent political action in the preceding chapters, to examine issues connected to the ethics of nonviolence and its relationship with pacifism.

An important aspect of the content and structure of the book as a whole is that the theorists and themes discussed and identified in the opening two chapters of the book are employed in response to core issues for nonviolence and political theory examined in subsequent chapters. These include power, violence, state sovereignty, war, political authority and individual autonomy. In this way, the book attempts to fulfill its objective of providing a more systematic analysis of the intersection between nonviolence as a form of political action and some of the central concerns of political theory.

Notes

1 See Gene Sharp, *The Politics of Nonviolent Action, Part Two: The Methods of Nonviolent Action* (Boston, MA: Porter Sargent Publishers, 1973). This is the second volume of Sharp's three-volume work *The Politics of Nonviolent Action*. The whole of this volume is dedicated to examining these three categories of nonviolent action, with specific methods discussed in connection with each of the three categories.

2 Gandhi discusses satyagraha in many places, but a useful volume is: Mohandas K. Gandhi, *Non-Violent Resistance (Satyagraha)*, Bharatan Kumarappa (ed.) (New York, NY: Schocken Books, 1961).

3 The analysis of Tolstoy, in terms of his three-part critique of the state, is my own, and this is discussed in detail in Chapter 3, 'Nonviolence, the state and civil resistance'. See, also, Leo Tolstoy, *Tolstoy's Writings on Civil Disobedience and Non-Violence* (New York, NY: The New American Library, 1968); Leo Tolstoy, *Government is Violence: Essays on Anarchism and Pacifism* (London: Phoenix Press, 1990).

4 See Antonio Gramsci, *Selections from the Prison Notebooks* (London: Lawrence and Wishart, 1971).

5 See Paul Rabinow (ed.), *The Foucault Reader: An Introduction to Foucault's Thought* (London: Penguin Books, 1991).

Chapter 1

THE THEORY AND PRACTICE OF
NONVIOLENT POLITICAL ACTION

INTRODUCTION

Nonviolent political action, civil resistance or 'people power' have become increasingly important mechanisms for achieving significant political and social change, especially where both conventional constitutional politics and political violence or armed force have failed. This has become particularly noticeable during the last century or so – a century devastated by war and armed conflict, but also characterised by a trend towards democratisation and popular sovereignty, as well as the recognition and protection of fundamental human rights and civil liberties. Recent examples of political change, achieved through nonviolent action or civil resistance, include the 'Arab spring' (especially regime change in Tunisia and Egypt), the so-called 'colour revolutions' in countries such as Georgia and the Ukraine and the end of Communist Party rule in the countries of Eastern and central Europe. Mahatma Gandhi and Martin Luther King pioneered the use of nonviolent political action in the twentieth century, and Gene Sharp subsequently developed a theory of strategic nonviolence to help explain its political effectiveness. Nonviolent political action has been used to resist and defeat authoritarian and undemocratic regimes, to challenge racial segregation and promote and protect human rights and to end colonial rule and achieve political independence.

Adam Roberts and Timothy Garton Ash recognised the importance of this form of political activity in their recent volume of case studies, *Civil Resistance and Power Politics: The Experience of Non-Violent Action from Gandhi to the Present*. The opening paragraph of the book states:

6

Civil resistance, which has occurred in various forms throughout history, has become particularly prominent in the past hundred years. Three great overlapping causes – decolonization, democratization, and racial equality – have been advanced by campaigns of civil resistance characterized by extensive use of non-violent action. So have many other causes: workers' rights, protection of the environment, gender equality, religious and indigenous rights, defence of national cultures and political systems against foreign encroachments, and opposition to wars and weaponry. Civil resistance was one factor in the ending of communist party rule in many countries in 1989–91, and hence in ending the Cold War. The world today has been shaped significantly by this mode of political action.[1]

Nonviolent political action and civil resistance involve a powerful confluence of ideological or philosophical concerns based on anti-war sentiment and moral opposition to the use of violence, and pragmatic considerations about the most effective way to mobilise popular power and to resist and replace authoritarian or undemocratic regimes and protect fundamental human rights.

Martin Luther King claimed that nonviolent political action provides a middle way, between acquiescence to an unjust or evil system and violent resistance to it. Acquiescence may seem like the easier way, but it 'is not the moral way. It is the way of the coward'. This is because to 'accept injustice or segregation passively is to say to the oppressor that his actions are morally right'.[2] Similarly, for King, violence 'as a way of achieving racial justice is both impractical and immoral'.[3]

> The third way open to oppressed people in their quest for freedom is the way of nonviolent resistance . . . With nonviolent resistance, no individual or group need submit to any wrong, nor need anyone resort to violence in order to right a wrong . . . Nonviolent resistance is not aimed against oppressors but against oppression.[4]

Nonviolent political action provides an effective form of mass mobilisation against injustice that avoids the immorality of both acquiescence and violent resistance, according to King.

Nonviolent political action can be 'understood as a set of methods with special features that are different from both violent resistance and institutional politics'.[5] Mark Garavan, for example, contrasts what he calls 'the politics of moral force' with 'conventional, parliamentary politics on the one hand and . . . physical force or violence on the other'.[6] Thus, a basic definition of nonviolent political action could be: collective action outside the formal institutions or procedures of the state that avoids the systematic or deliberate use of violence or armed force to achieve its political or social objectives.

Michael Randle uses the term 'civil resistance' to refer to nonviolent political action,[7] in order to emphasise its character as collective action on the part of ordinary citizens or civilians, outside conventional political structures or organisations (such as political parties).[8] In other words, as well as avoiding the systematic use of armed force or violence, nonviolent action is also collective political action on the part of ordinary citizens or civilians, organising themselves directly through civil society groups or social movements to achieve their political or social objectives. It tends to be based in the institutions or organisations of civil society, outside the established institutional or constitutional procedures of the state.

Furthermore, such collective action often involves popular resistance to the policies or structures of an oppressive state or government, which explains why it is based in civil society. This provides us with a positive definition of nonviolent action as involving not merely the absence of violence (negative), but also the strengthening of the capacity for popular power and popular resistance against oppression and injustice (positive).

The relationship between nonviolent political action and both political violence and constitutional politics is a complex and subtle one. Although the methods of nonviolent political action can be distinguished from these other two forms of political activity, it is often employed in tandem with one or both of them, in the context of specific campaigns for social and political change. Thus, the US civil rights movement relied upon the legal system and the federal government to alleviate racial segregation. Similarly, the ending of apartheid in South Africa involved both mass nonviolent civil resistance through the United Democratic Front and political violence through the armed wing of the African National Congress, Umkhonto we Sizwe, for example.

An important distinction is often made between those who use the methods of nonviolence political action for pragmatic reasons and those who have some underlying principled ethical or religious commitment to nonviolence. Pragmatic proponents of nonviolent political action use these methods, because they seem to be the most effective under the circumstances or because armed resistance or armed conflict are not realistic options. Principled proponents of nonviolence, on the other hand, attach some deeper ethical or religious significance to avoiding or replacing violence in political action and social relationships more generally.

The iconic figures of twentieth century nonviolence, such as Mahatma Gandhi and Martin Luther King, tend to be associated with principled nonviolence and, yet, as theorists and scholars of nonviolence (such as Gene Sharp and Adam Roberts) point out, the vast majority of the instances of nonviolent political action or civil resistance involve individuals or groups who are using it for pragmatic reasons. They may not even employ the language of nonviolence to describe what they are doing, and, in many cases, they are only dimly aware of the rich history of nonviolent political action in other parts of the world and of recent efforts to systematise and develop a theory of strategic nonviolent action. According to Sharp: 'There has been much variation in the degree to which people in these conflicts have been aware of the existence of a general nonviolent technique of action and have had prior knowledge of its operation'.[9]

The vast majority of those involved in any of the campaigns associated with nonviolent political action – from the struggle for Indian independence in the first half of the twentieth century through to the 'colour revolutions' in countries of the former Soviet Union in the first decade of this century and, even more recently, the 'Arab spring' in North Africa and the Middle East – would have a largely pragmatic commitment to the use of nonviolent methods. Gandhi certainly acknowledged that many, if not most, of his colleagues in the Indian National Congress and the majority of Indians who took part in *satyagraha* or campaigns of mass nonviolent civil disobedience employed these methods pragmatically, rather than for reasons of principle. He recognised it explicitly in his distinction between nonviolence as a policy (pragmatic) and the *dharma* (or ethical law) of nonviolence.[10]

Timothy Garton Ash, in the conclusion to *Civil Resistance and Power Politics*, states that the authors of the various case studies arrive 'separately but almost unanimously' at the same view,[11] concerning the preponderance of pragmatic over principled examples of nonviolent political action:

The choice of non-violence, we find them arguing again and again, was more pragmatic than principled, and often less unequivocal than is generally assumed. Even Gandhi countenanced the use of armed force in some circumstances. Only a very few of the leading actors in these histories are true pacifists, like the Theravada Buddhists of Burma . . .[12]

Like Gandhi and King, the Burmese monks have an ethical commitment towards the use of nonviolence, derived from Buddhism and their monastic code, but this places them among the few who employ the methods of nonviolent political action primarily for moral or religious reasons.

There are two important concerns of nonviolent political action that correspond to this distinction between pragmatic and principled reasons for employing it. These are power – the political dimension – and violence, which is the ethical dimension. Thus, we find pragmatic proponents of nonviolence, such as Gene Sharp, primarily concerned with developing theories of social power peculiar to civil resistance or nonviolent political action, which help explain its effectiveness in resisting even the most oppressive or authoritarian regimes. On the other hand, principled or ethical supporters of nonviolence are interested in promoting civil resistance or nonviolent action as an alternative to violence, where constitutional methods, for example, are unavailable, incomplete or insufficient, because of the harm to human beings (and, in some cases, all living beings) resulting from violent forms of political action, whether perpetrated by individuals, states or other social groups.

This is not to say that principled or ethical proponents of nonviolence are uninterested in its effectiveness, in issues of political power or in achieving or realising other ideals or values, such as democracy or human rights. Gandhi epitomises the connection between an underlying philosophical commitment to nonviolence and a concern with political effectiveness. It is more that their primary ethical concern is with replacing or eliminating violence as a feature of social life. Principled proponents of nonviolence are committed to the use of nonviolent methods because they assign it intrinsic value or significance as a political objective so that such methods are not merely extrinsic to some other valued political objective, such as political independence or democracy.

Similarly, it is not so much that pragmatic proponents of nonviolence lack principles or are unprincipled, but that their actions are aimed at achieving or realising a set of ideals or objectives, such as political independence, democracy or human rights, which are distinct or separable from nonviolence as such. In other words, civil resistance provides a useful and effective set of methods for achieving specific political objectives. Nonviolent action is seen as the means, but it is the achievement of political aims or ends extrinsic to, and logically distinct from, the use of nonviolence that is of real importance. One of the key issues for proponents and practitioners of pragmatic nonviolence, of course, concerns what counts as success or failure for achieving their ends. As Roberts points out: 'The very question of what constitutes success or failure may have no immediate or obvious answer'.[13]

Furthermore, in some cases, those who use nonviolent or peaceful methods appeal to a set of ideals or norms different from nonviolence, as such, as the primary moral motive for their actions. According to Merle Goldman, for example:

> Although Gandhi's methods may have had some influence . . . for the general public, including those who participated in the 1989 movement, the Chinese tradition of moral remonstrance – which seeks to exert moral pressure on political leaders to live up to their enunciated ideals – played an even greater role . . . Like their Confucian predecessors, they saw themselves as loyal followers, appealing to the authorities to live up to their promises.[14]

The norms or values that influenced pro-democracy protestors, in their use of peaceful or nonviolent methods, were derived from a Confucian interpretation of the relationship between rulers and the ruled and their moral responsibility to each other. Placing moral pressure upon Communist Party authorities involved peaceful methods of protest, but not an explicit commitment to the intrinsic moral worth of nonviolence as such.

Principled proponents of nonviolence, on the other hand, include replacing or eliminating violence as a feature of social and political life as one of their primary objectives or goals. Furthermore, they emphasise an intimate link between methods and outcomes, or means and ends, so that a nonviolent or peaceful society can only be achieved through the use of nonviolent or peaceful means. Nonviolence has intrinsic value or significance as an objective or goal of political action and also as a means or method for achieving social and political change.

Principled proponents of nonviolence, such as Gandhi, assign intrinsic value to the use of nonviolent methods, partly because of the intimate link between methods and outcomes, but also because we can control our actions (and, especially, their moral quality) much more directly than we can control their consequences or results. Gandhi, for instance, argued that the best way to achieve a goal was to concentrate on utilising the means appropriate to achieving it, rather than on the goal or objective itself, which otherwise remained indeterminate, uncertain and, most likely, unobtainable.

> The clearest possible definition of the goal and its appreciation would fail to take us there, if we do not know and utilize the means of achieving it. I have, therefore, concerned myself principally with the conservation of the means and their progressive use; I know if we can take care of them attainment of the goal is assured.[15]

The moral quality of the methods helps create and shape, in a very immediate way, the moral content of the outcomes of political action, and this is why a principled commitment to nonviolence is so important.

Thus, pragmatic proponents of nonviolence tend to distinguish between the value of the ends or objectives of political activity and the moral quality of the methods employed to obtain them, whereas principled proponents, such as Gandhi, tend to focus on the ethical or moral quality of the methods – in the form of nonviolence – as determining the value of the outcomes of political action. Pragmatic proponents of nonviolent action view it as the most effective way to achieve valued political ends, such as democracy and human rights. Principled proponents of nonviolence, on the other hand, emphasise the intrinsic moral significance of the use of nonviolent action, because of the intimate and direct connection between the moral quality of the methods employed and the political outcomes achieved.

This chapter continues with an exploration of themes associated with the ethical principles, or underlying philosophy, of nonviolence, derived primarily from Tolstoy, Gandhi and King. This is complemented by a discussion of pragmatic nonviolence, represented primarily by Gene Sharp, as a theorist and strategist of nonviolent political action.

PRINCIPLED NONVIOLENCE

Tolstoy locates the source of his ethical commitment to nonviolence and pacifism in his interpretation of Christian principles. The essence of Christ's teachings, according to Tolstoy, is love, which is the only moral law governing human life: 'That love – i.e. the striving for the union of human souls and the activity derived from this striving – is the highest and only law of human life'.[16]

Furthermore, violence contradicts this fundamental law – the law of love: 'The essential thing, however, is that the law given to us by God . . . distinctly forbids, not killing only but also every kind of violence'.[17] According to Tolstoy:

> Christ . . . knew . . . that the use of force is incompatible with love as the fundamental law of life, that as soon as violence is permitted . . . the insufficiency of the law of love is acknowledged . . . as soon as force was admitted into love it was no more, and there could be no love as the law of life, and as there was no law of life, there was no law at all except violence – i.e. the power of the strongest.[18]

There is only one law for Tolstoy – the law of love, which consists of the striving for human unity. This is directly contradicted and undermined by the use of violence, which represents only the power of the strongest.

This theme of love as the theological or cosmological source of an ethical commitment to nonviolence continues through a direct line of influence from Tolstoy to Gandhi and King. The core ethical principle behind Gandhi's ethical commitment to nonviolence is *ahimsa* (from the Sanskrit or Gujarati), which means non-harm or non-injury (*a-himsa*) to all living things in thought, word and deed. For Gandhi, however, this commitment to non-harm or harmlessness (non-maleficence) is complemented by a commitment to do good (or beneficence): 'Complete non-violence is complete absence of ill-will against all that lives . . . Non-violence is therefore in its active form good will towards all life. It is pure Love'.[19]

Martin Luther King, whose commitment to nonviolence was strongly influenced by Gandhi, also identified nonviolence with love, understood through a particular theological interpretation. 'At the center of nonviolence stands the principle of love', he wrote.[20] He deliberately identified love, in this sense, as an ethical or moral principle, rather than as some affectionate or sentimental emotion, because '[i]t would be nonsense to urge men to love their oppressors in an affectionate sense'.[21]

Instead, King distinguished between 'three words for love in the Greek New Testament'[22] – *eros, philia* and *agape*.[23] In Platonic philosophy, *eros* meant the yearning of the soul for the realm of the divine. It has now come to mean a sort of aesthetic or romantic love.[24] Such love is dependent upon some perceived quality in its object that prompts it in those who love. King contrasts *eros* with *philia*, which means: 'intimate affectionateness (sic) between friends. *Philia* denotes a sort of reciprocal love: the person loves because he is loved'.[25]

Finally, King refers to *agape* – the form of unconditional, universal or cosmopolitan love that provides the inspiration or motivation for nonviolence as a method to resist injustice and oppression.

> When we speak of loving those who oppose us we refer to neither *eros* nor *philia*; we speak of a love which is expressed in the Greek word *agape*. *Agape* means nothing sentimental or basically affectionate; it means understanding, redeeming good will for all men, an overflowing love which seeks nothing in return. It is the love of God working in the lives of men.[26]

This interpretation of love as *agape* has an explicitly Christian theological basis for King, just as *ahimsa* has its basis in Hinduism for Gandhi. It resembles the 'striving for the union of human souls'[27] that characterises the law of love for Tolstoy, as the fundamental ethical principle governing human behaviour and underlying, or requiring, a commitment to nonviolence.

Agape, as the basis for a principled or ethical commitment to nonviolence for King, resembles Gandhi's understanding of *ahimsa* as benevolence or active good-will towards all living beings. Even so, King often distinguished between the Christian inspiration for nonviolence as a religious and moral principle and the example provided by Gandhian methods or techniques of nonviolence. It was the fusion of the two that was most relevant to the situation of African-Americans, in their struggle for civil rights in the United States.

> I had come to see early that the Christian doctrine of love operating through the Gandhian method of nonviolence was one of the

most potent weapons available to the Negro in his struggle for freedom . . . Nonviolent resistance had emerged as the technique of the movement, while love stood as the regulating ideal. In other words, Christ furnished the spirit and motivation, while Gandhi furnished the method . . .[28]

Gandhi's methods and tactics were immediately useful, even if they had to be explained or justified by using a moral, religious and cultural discourse more directly relevant to the African-American context. As King recounted about the Montgomery bus boycott of 1955–6: 'We had to use our mass meetings to explain nonviolence to a community of people who had never heard of the philosophy and in many instances were not sympathetic with (sic) it'.[29]

The significance of Gandhi's example in restoring King's faith in the power of love to achieve social change should not be underestimated, however. He explains that he had 'almost despaired of the power of love in solving social problems'.[30]

> The 'turn the other cheek' philosophy and the 'love your enemies' philosophy are only valid, I felt, when individuals are in conflict with other individuals; when racial groups and nations are in conflict a more realistic approach is necessary. Then I came upon the life and teachings of Mahatma Gandhi . . . and I came to see for the first time that the Christian doctrine of love operating through the Gandhian method of nonviolence was one of the most potent weapons available to oppressed people in their struggle for freedom.[31]

Gandhi's methods of nonviolence provided King with the opportunity and the means for expressing his moral and theological commitment to *agape* and Christian love through effective action to resist and dismantle social and economic injustice in the United States, in the form of segregation, poverty and militarism.

The benevolence derived from *agape* is both universal and disinterested. It does not distinguish between political opponents and political allies or between friend and enemies. This is why it is such a powerful source of, and inspiration for, nonviolence, in the context of acute social conflict.

> *Agape* ... is not set in motion by any quality or function of its object
> ... *Agape* is disinterested love. It is a love in which the individual
> seeks not his own good, but the good of his neighbor (1 Cor. 10:
> 24). *Agape* does not begin by discriminating between worthy and
> unworthy people, or any qualities people possess. It begins by
> loving others *for their sakes* ... Therefore, *agape* makes no distinc-
> tion between friends and enemy; it is directed toward both.[32]

Agape provides the moral basis for dealing with conflict in such a way
that not only does one's opponent remain unharmed, but a solution is
sought that will somehow be of benefit to all sides involved in the conflict, through responding to their shared and common humanity and
their underlying human needs.

A fundamental need for human beings, according to King, is a sense
of belonging and community so that a fundamental role for *agape* in
human relationships is to create or restore community:

> *Agape* is love seeking to preserve and create community ... *Agape*
> is a willingness to go to any length to restore community ... crea-
> tion is so designed that my personality can only be fulfilled in the
> context of community.[33]

Community can be interpreted in a cosmopolitan sense to mean the
moral community of all human beings, based on our common humanity. Thus, King states that *agape* 'springs from the need of the other
person – his need for belonging to the best in the human family'.[34]
Segregation not only harms African-Americans in a direct and egregious way, according to King, it also harms 'the white man's personal-
ity',[35] through excluding him from this universal, or shared, human
community. Nonviolent political action can be effective in political
campaigns for civil rights and against segregation, but *agape* – as the
moral motive – can heal or restore this broken community as the ultimate, underlying objective.

A constant theme, or trope, for King is his view that the ultimate
purpose of social and political action is the creation of, what he
referred to as, 'the beloved community' and that this can only be
achieved through nonviolence: 'The end is redemption and recon-
ciliation. The aftermath of nonviolence is the creation of the beloved
community'.[36]

Thus, the ethical commitment to nonviolence has a profoundly religious, philosophical and, even, cosmological significance for both King and Gandhi. It involves much more than selecting the methods of nonviolent action for reasons of effectiveness or convenience. As King writes:

> the method of nonviolence is based on the conviction that the universe is on the side of justice . . . This belief that God is on the side of truth and justice comes down to us from the long tradition of our Christian faith.[37]

Although both Gandhi and King aimed to achieve significant political and social change, their motives for using nonviolence to obtain their objectives transcended strategic or pragmatic considerations. Thus, according to King, 'nonviolence in the truest sense is not a strategy that one uses simply because it is expedient at the moment; nonviolence is ultimately a way of life that men live by because of the sheer morality of its claim'.[38]

REDEMPTIVE SUFFERING

Nonviolence understood through either *ahimsa* or *agape*, according to both Gandhi and King, requires a willingness to accept suffering, without inflicting harm or suffering upon others. Principled proponents of nonviolence retain their moral commitment to the point of arrest, injury or even death, because this unswerving allegiance demonstrates the sincerity of their commitment to their cause and becomes a major component of the impact of nonviolent action upon the opponent or the oppressor.

Both *ahimsa* and *agape* (as both non-harm and benevolence) imply or require non-cooperation with evil, as well as full acceptance of the consequences of such non-cooperation. Such non-cooperation with evil is at the basis of any genuinely ethical response to systems of oppression and injustice and provides a consistently strong and, ultimately, effective challenge to such systems. Both Gandhi and King followed Henry David Thoreau, in his famous essay 'On civil disobedience', in identifying non-cooperation with evil and the concomitant voluntary acceptance of any suffering that results, as the core ethical requirements of a principled commitment to nonviolence:

What, then, is the meaning of non-co-operation in terms of the Law of Suffering? We must voluntarily put up with the losses and inconveniences that arise from having to withdraw our support from a government that is ruling against our will. Possession of power and riches is a crime under an unjust government . . . says Thoreau. We must not, for fear of ourselves or others having to suffer, remain participators in it. But we must combat the wrong by ceasing to assist the wrong-doer directly or indirectly.[39]

A willingness to accept the negative consequences of non-cooperation with evil is an important element of the voluntary acceptance of suffering required by an ethical commitment to nonviolence.

One of the reasons for the significance of the voluntary acceptance of suffering as a component of nonviolence, according to Gandhi, is that only those initiating or employing nonviolent political action or civil resistance suffer any negative or harmful consequences resulting from their actions.[40] This is the opposite of armed resistance or armed conflict, of course, where the purpose of military action is to inflict maximum damage upon the enemy, while minimising the damage to oneself. A core ethical principle for Gandhi, in particular, however, is a willingness to accept the consequences of one's actions, rather than displacing or inflicting them upon others. The voluntary acceptance of suffering and nonviolence require this, whereas the purpose of armed force is to protect oneself as much as possible from the consequences of engaging in military action: 'Passive resistance is a method of securing rights by personal suffering; it is the reverse of resistance by arms'.[41]

This is connected to a kind of ethical and epistemological humility central to Gandhi's approach to social and political conflict. No one can be absolutely certain of the moral correctness of their position and the moral wrongness of their opponent: 'No man can claim that he is absolutely in the right or that a particular thing is wrong because he thinks so'.[42] Therefore, if nonviolence 'is used in a cause that is unjust, only the person using it suffers. He does not make others suffer for his mistakes'.[43] The voluntary acceptance of suffering ensures that those engaging in nonviolent political action or civil resistance accept the consequences of their actions, including the consequences of any mistaken moral or political judgements.

The voluntary acceptance of suffering as a consequence of one's actions also demonstrates the sincerity of one's commitment to a particular moral or political position, even if it also reveals an intellectual humility or a willingness to accept the incorrectness of this position, if this can be shown. The purpose of one's actions is to achieve a particular goal or objective, even at a high personal cost, rather than to inflict harm or suffering upon one's opponent. This sincerity of purpose through the voluntary acceptance of suffering helps to persuade one's opponent that this objective is being pursued for the sake of justice and mutual benefit and not out of self-interest at their expense. Thus, nonviolence, combined with the acceptance of suffering, can move a conflict beyond mutually exclusive antagonism to a shared sense of responsibility for resolving the conflict. Nonviolence, then, 'is a case of appealing to the reason and conscience of the opponent by inviting suffering on oneself. The motive is to convert the opponent and make him one's willing ally and friend'.[44] Gene Sharp also identified 'self-suffering' as a mechanism for persuading or converting one's opponent to the justice of the cause, even if he remained sceptical about the ultimate efficacy of such processes, as a pragmatic proponent of nonviolent political action: 'Self-suffering is often considered important in triggering conversion . . . Suffering then is no longer only a risk, it also becomes a weapon'.[45]

Martin Luther King also identified the voluntary acceptance of suffering, or what he sometimes referred to as redemptive suffering, as a central component of nonviolence. According to King, one of the basic characteristics of 'nonviolent resistance is a willingness to accept suffering without retaliation, to accept blows from the opponent without striking back'.[46]

> The nonviolent resister is willing to accept violence if necessary, but never to inflict it . . . unearned suffering is redemptive. Suffering, the nonviolent resister realizes, has tremendous educational and transforming possibilities.[47]

Redemptive suffering, for example, can transform the conflict from one of mutual hostility towards cooperation to achieve a mutually agreeable outcome.

King also contrasted the intended consequences of violence with those of nonviolence, in terms of suffering.

> Another thing that stands at the center of this movement is another idea: that suffering can be a most creative and powerful

social force . . . violence says that suffering can be a powerful social force by inflicting the suffering on somebody else: so this is what we do in war . . . It believes that you achieve some end by inflicting suffering on another. The nonviolent say that suffering becomes a powerful social force when you willingly accept that violence on yourself, so that self-suffering stands at the center of the nonviolent movement . . . feeling that unearned suffering is redemptive, and that suffering may serve to transform the social situation.[48]

Thus, the Christian principles of 'turn the other cheek' and 'love thine enemy' are not prescriptions for the passive acceptance of injustice and oppression, but, instead, become powerful instruments of achieving social and political change through nonviolent civil resistance.

King suggests another reason for accepting suffering without inflicting it in return, as a component of nonviolence. The purpose of nonviolent action is 'to defeat the unjust system, rather than individuals who are caught in that system'.[49] Retaliatory violence and suffering does quite the opposite, however, targeting human beings, rather than systems or structures of injustice, inequality and oppression, such as racial segregation, colonialism and authoritarian political regimes. Such violence may, in fact, undermine the capacity of the resistance to change systems or structures, through deflecting their actions into unproductive and harmful directions and alienating both potential allies and those elements of the opponent group with whom they will eventually need to achieve some sort of negotiated settlement.

SATYAGRAHA

Gandhi coined the term *satyagraha* to replace the term passive resistance to refer to nonviolent political action.[50] He found the term passive resistance, which was then in common use, unsatisfactory, for at least two reasons. Firstly, according to Gandhi, nonviolence was not passive, but was very active, both spiritually and politically, in terms of the engagement of opposing groups with each other. Secondly, the term passive resistance did not include the principled ethical, religious or philosophical elements of nonviolence, so basic to Gandhi's understanding of it. It may involve the avoidance of violence, but it does not include a positive commitment to the values Gandhi associated with nonviolence that transcend and supersede pragmatic considerations:

Passive resistance is used in the orthodox English sense and covers the suffragette movement as well as the resistance of the Non-conformists . . . Whilst it avoids violence . . . it does not exclude its use if, in the opinion of a passive resister, the occasion demands it.[51]

He coined the term *satyagraha* to overcome both these defects of the term passive resistance, when describing his own methods and philosophy of nonviolent action.

Gandhi used the terms *satyagraha* and passive resistance to distinguish between principled and pragmatic nonviolence (or 'nonviolence as a policy'). Kumarappa claims, then, that passive resistance is not nonviolence in the full Gandhian sense, because it does not involve a moral or philosophical commitment that transcends more immediate pragmatic considerations:

The passive resister, or the one who adopts non-violence as policy, on the other hand, is really not non-violent, for he would be violent if he could, and is nonviolent (sic) only because he does not for the time being have the means or the capacity for violence. It is a far cry, therefore, from passive resistance to Satyagraha.[52]

Passive resistance, like pragmatic nonviolence, is contingent upon the effectiveness of nonviolent methods and the availability or usefulness of violence.

Thus, the term *satyagraha* combined Gandhi's concern with the ethical, epistemological and philosophical aspects of nonviolence and the use of nonviolent methods to achieve social and political change. As a method (or collection of methods) of nonviolent political action, *satyagraha* 'means mass resistance on a non-violent basis against the Government when negotiations and constitutional methods have failed'.[53]

In philosophical terms, on the other hand, *satyagraha* derives its moral and political impetus from its connection to 'Truth', understood in its cosmological, epistemological and ethical dimensions: '*Satyagraha* is, literally, holding on to Truth, and it means, therefore, Truth-force. Truth is soul or spirit. It is, therefore, known as soul-force'.[54] *Satyagraha* is conventionally translated into English as truth-force or soul-force, because Gandhi equated truth with God, and God, in accordance with

Hinduism, was equated with both a universal or cosmological soul and the soul of each individual (connecting the transcendent and the imma- nent). 'Satyagraha means literally "clinging to truth", and as Truth for Gandhiji was God, Satyagraha in the general sense of the word means the way of life of one who holds steadfastly to God'.[55]

Truth, for Gandhi, has both cosmological or metaphysical and ethical significance, and these are connected. Furthermore, 'since the greatest truth is the unity of all life, Truth can be attained only by loving service of all, i.e. by non-violence. The weapon of the Satyagrahi is therefore non-violence'.[56] The 'unity of all life' is a cosmological or metaphysical claim, with huge implications concerning *ahimsa* as the basis of a moral commitment to nonviolence, understood not merely as non-harm to all living things, but also as active benevolence towards them.

The epistemological dimension of truth, or the limits of human knowledge, is also an important basis for *satyagraha* and nonviolence. *Satyagraha*, therefore, 'excludes the use of violence because man is not capable of knowing the absolute truth and, therefore, not competent to punish'.[57] *Satyagraha* is a method for pursuing truth, especially moral or ethical truth, realised through human relationships and forms of social and political organisation. Human knowledge is finite, rather than absolute, however, so we must always allow for error. This is why truth must be pursued nonviolently, in a spirit of epistemological humility, so that we do not inflict suffering or harm upon others and force them to accept the negative consequences of our moral mistakes.

Satyagraha cannot be used in the service of an unjust cause, accord- ing to Gandhi, precisely because of the intimate connection between its nonviolent methods and its pursuit of truth, including moral truth.[58] Nonviolence is more than a collection of tactics or methods. It must be infused with the spirit of the search for truth. Gene Sharp, on the other hand, as a proponent and theorist of pragmatic nonviolence, concedes that that there is no direct or necessary connection between the moral status of the methods and the political objectives of nonviolent political action, understood in purely practical and strategic terms: 'Methods of nonviolent action have also been applied for purposes that most demo- crats and supporters of social justice would reject'.[59] Mass nonviolent protests have been deployed in support of, or to install, autocratic or theocratic regimes (such as Iran in 1979), and the Nazis employed boy- cotts against Jewish shopkeepers, for example.

Another significant point for *satyagraha* as nonviolent political action is that it is available to every human being, because it is based on a moral commitment to the pursuit of truth, rather than specific knowledge as such (or access to material weapons). It is not an elite-based method of political action, nor does it depend upon hierarchical forms of political organisation, because it is derived from a commitment to the pursuit of truth on the part of each individual: 'The striving does not require any quality unattainable by the lowliest among us. For Satyagraha is an attribute of the spirit within. It is latent in every one of us'.[60] *Satyagraha* is available to all individuals or social groups in the form of nonviolent political action and civil resistance.

Gandhi's so-called 'constructive programme' was also an important component of both his vision and his practice of *satyagraha*. Gandhi always put equal effort into rectifying numerous social problems, parallel to his political efforts to achieve independence from British colonial rule. He campaigned on issues as diverse as village hygiene, caste-based discrimination against dalits (so-called 'untouchables' or harijans, as Gandhi called them) and sectarian divisions between Hindus and Muslims. He claimed that Indians must be capable of demonstrating their capacity for self-rule, or *hind swaraj*, through dealing with these issues, and, in some ways, he viewed political independence as significant, primarily because it would facilitate Indians in resolving these social problems. According to Kumarappa:

> Gandhiji showed that non-violence to be effective requires constructive effort in every sphere of life, individual, social, economic and political . . . the practice of non-violence in the political sphere . . . involves building up brick by brick with patience and industry a new non-violent social and economic order.[61]

Satyagraha is a form of mass nonviolent political action or civil resistance to oppression and injustice, but it is also a positive programme for building a new society, in tandem with challenging and changing the old.

PRAGMATIC NONVIOLENCE

Gandhi referred to pragmatic nonviolence as 'non-violence as a policy', which was the minimum commitment to nonviolence he expected from those who participated in the campaigns he led, through the Indian National Congress, against British rule in India.

I have not put before India the final form of non-violence. The
non-violence that I have preached from Congress platforms is
non-violence as a policy. But even policies require honest adher-
ence in thought, word and deed . . . Non-violence being a policy
means that it can upon due notice be given up when it proves
unsuccessful or ineffective. But simple morality demands that,
whilst a particular policy is pursued, it must be pursued with all
one's heart.[62]

In other words, even pragmatic nonviolence, or 'nonviolence as a
policy', requires a consistency of commitment and application. He
often stated that those who could not support the consistent use of
nonviolent methods, even in the context of a specific campaign, should
abandon the use of nonviolence altogether:[63] 'Our non-violence need
not be of the strong, but it has to be of the truthful'.[64]

Pragmatic nonviolence, or nonviolence as a policy, is selected
because of its effectiveness or appropriateness to achieve the objectives
of a specific campaign, and while it needs to be used consistently in the
context of that campaign, unlike principled nonviolence, it does not
imply some deeper moral commitment that transcends the tactical and
strategic requirements of the campaign: 'A particular practice is a policy
when its application is limited to time or space. Highest policy is therefore fullest practice'.[65] Highest policy is fullest practice, in the sense
that the more consistently nonviolent methods were used, even in the
context of a particular struggle, the more it conformed to the criteria of
nonviolent political action. Gene Sharp, as a proponent of pragmatic
nonviolence, also insisted upon the need for consistency in its application or use, not for moral reasons, but because this was essential for its
effectiveness.

Gene Sharp is very clear on the distinction between principled and
pragmatic nonviolence, both in terms of understanding the dynamics
of the vast majority of situations in which nonviolent methods have
been used and for developing an effective theory of strategic nonviolent
political action. According to Sharp, pragmatic nonviolence focuses on
actions, rather than on beliefs, ideals or principles:

Nonviolent struggle is identified by what people do, not by what
they believe. In many cases, the people using these nonviolent
methods have believed violence to be perfectly justified in moral

or religious terms. However, for the specific conflict that they currently faced they chose, for pragmatic reasons, to use methods that did not include violence. Only in rare historical instances did a group or a leader have a personal belief that rejected violence in principle . . . It is the type of activity that identifies the technique of nonviolent action, not the belief behind the activity.[66]

Sharp is primarily concerned with nonviolent political action, or civil resistance, as a functional substitute for political violence. A theory or ideology of nonviolence is of interest or benefit only insofar as it contributes to an effective strategy of nonviolent political action.

According to Sharp, pragmatic nonviolence refers to 'forms of mass action' and should not be confused with 'beliefs in ethical or religious nonviolence ("principled nonviolence")'.[67] These beliefs, 'which have their merits, are different phenomena that usually are unrelated to mass struggles conducted by people who do not share such beliefs'.[68] Sharp emphasises that in the majority of instances of the use of nonviolent political action, 'nonviolent means appear to have been chosen because of considerations of anticipated effectiveness',[69] that is, for pragmatic reasons. A commitment to nonviolence for ethical or moral reasons plays, at most, a subservient role to these pragmatic considerations, leading those involved in the struggle to choose nonviolent over violent methods, where both might be practical options for achieving political objectives: 'In some cases, there appear to have been mixed motives, with practical motives predominating but with a relative moral preference for nonviolent means'.[70]

Many campaigns of civil resistance choose nonviolent methods based on practical, strategic calculations, due to the unavailability of formal constitutional or institutional channels, and the unattractiveness of political violence, because of the overwhelming military or 'material power' of the opponent, for example, which, in the case of governments or ruling regimes, often have the full resources of the state at their command. Merle Goldman refers to these considerations in his analysis of the pro-democracy protests in China in 1989, for instance:

With official channels being closed to them, and violent resistance lacking any serious appeal, for those who wanted to express their views openly peaceful action was the only choice . . . because of the public reaction against the violence and turmoil of the Mao

era, non-violent and peaceful methods were the most likely to
win wide popular support. So, for the student organizers, these
methods were the most rational strategies for achieving their goal
of political reform.[71]

Recent political history and political culture also influenced the choice
of nonviolent methods by the Chinese protestors, in addition to the
government's access to overwhelming military force, which it eventually used to crush the protests. As Roberts points out, in this, as in
many other cases: 'Often the reasons for a movement's avoidance of
violence are related to the context rather than to any absolute ethical
principle',[72] even if there might be a 'relative moral preference' for the
use of nonviolent methods. Thus, according to Goldman, the protestors
'remained firm in their commitment to the principle of non-violence
and dialogue even as the troops used force to repress them violently'.[73]

The issue of violence versus nonviolence in human affairs and forms
of social organisation is primarily a practical and political problem,
rather than a moral one, according to Sharp:

> Our failure to resolve the problems of institutionalized political
> violence, and various sub-problems such as war, has been largely
> rooted in our failure to perceive that violent sanctions are not the
> only possible ones, and that we can explore the potential of alter-
> native nonviolent sanctions. This type of analysis, however, points
> the way to examination of functional alternatives, of functional
> substitutes . . . Alternative nonviolent sanctions . . . do exist. This
> opens the way for basic change to the extent that they are substi-
> tuted for violent sanctions . . . A series of such substitutions would
> contribute to systemic change.[74]

In situations where sanctions or even coercive force are required, the
methods of nonviolent political action can become an effective alternative to all forms of political violence, including war, through a process
of progressive substitution, according to Sharp.

Nonviolent methods can be employed both internally – to deal with
issues of conflict, social order and justice within a country or a society
– and, also, externally – in the form of 'national defense against foreign
invasions and occupations',[75] for example. Societies or countries currently depend upon various forms of political violence for multifarious

purposes or reasons, such as law enforcement (police and prisons) and defence against external aggression (armies), so that their replacement by nonviolent sanctions can occur incrementally, on a function-by-function basis. This does not require a sudden, revolutionary transformation of society, according to Sharp:

> The change in sanctions therefore would *not* be a sweeping adoption of a new way of life by the whole population, nor a sudden sweeping transformation the whole society. It would instead be a phased comprehensive attempt over some years or decades to develop and substitute nonviolent sanctions for violent ones . . . for those functions for which our society legitimately requires effective sanctions and today relies upon political violence.[76]

The change to exclusively nonviolent methods and sanctions for dealing with issues of conflict, social order and, even, survival (in the face of external threats) for a society would occur progressively and pragmatically, through providing effective functional substitutes for current mechanisms of institutionalised political violence.

Adam Roberts refers to this as a policy of 'progressive substitution' of civil resistance, 'for the threat and use of force'. This policy 'recognizes that force has served important functions in society – for example in policing and in defence'.[77]

> The hope is that [civil resistance] will replace reliance on force progressively in a succession of issue-areas. The central idea is that only if there is a viable substitute can force be effectively renounced. Implicitly, this tradition could be compatible with support for particular uses of armed force in circumstances where civil resistance appears impractical.[78]

Roberts claims that 'Gandhi and Martin Luther King . . . arguably leaned toward the concept of "progressive substitution"' and, also, that 'Gene Sharp has done most to develop this tradition of thought into a coherent theory'.[79]

However, the use of nonviolence for purely pragmatic or strategic reasons may limit its ability to influence political policy and political structures after the immediate political objectives of the civil resistance groups employing it have been met. Even some of the groups and movements involved in some of the more successful examples of civil resistance and associated ideas around nonviolence quickly became marginalised and politically impotent or insignificant in their home societies, at least, following the attainment of campaign goals. Their lasting influence on political ideology, practice and institutions seems diluted or even irrelevant. This seems to be the case with the New Forum in East Germany, Otpor in Serbia and Kmara in Georgia, for example. In East Germany, for example, Charles S. Maier writes:

> The protesters of 1989 opened a civic space, they enabled the apparent triumph of what we call civil society, but they did not continue to prevail . . . The New Forum and other groups, allied together as Alliance-90 won only about 3 per cent in the last and finally free elections to the GDR's *Volkskammer*.[80]

Similarly, 'Otpor received a mere 1.76 per cent of the votes and attained no seats' when it contested 'elections to the Serbian Parliament in December 2003'.[81]

In the case of the 'Rose Revolution' in Georgia, the impact of non-violent political action on state practice was also severely limited. According to Stephen Jones, 'the practice of non-violence in November 2003 was a strategic decision'.[82]

> This explains, as does Georgia's unstable regional environment and the demands of state-building, why Georgia's Rose Revolutionaries have spent their energies since 2003 on the creation of a powerful army. Georgia in 2007, where the ideas of civil resistance along with the influence of civil society have been marginalized by a government-inspired martial patriotism, suggests the legacy of successful civil resistance on a state's administrative practice and foreign policy is a limited one.[83]

Even in India, as C. Douglas Lummis notes, 'the greatest nonviolent force the world had ever known, the Indian National Congress, metamorphosed, with independence, into the builder of a "normal" violent state'.[84] There are many reasons for this limited long-term impact of civil resistance on the practices of states and societies, even where they have been successful in achieving specific political objectives in highly difficult circumstances.

This is partly to do with the nature of these objectives, which are often reformist, rather than transformational or revolutionary. Civil resistance groups often seek to establish, restore or protect the institutions of liberal democratic states, in the form of transparent and genuinely democratic election processes, for instance, or respect for fundamental human rights. In the case of the 'Rose Revolution' in Georgia and the 'Orange Revolution' in the Ukraine, for example, the civil resistance campaigns of 2003 (Georgia) and 2005 (Ukraine) could be seen as attempts to ensure that processes of democratic transition, already initiated some years previously, were completed so that the procedures and institutions of a liberal democratic state were observed and respected by competing political elites and political parties. As Jones points out, 'the Rose Revolution made no demands for major economic, social or systemic change'.[85]

> There was no ideological innovation . . . and no expectation of socio-economic transformation. Non-violence was a strategy, not an ideological goal . . . It sought to improve market democracy and return to liberalism's constitutional principles.[86]

The Rose Revolution was part of a much broader process of political change, beginning with the break-up of the Soviet Union and the end of Communist Party rule. The innovations it introduced were methodological, in the form of mass nonviolent mobilisation of parts of the population, rather than ideological or structural.

Even where civil resistance groups have been involved at the beginning of processes of profound and, perhaps, revolutionary change, such as East Germany and other Eastern bloc countries in 1989, their influence often diminishes rapidly once these changes have been achieved. This is because of the characteristics of social movements and civil society groups directly inspired by, and employing, the ideas and methods of nonviolent political action. Such groups are goal-orientated, finite and almost ephemeral by nature and, as such, are quite distinct from the durable and institutionalised structures of the state (and, to a lesser extent, from the political parties that compete or contend for government power, in order to control the state). As Maier points out, 'the movements generated in the course of civil protest may be ill suited for the routines of power sharing in a day-to-day modern democracy'.[87]

Public life, after all, is conducted by means of institutions. The interval in which some dissolve and others are created to take their place comes rarely and, as we can see in the case of earlier upheavals, is usually brief.[88]

Protestors and civil resistance groups may be able to help engineer a process of transition from one regime to another or even from one type of state to another, but the on-going demands of governance require a different type of political organisation and a different sort of commitment to formal, institionalised politics. As Maier concludes: 'Civil resistance is powerful and heartening but when it is successful it leaves those who organized it to carry on in the post-heroic world of party politics'.[89]

CONCLUSION

The recent history of nonviolent political action suggests that most of those who engage in civil resistance use these methods for pragmatic reasons, rather than out of any profound ethical commitment to the principles of nonviolence. Pragmatic nonviolence, epitomised by proponents such as Gene Sharp, is characterised by an over-riding concern with its effectiveness as a method of political action. Nonviolence as such has no intrinsic value, apart from this concern with its efficacy. Nonviolent action is seen primarily as a set of methods or techniques, which can be used to achieve a wide variety of political objectives or goals.

Proponents of principled nonviolence, such as Gandhi and King, on the other hand, may have a high historical profile, partly because of their charisma as individuals and as leaders, but they represent a minority of those who have used these methods. Nonviolence has intrinsic value or worth as a central objective of political action, in the form of King's beloved community, for example, and is not merely a means to other valued goals, such as democracy and human rights. Furthermore, there is an intimate connection between the use of the methods of nonviolent action and the achievement of a society or, even, a world community characterised by peaceful social and political relations.

Notes

1 Roberts, 'Introduction', p. 1.
2 King, 'Stride toward freedom', p. 482.
3 Ibid. p. 482.
4 Ibid. p. 483.
5 Schock, 'Nonviolent action and its misconceptions', p. 705. See, also, Schock, *Unarmed Insurrections: People Power Movements in Nondemocracies*, p. 6. Schock's book provides a thorough discussion and evaluation of conditions for effective uses of pragmatic nonviolent political action.
6 Garavan, *The Politics of Moral Force*, no page numbers.
7 For an initial discussion of basic characteristics of civil resistance, see Randle, *Civil Resistance*, pp. 9–10.
8 Randle, *Civil Resistance*.
9 Sharp, *Waging Nonviolent Struggle: 20th Century Practice and 21st Century Potential*, p. 20.
10 Gandhi, *Selected Writings of Mahatma Gandhi*, p. 69.
11 Ash, 'A century of civil resistance: Some lessons and questions', p. 367.
12 Ibid. p. 372.
13 Roberts, 'Introduction', p. 1.
14 Goldman, 'The 1989 demonstrations in Tiananmen Square and beyond: Echoes of Gandhi', pp. 258–9.
15 Gandhi, *Selected Writings of Mahatma Gandhi*, p. 276.
16 Tolstoy, 'A letter from Tolstoy to Gandhi', p. 62.
17 Tolstoy, 'Two wars', p. 20.
18 Tolstoy, 'A letter from Tolstoy to Gandhi', p. 62.
19 Gandhi, *Selected Writings of Mahatma Gandhi*, p. 69.
20 King, 'Nonviolence and racial justice', p. 8.
21 Ibid. p. 8.
22 Ibid. p. 8.
23 According to James Melvin Washington, 'King relied heavily on the systematic analysis of the Christian concept of "love" in the work of Anders Nygren, a noted Swedish theologian', in his book *Agape and Eros* (1953). See King 'An experiment in love', p. 16.
24 King, 'Nonviolence and racial justice', p. 8.
25 Ibid. p. 8.
26 Ibid. p. 8.
27 Tolstoy, 'A letter from Tolstoy to Gandhi', p. 62.
28 King, 'An experiment in love', pp. 16–17.
29 King, 'The power of nonviolence', p. 12.
30 King, 'Pilgrimage to nonviolence', p. 38.
31 Ibid. p. 38.

32 King, 'An experiment in love', p. 19.
33 Ibid. p. 20.
34 Ibid. p. 19.
35 Ibid. p. 19.
36 King, 'Nonviolence and racial justice', p. 8.
37 Ibid. p. 9.
38 King, 'An experiment in love', p. 17.
39 Gandhi, *Selected Writings of Mahatma Gandhi*, p. 133.
40 Gandhi, *Non-Violent Resistance (Satyagraha)*, p. 17.
41 Ibid. p. 17.
42 Ibid. p. 17.
43 Ibid. p. 17.
44 Kumarappa, 'Editor's note', p. iii.
45 Sharp, *Waging Nonviolent Struggle: 20th Century Practice and 21st Century Potential*, p. 416.
46 King, 'An experiment in love', p. 18.
47 Ibid. p. 18.
48 King, 'Love, law, and civil disobedience', p. 47.
49 Ibid. p. 47.
50 For a useful passage where Gandhi contrasts *satyagraha* with passive resistance and provides brief definitions of both terms, see Gandhi, *Non-Violent Resistance (Satyagraha)*, p. 3.
51 Gandhi, *Non-Violent Resistance (Satyagraha)*, p. 3.
52 Kumarappa, 'Editor's note', p. iv.
53 Ibid. p. iv.
54 Gandhi, *Non-Violent Resistance (Satyagraha)*, p. 3.
55 Kumarappa, 'Editor's note', p. iii.
56 Ibid. p. iii.
57 Gandhi, *Non-Violent Resistance (Satyagraha)*, p. 3.
58 Ibid. p. 56.
59 Sharp, *Waging Nonviolent Struggle: 20th Century Practice and 21st Century Potential*, p. 510.
60 Gandhi, *Non-Violent Resistance (Satyagraha)*, p. 176.
61 Kumarappa, 'Editor's note', p. v.
62 Gandhi, *Selected Writings of Mahatma Gandhi*, p. 67.
63 Ibid. p. 68.
64 Ibid. p. 71.
65 Ibid. p. 70.
66 Sharp, *Waging Nonviolent Struggle: 20th Century Practice and 21st Century Potential*, pp. 19–20.
67 Ibid. p. 20.
68 Ibid. pp. 20–1.

69 Ibid. p. 20.

70 Ibid. pp. 20–1.

71 Goldman, 'The 1989 demonstrations in Tiananmen Square and beyond: Echoes of Gandhi', p. 248.

72 Roberts, 'Introduction', p. 3.

73 Goldman, 'The 1989 demonstrations in Tiananmen Square and beyond: Echoes of Gandhi', p. 255.

74 Sharp, *Social Power and Political Freedom*, p. 257.

75 Ibid. p. 374.

76 Ibid. p. 374.

77 Roberts, 'Introduction', p. 8.

78 Ibid. p. 8.

79 Ibid. pp. 8–9.

80 Maier, 'Civil resistance and civil society: Lessons from the collapse of the German Democratic Republic in 1989', p. 272.

81 Nenadić and Belčević, 'Serbia – Nonviolent struggle for democracy: The role of Otpor', p. 34.

82 Jones, 'Georgia's "Rose Revolution" of 2003: Enforcing peaceful change', p. 333.

83 Ibid. p. 333.

84 Lummis, 'The smallest army imaginable', p. 326.

85 Jones, 'Georgia's "Rose Revolution" of 2003: Enforcing peaceful change', p. 318.

86 Ibid. p. 318.

87 Maier, 'Civil resistance and civil society: Lessons from the collapse of the German Democratic Republic in 1989', p. 273.

88 Ibid. p. 273.

89 Ibid. p. 276.

Chapter 2

POLITICAL THEORY, VIOLENCE
AND THE STATE

INTRODUCTION

The relationship between violence and social order is a central concern of Western political theory, epitomised by the social contract theorists of the seventeenth and eighteenth centuries – Thomas Hobbes, John Locke and Jean-Jacques Rousseau. Ideas, concepts and theories furnished by these political philosophers continue to dominate Western political discourse, concerning the role of the state and the importance of the rule of law for containing and minimising political violence within, and between, societies. Any discussion of the place of nonviolence, civil resistance and nonviolent political action in Western political theory must occur in the context of justifications of state sovereignty, and the state's monopoly over the legitimate use of violence, provided by the social contract theorists.

HOBBES AND LOCKE AS PHILOSOPHERS OF PEACE

An explicit and central normative concern of the political theories of these three social contract theorists is the achievement of peace, by which they mean minimising, containing or circumscribing violence as a feature of human interaction. This does not mean that Hobbes, Locke and Rousseau can be considered unequivocal proponents of nonviolence, since the price of peace involves the legitimisation of some violence, domestically – in terms of law enforcement – and internationally – in terms of the use of armed force for self-defence.

Hobbes begins his argument in favour of peace in the state of nature, which is also, famously, for Hobbes, a state or condition of war:

during the time men live without a common Power to keep them all in awe, they are in that condition which is called Warre; and such a warre, as is of every man, against every man . . . In such condition, there is . . . worst of all, continuall feare, and danger of violent death; And the life of man, solitary, poore, nasty, brutish and short . . . And thus much for the ill condition, which man by meer Nature is actually placed in . . .[1]

Nonetheless, Hobbes states that 'Reason suggesteth convenient Articles of Peace' that can pull human beings out of this state of nature or condition of war (of all, against all) for basic survival: 'These articles, are they, which otherwise are called the Lawes of Nature . . .'[2]

Hobbes begins his elaboration of these 'laws of nature' with a fundamental 'right of nature', which forms the basis for his political philosophy and is also derived from his theory of human nature, as developed in *Leviathan*:

The Right of Nature, which Writers commonly call *Jus Naturale*, is the Liberty each man hath, to use his own power, as he will himselfe, for the preservation of his own Nature; that is to say of his own life; and consequently, of doing any thing, which in his own Judgement, and Reason, hee shall conceive to be the aptest means thereunto.[3]

The fundamental right of every human being, in other words, is the right of self-preservation, by any means necessary. From this fundamental right, Hobbes derives his 'first, and Fundamentall Law of Nature; which is, *to seek peace and follow it*'.[4] In other words, the best way to achieve self-preservation is through peace or an absence of violence between human beings. This first and fundamental law of nature is the 'first branch' of 'a precept, or generall rule of Reason, *That every man, ought to endeavour Peace, as farre as he has hope of obtaining it; and when he cannot obtain it, that he may seek, and use, all helps and advantages of Warre*'.[5] It is not within our power to forfeit this fundamental right, which is why we must revert to war and the state of nature when we fail to obtain peace. Both peace and war are derived from the right of nature, aimed at self-preservation, but war becomes necessary only when we fail to obtain peace. The primary requirement (and first and fundamental law of nature) is 'to seek peace, and follow it', in order to achieve self-preservation. Peace leads us out of the state of nature into what social contract theorists call civil society, whereas, for Hobbes, war is synonymous with the state of nature, in which we retain our fundamental right to use all means necessary for self-preservation.

In order to obtain peace, as our primary obligation and require-ment for self-preservation, however, human beings must reciprocally renounce their right to use every means available, including violence, for self-defence. This reciprocal arrangement, for the achievement of peace, forms the basis of the social contract and civil society:

> From this Fundamentall Law of Nature, by which men are com-mended to endeavour Peace, is derived this second Law; *That a man be willing, when others are so too, as farre-forth, as for Peace, and defence of himselfe he shall think it necessary, to lay down this right to all things; and be contented with so much liberty against other men, as he would allow other men against himselfe.* For as long as every man holdeth this Right, of doing any thing he liketh; so long are all men in the condition of Warre.[6]

Hobbes stresses that this renunciation must be mutual for it to be effective in achieving its objective of peace and, also, for it to become binding: 'But if other men will not lay down their right, as well as he; then there is no Reason for any one to devest himselfe of his: For that were to expose himselfe to Prey, (which no man is bound to) rather than to dispose himselfe to Peace'.[7] Such a unilateral renunciation of the right to self-defence would also violate the fundamental right of nature, which is to use all means necessary (or the best means neces-sary) to achieve self-preservation.

Thus, peace, understood as the absence of violence between human beings, has instrumental value, because it is the primary means for ful-filling our fundamental 'right of nature' – the right of self-preservation or survival. The first and fundamental law of nature is that we must seek peace and follow it, in order to fulfill this right. The second law of nature is that we must renounce, equally and reciprocally, our use of all means necessary (including violence) for self-defence, in order to obtain peace. It is only if we fail to achieve peace that we revert to a state of nature and retain the use of all means necessary (including violence) in our attempts to defend or preserve ourselves.

John Locke also invokes characteristics of the state of nature to support peace as a law of nature for human beings: 'The State of Nature has a Law of Nature to govern it, which obliges every one: and Reason, which is that Law, teaches all mankind, who will but consult it, that being all equal and independent, no one ought to harm another in his Life, Health, Liberty, or Possessions'.[8] If all are equal in the state of nature, then it follows (according to reason): 'Every one as he is *bound to preserve himself* . . . ought he, as much as he can, *to preserve the rest of Mankind*'.[9] If we owe an obligation of self-preservation to ourselves, we also owe it to all other human beings: 'being furnished with like Faculties, sharing all in one Community of Nature, there cannot be supposed any such *Subordination* among us, that may Authorize us to destroy one another'.[10] It is 'the Law of Nature', or reason applied to the characteristics of human beings in the state of nature, 'which willeth the Peace and *Preservation of all Mankind*'.[11] Alexander Moseley refers to 'Locke's pacifism', because he indicates 'the rational, peaceful order that is morally and naturally man's by right'.[12]

Unlike Hobbes, however, Locke does differentiate between war, which necessarily involves the use of violence, and the state of nature, which does not. Those living in a state of nature may lack an agreed or common sovereign, but while this creates the conditions for war, it is not synonymous with war. Wars can occur whether or not human beings are in a state of nature, according to Locke:

> *And here we have the plain difference between the State of Nature, and the State of War* . . . Men living together according to reason, without a common Superior on Earth, with Authority to judge between them, is *properly the State of Nature* . . . *Want of a common Judge with Authority, puts all Men in a State of Nature: Force without Right, upon a Man's Person, makes a State of War.*[13]

The defining characteristic of the state of nature is the lack of a common authority or sovereign, while the defining characteristic of war is aggression or the unlawful use of force or violence.

Nonetheless, the state of nature does not provide the mechanisms necessary to end wars once they have begun, precisely because it lacks a common authority or agreed set of laws to which those in conflict can appeal. According to Locke, 'in the State of Nature, for want of positive Laws, and Judges with Authority to appeal to, *the State of War once begun, continues*, with a right to the innocent Party, to destroy the other whenever he can, until the aggressor offers Peace'.[14] In other words, without a common authority or judge to which they can appeal, those who are engaged in war can only persist until they agree to end it or one side or the other is defeated.

Even so, war is not unique to the state of nature. It can also occur where lawful authority has been usurped for self-interested reasons:

> nay where an appeal to the Law, and constituted Judges lies open, but the remedy is deny'd by a manifest perverting of Justice, and a barefaced wresting of the Laws, to protect or indemnifie the violence or injuries of some Men, or Party of Men, *there* it *is* hard to imagine any thing (sic) but *a State of War*. For wherever violence is used, and injury done, though by hands appointed to administer Justice, it is still violence and injury, however colour'd with the Name, Pretences, or Forms of Law, the end whereof being to protect and redress the innocent, by an unbiassed application of it, to all who are under it; wherever that is not *bona fide* done, *War is made* upon the Sufferers . . .[15]

The mechanisms and coercive powers of the state must be applied in an unbiased and disinterested fashion, according to principles of equity and justice. Otherwise, those employing state power engage in aggression and war, promoting self-interest, rather than equal treatment, despite the veneer or appearance of the rule of law.

Thus, as Peter Laslett points out, for Locke: 'War, in fact, is not a state but an incident'[16] or a specific occurrence of violence between individuals or communities acting outside of the rule of law. In other words, war is not a perpetual or uniform condition of human beings living in the state of nature, as it is for Hobbes. Instead, it consists of specific incidents that can occur in the state of nature, but also in civil society:

> It is to be expected that war should be much closer to the surface in a state of nature, as witness the frequency and importance of war in the international state of nature, but this cannot mean that war describes the state of nature, or that it is otherwise relevant to the distinction between the state of nature and the state of society.[17]

War – understood as the unlawful or unregulated use of violence – is not synonymous with the state of nature, even if it can be expected to be a common occurrence there, because of the lack of a common authority and shared, agreed laws.

The propensity and, perhaps, inevitability of the state of nature to result in unending war provides the incentive for human beings to leave it, according to Locke, despite its apparent benefits of liberty and natural equality, for political society: 'To avoid this State of War (wherein . . . every the least difference is apt to end, where there is no Authority to decide between the Contenders) is *one great reason of Mens* (sic) *putting themselves into Society*, and quitting the State of Nature'.[18]

MORAL AUTONOMY AND POLITICAL SOCIETY

There is a tension between freedom and security and the need for social order in the social contract theorists and in Locke and Rousseau, in particular. This is reflected, to some extent, in their attitude towards the state and its control over violence. Laslett, for example, claims that with Locke:

> there were in his attitude recognizable anarchist elements, a disposition found in all individualists to regard state, society and government as unnecessary, or accidental, or just unfortunate. It is to be seen in his aside declaring that it was only corruption, viciousness, degeneracy in some men which made it necessary for humanity to set up communities 'separate from this great and natural Community' of all mankind.[19]

This is based on Locke's view of the state of nature as a state of equality and freedom, rather than a condition of war and insecurity. Moseley also refers to 'Locke's characterisation of the state of nature' as 'a state of perfect freedom and equality, which is a generally benevolent condition of peaceful individualism . . . in which conscience guides actions . . .'[20]

Laslett is referring to Locke's view that, in the state of nature, all human beings share the fundamental '*Law of Nature*' – self-preservation – which they apply equally to themselves and all others and 'by which Law common to them all, he and all the rest of *Mankind are one Community*'.[21]

> And were it not for the corruption, and vitiousness (sic) of degenerate Men, there would be no need of any other; no necessity that

Men should separate from this great and natural Community, and by positive agreements combine into smaller and divided associations.[22]

Separate states, communities or commonwealths are modifications of an original, single, moral community, required only because of the propensity of individual human beings for moral corruption that prevents them from living cooperatively.

Hobbes makes a similar point about the instrumental value of the state or commonwealth. If human beings were able to behave virtuously, in accordance with the laws of nature, and maintain justice and achieve peace without enforcement, then there would be no need for them to covenant or agree to live under separate states or governments:

if we could suppose a great Multitude of men to consent in the observation of Justice, and other Lawes of Nature, without a common Power to keep them all in awe; we might as well suppose all Man-kind to do the same; and then there neither would be, nor need to be any Civill Government, or Common-wealth at all; because there would be Peace without subjection.[23]

Hobbes' point, of course, is that the state or commonwealth, backed up by sufficient coercive power or violence to enforce the rule of law, is needed to protect the covenant or social contract that provides the only secure basis of social peace: 'Covenants, without the Sword, are but Words, and of no strength to secure a man at all'.[24] The only alternative to the state or commonwealth is not unforced or uncoerced social harmony and cooperation, but a state of nature, in which 'every man will and may lawfully rely on his own strength and art, for caution against all other men'.[25]

Rousseau agrees that while there may be:

a universal justice which springs from reason alone . . . the laws of natural justice, lacking any natural sanction, are unavailing among men. In fact, such laws merely benefit the wicked and injure the just, since the just respect them while others do not do so in return. So there must be covenants and positive laws . . .

These convenants and positive laws can be enforced by the state, and we cannot rely on any natural justice that might exist outside of, or prior to, political society.[26]

This raises the question as to whether the political obligations established by the social contract, especially in terms of obedience to the sovereign state, are genuinely moral or merely prudential, based on a long-term consideration of individual self-interest.[27] Moseley claims, for example, that, for Locke, the 'move to a political society is . . . prudential rather than necessary', based on a calculation that the inconveniences of the state of nature outweigh its benefits in terms of natural liberty so that 'the advantages of "perfect freedom and equality" are offset by the worries of aggression'.[28] Moseley refers to three inconveniences, in particular:

> a lack of knowledge of or agreement concerning laws; the absence of executive powers and the subsequent vulnerability of small groups; and agents judging their own cases with little regard to impartiality . . . for Locke, the state is a tool that provides useful services that are allegedly absent in the state of nature.[29]

This is different from Hobbes' view that equates the state of nature with a state of war, so that self-preservation and the 'Law of Nature' compel human beings to join together into political society and the commonwealth.[30] For both Hobbes and Locke, however, the moral status of the political obligations resulting from the social contract can be queried, since the social contract results from decisions based on either necessity and self-preservation (Hobbes) or calculations of self-interest or 'convenience' (Locke), rather than the disinterested application of universal moral principles as such.

A characteristic of law that distinguishes it from arbitrary action is its impartiality and generality, so that the laws themselves (as distinct from specific legal decisions) formulate general principles to be applied uniformly in all simlar cases. According to Rousseau, for example, 'the law considers all subjects collectively and all actions in the abstract; it does not consider any individual man or any specific action'.[31] This is because the law is the expression of what Rousseau famously refers to as the 'general will' or the collective or shared interest of all citizens as members of the state or commonwealth as a collective, shared political entity (see below).[32]

Rousseau seems to imply that the rule of law and political society provide the conditions under which morality can operate, because moral obligations (like law) depend on general (or universal) principles that can be applied to individual cases. Where only individual cases or relationships between individual human beings exist, as in the state of nature, there can be no general obligations characteristic of the rule of law: 'In the state of nature . . . I owe nothing to those to whom I have promised nothing, and I recognize as belonging to others only those things that are of no use to me'.[33] As he says elsewhere in *The Social Contract*:

> The passing from the state of nature to the civil society produces a remarkable change in man; it puts justice as a rule of conduct on the place of instinct, and gives his actions the moral quality they previously lacked . . . We might also add that man acquires with civil society, moral freedom . . . for to be governed by appetite alone is slavery, while obedience to a law one prescribes to oneself is freedom.[34]

Appetite or instinct are characteristic of the state of nature and can only react to situations individually or on a case-by-case basis. Morality and law, on the other hand, allow deliberate choice, through the application of agreed general rules or principles. Freedom is achieved through obeying mutually agreed laws, not through the individual pursuit of autonomous goals or objectives.

STATE SOVEREIGNTY, CONSENT AND CIVIL LIBERTY

The social contract or covenant that forms the basis of the state depends upon a real unity of all its members into a single body or political entity, according to Hobbes:

> The only way to erect such a Common Power . . . is, to conferre all their power and strength upon one Man, or upon one Assembly of men, that may reduce all their Wills, by plurality of voices, unto one Will . . . This is more than Consent, or Concord; it is a reall Unitie of them all, in one and the same Person, made by Covenant of every man with every man . . . This done, the Multitude so united in one Person, is called a COMMON-WEALTH, in latine CIVITAS.[35]

All those who are members of this commonwealth equally agree to give up their right of self-preservation to the state, which now governs them, in order to achieve 'Peace at home' and to provide 'mutual ayd against their enemies abroad'.[36] This unity and authority of the state is the basis of its sovereignty (and also its power).[37] As Macpherson says: 'The person or body of persons to whom these rights were transferred would be the sovereign'.[38] Those who remain outside the covenant, and thus the sovereignty and authority of the state, remain in the state of nature 'or the condition of warre he was in before; wherein he might without injustice be destroyed by any man whatsoever'.[39]

State sovereignty is absolute, because it is derived from the transfer of the fundamental right of nature – to self-protection – of each individual to the state or commonwealth, and 'when a man hath . . . granted away his Right; then is he said to be OBLIGED, or BOUND, not to hinder those, to whom such Right is granted'.[40] Individual freedom or liberty, interpreted as a lack of constraint on action, remains only where the state has not legislated to govern an activity: 'In cases where the Soveraign (sic) has prescribed no rule, there the Subject hath the liberty to do, or forbeare, according to his own discretion'.[41] Furthermore, according to Macpherson: 'it would have to be left to the sovereign to decide how much of men's powers the sovereign would need to have, for otherwise the sovereign could not be sure of enough power to enforce the contract and maintain peace'.[42]

We need to distinguish, however, between the sovereignty of the state or commonwealth and absolute obedience to the sovereign or government. In other words, we can recognise the authority of the state as the sole source of law (or equally binding rules) for all its citizens or subjects, on the basis of the social contract, but distinguish this from obedience to a specific government or regime controlling the state. As Locke points out, it is worse to obey an unjust, oppressive and tyrannical regime, than to be in the state of nature, because at least in the state of nature, we retain the right of self-protection:

> . . . *Absolute Monarchs* are but Men, and if Government is to be the Remedy of those Evils, which necessarily follow from mens being Judges in their own Cases, and the State of Nature is therefore not to be endured, I desire to know what kind of Government that is, and how much better it is than the State of Nature, where one Man commanding a multitude, has the Liberty to be Judge in

his own Case, and may do to all his Subjects whatever he pleases
. . . Much better it is in the State of Nature wherein men are not
bound to submit to the unjust will of another . . .[43]

Such regimes do not eliminate the arbitrary nature of power that
obtains in the state of nature, since they are, instead, subject to the
arbitrary judgements of those in control of an unrepresentative government, who have exempted themselves from the social contract and
who rule by decree, rather than by law.

Rousseau points out – in common with the other social contract
theorists – that the social contract alone requires the consent of all:

There is only one law which by its nature requires unanimous
assent. This is the social pact . . . every man having been born free
and master of himself, no one else may under any pretext whatever subject him without his consent.[44]

Having agreed to establish the state by means of the social contract,
however, every citizen agrees to all the laws made in accordance with
the legitimate decision-making procedures of that state: 'After the state
is instituted, residence implies consent: to inhabit the territory is to
submit to the sovereign'.[45]

Locke expands upon and, perhaps, clarifies this point, with his distinction between express and tacit consent:

it is to be considered, what shall be understood to be *a sufficient
Declaration of a* Mans *Consent, to make him subject* to the Laws of
any Government. There is a common distinction of an express and
a tacit consent . . . The difficulty is, what ought to be look'd upon
as a *tacit Consent*, and how far it binds . . . every man, that hath
any Possession, or Enjoyment, of any part of the Dominions of
any Government, doth thereby give *his tacit consent*, and is as far
forth obliged to Obedience to the Laws of that Government . . .
in Effect, it reaches as far as the very being of any one within the
Territories of that Government . . .[46]

This is an important point, because it illuminates the nature of agreement constituting the social contract. The social contract does not
require an explicit agreement between every individual citizen of a

state to subject themselves equally to the laws of that state. Those who benefit from the security and stability provided from living within the boundaries of a state have tacitly agreed to a social contract, with others doing the same.

In other words, each individual agrees to obey all the laws of the state of which they are a citizen, whether or not they agree with every single law or piece of legislation. They have consented to the institution of the state and its decision-making procedures and, therefore, they also consent to the outcomes of those procedures: 'The citizen consents to all the laws', according to Rousseau, 'even to those that are passed against his will, and even to those which punish him when he dares to break any one of them'.[47]

It is important, for Locke, that the law expresses 'the consent of the Society' or commonwealth, because this distinguishes it from the arbitrary exercise of power, for example, or 'any Edict of any Body', which do not have 'the force and obligation of a Law'.[48] The law expresses 'the consent of the Society' or commonwealth, because it comes from the legislative power of the state, which is established on the basis of such consent, through the social contract.

Locke carefully distinguishes between what he calls 'the *Natural Liberty* of Man' in the state of nature, where human beings 'have only the Law of Nature for his Rule', and '*the Liberty of Man, in Society*',[49] which can be reconciled with state sovereignty and the laws of civil or representative government. 'The *Liberty of Man, in Society*, is to be under no other Legislative Power, but that established, by consent, in the Common-wealth',[50] so that:

> *Freedom of Men under Government*, is, to have a standing Rule to live by, common to every one of that Society, and made by the Legislative Power erected in it; A Liberty to follow my own Will in all things, where the Rule prescribes not; and not to be subject to the inconstant, uncertain, unknown, Arbitrary Will of another Man.[51]

Thus, the 'liberty of man in society', for Locke, is synonymous with equality before the law in the sovereign state and not with absolute freedom from all external constraints.

This concurs with Rousseau's brilliant analysis of the way in which the social contract combines freedom with security for every individual who is a part of it, through transforming natural liberty into civil liberty. Rousseau refers to the difficulty with reconciling freedom (and equality) with security:

> This difficulty . . . may be expressed in these words: 'How to find a form of association which will defend the person and goods of each member with the collective force of all, and under which each individual, while uniting himself with the others, obeys no one but himself, and remains as free as before'. This is the fundamental problem to which the social contract holds the solution.[52]

The social contract allows and requires each individual to preserve and secure themselves equally, by means of an institution – the state – to which they have each consented from their original position of natural liberty in the state of nature.

This does not involve a loss of liberty, because all are equally a part of the social contract:

> since each man gives himself to all, he gives himself to no one; and since there is no associate over whom he does not gain the same rights as others gain over him, each man recovers the equivalent of everything he loses, and in the bargain he acquires more power to preserve what he has.[53]

This creates an indivisible political community, of which all are equally members and to which all are equally subject. This entails no loss of liberty, because all citizens participate equally in its decision-making and, especially, its legislative (or law-making) functions. 'In its passive role', this collective political entity 'is called the *state*, when it plays an active role it is the *sovereign*; and when it is compared to others of its own kind, it is a *power*'.[54]

This argument in favour of the social contract and the state depends on Rousseau's crucial distinction between natural and civil liberty and also on his concept of the general will:

> And although in civil society man surrenders some of the advantages that belong to the state of nature, he gains in return far greater ones . . . What man loses by the social contract is his natural liberty and the absolute right to anything that tempts him

and that he can take; what he gains by the social contract is civil liberty and the legal right of property in what he possesses . . . we must clearly distinguish between *natural* liberty, which has no limit but the physical power of the individual concerned, and *civil* liberty, which is limited by the general will; and we must distinguish also between *possession*, which is based only on force or 'the right of the first occupant', and *property*, which must rest on a legal title.[55]

By 'general will', Rousseau means the capacity of the state, as a collective political entity, to make decisions and pass laws for the benefit of all its citizens, taken as an indivisible whole and not merely as an amalgamation of individual interests: 'There is often a great difference between the will of all [what all individuals want] and the general will; the general will studies only the common interest while the will of all studies private interest'.[56]

The social contract creates the conditions for civil liberty, according to which citizens are free to make the laws they must obey. This corresponds to Rousseau's distinction between the people in their capacity as citizens and as subjects: 'Those who are associated in it [the social contract] take collectively the name of a *people*, and call themselves individually *citizens*, in so far as they share in the sovereign power, and *subjects*, in so far as they put themselves under the laws of the state'.[57] Or, as Maurice Cranston says, '. . . laws . . . are rules made by a people in its capacity of sovereign (sic) and obeyed by the same people in its capacity as subject'.[58] This is what Rousseau means by his famous comment: 'that whoever refuses to obey the general will shall be constrained to do so by the whole body, which means nothing other than that he shall be forced to be free'.[59] In other words, those citizens who break the law can be punished and coerced into obeying it, because they have freely agreed to the laws of the state as participants in the social contract. The laws are the outcomes of the exercise of the people's freedom, and, therefore, they can be 'forced to be free', through obedience to these laws.

POPULAR SOVEREIGNTY, STATE AUTHORITY AND POLITICAL POWER

The conditional, or instrumental, value of the state is demonstrated by Hobbes' attitude toward the limits of state authority:

> The Obligation of Subjects to the Soveraign, is understood to last as long, and no longer, than the power lasteth, by which he is able to protect them. For the right men have by Nature to protect themselves, when none else can protect them, can by no Covenant be relinquished . . . The end of Obedience is Protection . . .[60]

The obligation of subjects or citizens to obey the state and the sovereign, as the representative of the state, is contingent upon state capacity (or willingness) to protect or provide security for them. Law, as the result of the legislative power of the sovereign or government (representing the state or commonwealth), has similar instrumental value: 'And Law was brought into the world for nothing else, but to limit the naturall liberty of particular men, in such manner, as they might not hurt, but assist one another, and joyn together against a common Enemy'.[61]

Locke, in particular, points to the limits to the sovereignty or authority of the state. Authority is an explicitly normative concept and, in this sense, can be distinguished from power. Hobbes, for example, says that '. . . by Authority, is always understood a Right of doing any act: and *done by Authority*, done by Commission, or Licence from him whose right it is'.[62] Thus, Locke writes that the authority, or right to command, of the state is limited by the Law of Nature that governs all individuals in the state of nature. This Law of Nature concerns the fundamental right of every individual to self-preservation or survival. This right of self-preservation is all that can be delegated to the state by means of the social contract and forms the basis of its authority or legimate action, so that no state has the right to absolute or arbitrary power. According to Locke:

> . . . having in the State of Nature no Arbitrary Power . . . but only so much as the Law of Nature gave him for the preservation of himself, and the rest of Mankind; this is all he doth, or can give up to the Common-wealth, and by it to the *Legislative Power* . . . It is a Power, that hath no other end but preservation, and therefore can never have a right to destroy, enslave, or designedly to impoverish the Subjects . . . Thus the Law of Nature stands as an Eternal Rule to all men, *Legislators* as well as others.[63]

Thus, the state may be the supreme power in the political community, under the terms of the social contract, but this does not give it absolute or arbitrary power 'over the Lives and Fortunes of the People'.[64] It can only acquire as much authority as the people themselves had in the state of nature, because this is the ultimate source of its sovereignty and authority and this concerns the right to do whatever is necessary for their preservation and no more. As Locke says, 'it can be no more than those persons had in a State of Nature before they enter'd into Society, and gave up to the Community. For no Body (sic) can transfer to another more power than he has in himself'.[65]

The normative source of the authority of the state is the free consent or agreement of individuals exercising their liberty in the state of nature: 'Locke's political vision is thus of a minimal state whose justi-fication can only be that of consent, which must not possess arbitrary, absolute powers over the lives and property of the civilians'.[66] This is because 'man . . . owns himself. He is thus beholden to no one except by consent'.[67]

In political society, freedom 'can be negatively defined, therefore, as being under no other legislative power but that established by consent in the commonwealth, and positively as the progressive elimination of the arbitrary from political and social regulation'.[68] As Locke points out, freedom does not really exist in the state of nature, despite the appear-ance that we can do what we wish without constraint: 'For who could be free when every other Man's Humour might domineer over him?'[69] Freedom exists, instead, under the conditions of political society, where we can act in accordance with, and under, the protection of those laws to which we have consented, by means of the legislative branch of the state, freed from the arbitrary actions of others, by the protection of those same laws. Freedom is 'a *Liberty* to dispose, and order, as he lists, his Person, Actions, Possessions, and his whole Property, within the Allowance of those Laws under which he is; and therein not to be subject to the arbitrary Will of another, but freely follow his own'.[70] Similarly, for Rousseau, as Cranston points out, in political society, a free people obeys the laws, but not men: 'it has magistrates, but not masters'.[71] Liberty requires equity or justice, in the form of equal-ity before the law, so that all citizens are equally free of the arbitrary behaviour of others. As Cranston says, 'dependence on the state guar-antees men against all dependence on men'.[72]

Similarly, for Rousseau, the state can only acquire its authority in a normative sense, through the free agreement of human beings, by means of the social contract: 'Since no man has any natural authority over his fellows, and since force alone bestows no right, all legitimate authority among men must be based on covenants'.[73]

Under the terms of the social contract, the state has instrumental value, aimed at the preservation of the people, and when the state does not fulfill this function, the people retain the right to alter it or at least change those who control the legislative power of the state. According to Locke:

> there remains still *in the People a Supream Power* to remove or *alter the Legislative*, when they find the *Legislative* act contrary to the trust reposed in them. For all *Power given with trust* for the attaining an *end* . . . whenever that *end* is manifestly neglected, or opposed, the *trust* must necessarily be *forfeited*, and the Power devolve into the hands of those that gave it, who may place it anew where they shall think best for their safety and security. And thus the *Community* perpetually *retains a Supream Power* of saving themselves from the attempts and designs of any Body, even of their Legislators . . .[74]

Authority and sovereignty are derived from the Law of Nature, or the right of the people to ensure their survival, and they can exercise their 'supreme power' to change the government or even the form of government if the state fails to fulfill its central function of providing them with safety and security.

The authority of the state does not exceed this power of preservation, and the authority of a government (or the executive branch of the state) does not exceed the laws enacted by the legislative component of the state. Any government that transgresses the law can also be opposed by the people, because it has violated the limits of its authority: 'whosoever in Authority exceeds the Power given him by the Law, and makes use of the Force he has under his Command, to compass that upon the Subject, which the Law allows not . . . acting wtihout (sic) Authority, may be opposed'.[75] The authority of a government is circumscribed by the laws of the state, as decided upon by its legislative component, and the state derives its authority (including its right to enact and enforce laws) from its capacity to ensure the safety and survival of its citizens.

Locke states that the supreme or ultimate right of the people to resist and change a government that exceeds its authority is '*the best fence against Rebellion* . . . Rebellion being an Opposition, not to Persons, but

Authority'.[76] In other words, the people are protecting the integrity of the state and the rule of law, through resisting those who have transgressed their legitimate authority. As Locke says, '. . . exceeding the Bounds of Authority is no more a right in a great, than a petty Officer; no more justifiable in a King, than a Constable'.[77] Anyone who challenges the authority of a legitimate state undermines political society and places themselves in a state of war against the people:

> For when Men by entering into Society and Civil Government, have excluded force, and introduced Laws for the preservation of Property, Peace, and Unity amongst themselves; those who set up force again in opposition to the Laws, do *Rebellare*, that is, bring back again the state of War, and are properly Rebels . . .[78]

This includes legislators or those in government who abuse their authority, as much as 'those, who by force take away the Legislative'.[79] This is because: 'Whosoever uses *force without Right*, as every one does in Society, who does it without Law, puts himself into a *state of War* with those, against whom he so uses it'.[80]

Locke makes it clear that this right of rebellion extends to resistance against a conquering power, because it imposes itself by force and without the consent of the occupied state. There are specific limits to the right of conquest, even if the conquering power had a just cause, such as self-defence or responding to aggression.[81] In the case of occupation by an outside power with a just cause, those who did not participate in the aggressive war retain the right to form their own government to replace the one that has been overthrown: 'Over those . . . of the subdued Countrey that opposed him not, and the Posterity even of those that did, the Conqueror, even in a just War, hath, *by* his *Conquest, no right of Dominion* . . . and if their former Government be dissolved, they are at liberty to begin and erect another to themselves'.[82]

There is an important difference between the normative dimension of authority and its empirical or power dimension, exemplified by the capacity of those with authority to exercise it. This empirical or practical dimension of authority is especially important for nonviolent political action or civil resistance. The normative and empirical dimensions of authority are interdependent or intertwined, however, so that the capacity of the state, for example, to exercise its power, depends ultimately on the people's acceptance of its authority or its right to govern.

As Cranston writes, 'authority is a form of potency which rests on the credence and acceptance of those who respect it'.[83] And, according to Rousseau:

> The strongest man is never strong enough to be master all the time, unless he transforms force into right and obedience into duty . . . 'Obey those in power'. If this means 'yield to force' the precept is sound, but superfluous . . . might does not make right, and . . . the duty of obedience is owed only to legitimate powers.[84]

The power of the state and its capacity to rule can be ensured only if those it governs accept its authority in a normative sense. The use of force or violence to achieve control over a people, and the exercise of authority or governance over that people, are two quite different functions: 'There will always be a great difference between subduing a multitude and ruling a society'.[85]

Power, or the capacity to rule or govern, depends ultimately upon the authority of a state or government, which, in turn, is derived from the consent of those who are governed. Power is the result of people coming together, on the basis of consent, to achieve a common purpose. As Laslett says, 'when men come together politically they create power, which is available to them in institutional form for the purposes of their association, and which will find its first and highest expression in the making of law'.[86] Political society, or the state, is the highest expression of this power, because it creates the conditions under which human beings can achieve all their other objectives, whether individually or collectively, by means of the rule of law.

THE STATE, VIOLENCE AND WAR

Hobbes famously equates the state of nature, outside the commonwealth achieved by means of the social contract, with a state of war. War, for Hobbes, includes any use of violence ungoverned by the rule of law to achieve one's objectives, at both the personal or individual and political or collective levels:

> Whatsoever therefore is consequent to a time of Warre, where every man is Enemy to every man; the same is consequent to the time, wherein men live without other security, than what

their own strength, and their own invention shall furnish them withall.[87]

Furthermore, 'WARRE, consisteth not in Battell onely, or the act of fighting; but in a tract of time, wherein the Will to contend by Battell is sufficiently known . . . So the nature of War, consisteth not in actual fighting; but in the known disposition thereto, during all the time there is no assurance to the contrary. All other time is PEACE'.[88] Thus, war for Hobbes consists not only of fighting, but in the constant disposition or readiness to fight for self-preservation, characteristic of, and required by, the state of nature. Peace obtains only when this disposition can be set aside, and this can be achieved only in the context of a commonwealth and the rule of law.

According to Hobbes, the state of nature pertains in international relations, because states or commonwealths are not subject to a higher sovereign and, thus, cannot be subject to the rule of law:

> For as amongst masterlesse men, there is perpetuall war, of every man against his neighbour . . . So in States, and Common-wealths not dependent on one another, every Common-wealth, (not every man) has an absolute Libertie, to doe what it shall judge . . . most conducing to their benefit. But withall, they live in the condition of a perpetuall war . . . Whether a Common-wealth be Monarchicall, or Popular, the Freedome is still the same.[89]

Just as individual human beings would be, each state or common-wealth is in a state of perpetual war, because international relations are the equivalent of a state of nature.

Furthermore, individuals who are not citizens of a particular state, or who are rebel subjects, can be treated as enemies by that common-wealth or state, because they are either not part of the social contract that created that commonwealth or have removed themselves from it:

> But the Infliction of what evill soever, on an Innocent man, that is not a Subject, if it be for the benefit of the Common-wealth, and without violation of any former Covenant, is no breach of the Law of Nature. For all men that are not Subjects, are either Enemies, or else they have ceased from being so, by some precedent covenants. But against Enemies, whom the Common-wealth judgeth capable

to do them hurt, it is lawfull by the originall Right of Nature to make warre; wherein the Sword Judgeth not . . . than as it conduceth to the good of his own People. And upon this ground it is, that also in subjects, who deliberatly (sic) deny the Authority of the Common-wealth established, the vengeance is lawfully extended . . . because the nature of this offence, consisteth in the renouncing of subjection; which is a relapse into the condition of warre, commonly called Rebellion; and they that so offend, suffer not as Subjects, but as Enemies. For *Rebellion*, is but warre renewed.[90]

In other words, each sovereign state treats not only other states or commonwealths as its enemy in war, but also each individual subject of those states.

The right of each sovereign state to employ all means necessary against its enemies, including violence and armed force, is grounded in the fundamental right of self-preservation that pertains in the state of nature. According to Hobbes, 'every Soveraign hath the same Right, in procuring the safety of his People, that any particular man can have, in procuring the safety of his own Body' in the state of nature.[91]

Locke concurs with Hobbes that international relations is a state of nature, but we must remember that Locke distinguished between the state of nature and a state or condition of war:

all *Princes* and Rulers of *Independent* Governments all through the World, are in a State of Nature . . . for 'tis not every Compact that puts an end to the State of Nature between Men, but only this one of agreeing together mutually to enter into one Community, and make one Body Politick; other Promises and Compacts, Men may make one with another, and yet still be in the State of Nature.[92]

Independent governments or sovereign states are in a state of nature with regards to one another, because they have not agreed to a social contract that subjects them uniformly to a single sovereign and a common set of laws. Nonetheless, they can sign specific treaties or agree particular 'compacts' to regulate specific aspects of their relations with each other, either individually (bilaterally) or collectively (multilaterally).

Locke does agree with Hobbes that the state of war is a condition in which all means necessary, up to and including the destruction of one's enemy, can be used to achieve self-preservation. 'The *State of War* is a State of Enmity and Destruction;' and 'it being reasonable and just I should have a Right to destroy that which threatens me with Destruction', for it is *'the Fundamenatl Law of Nature man being to be preserved'*.[93] This 'fundamental law' of Locke's equates to Hobbes' fundamental right of nature.

Those who commit aggression have forfeited their right of self-preservation, so that 'one may destroy a Man who makes War upon him' and threatens his survival. Threatening 'another Mans Life, *puts him in a State of War* with him . . . and so has exposed his Life to the others Power to be taken away by him . . . it being reasonable and just I should have a Right to destroy that which threatens me with Destruction'.[94] Furthermore, 'when all cannot be preserv'd, the safety of the Innocent is to be preferred'.[95] Thus, war seems to involve a combination of aggression and self-defence for Locke, with only those engaged in self-defence maintaining their right of self-preservation.

Alexander Moseley agrees that for Locke, 'the initiator of aggression *absolutely* loses his rights',[96] including the right of self-preservation. 'This implies', Moseley points out, that a prisoner from the unjust or aggressive side in a war 'remains at the whim of his captor – he has lost all of his rights to his captor and may justly be killed or enslaved by him. In modern parlance, the initiator of aggression loses his "personhood"'.[97] This also implies, as Moseley points out, 'the possibility of wielding disproportionate force against transgressors, which stands contrary to the commonly held just war convention that retaliation ought to be proportional to the level of attack and intent'.[98] It also contradicts one element of the *jus in bello* principle of non-combatant immunity (and contemporary international law, in the form of the Geneva Conventions), according to which, captured and disarmed enemy soldiers have not forfeited their fundamental rights and are no longer legitimate targets in warfare, even if they have been fighting for an aggressive power.

Such aggression can consist not merely of direct threats to another person's life, but to any attempt to subjugate them and control them, because such subjugation denies them their capacity for self-preservation:

And hence it is, that he who attempts to get another Man into his Absolute Power, does thereby *put himself into a State of War* with him; It being to be understood as a Declaration of a Design upon his Life . . . To be free from such force is the only security of my Preservation . . . so that he who makes *an attempt to enslave* me, thereby puts himself into a State of War with me.[99]

In other words, attempts at subjugation can be considered aggression and its victims or targets retain the right to respond by all means necessary, up to and including the use of violence.

Rousseau restricts the domain of war, so that it is a function of the social contract, rather than the state of nature, and applies only to governments and international relations and not to relations between individuals. This is because war concerns conflicts over property, and property (as distinct from possession, achieved through power) exists only in the context of the state, through the rule of law:

> It is conflicts over things, not quarrels between men which constitute war, and the state of war cannot arise from mere personal relations, but only from property relations. Private wars between one man and another can exist neither in a state of nature, where there is no fixed property [because there is no law], nor in society, where everything is under the authority of law . . .[100]

War cannot occur between individuals, either in the state of nature – which lacks property relations – or in society, where individuals can appeal to law to settle disputes over property.

Thus, war can be a characteristic of international relations, but not of personal relations:

> War, then, is not a relation between men, but between states; in war individuals are enemies wholly by chance, not as men, not even as citizens, but only as soldiers; not as members of their country, but only as its defenders. In a word, a state can have as an enemy only another state, not men, because there can be no real relation between things possessing different intrinsic natures.[101]

Human beings feature in war in their role as soldiers, or agents of the state, and not as individual persons, as such.

Rousseau uses his point concerning war as a function of states, rather than personal relations, to provide a clear argument resembling the principle of non-combatant immunity in just war theory:

Since the aim of war is to subdue a hostile state, a combatant has the right to kill the defenders of that state while they are armed; but as soon as they lay down their arms and surrender, they cease to be either enemies or instruments of the enemy; they become simply men once more, and no one has any longer the right to take their lives. It is sometimes possible to destroy a state without killing a single one of its members, and war gives no right to inflict any more destruction than is necessary for victory.[102]

The clear implication of this passage is that human beings can be targeted only as agents of the state, while they are active enemy combatants, and this excludes both civilians and ex-combatants, including disarmed or captured soldiers. Furthermore, states can persist in war only until they succeed in defeating an aggressive enemy state, and they are not entitled to kill enemy soldiers, beyond what is required to achieve this. This contradicts Locke's position, noted earlier, that those involved in a war of aggression forfeit their rights, including their right of self-preservation, absolutely and unconditionally.

Nonetheless, Rousseau points out that soldiers are risking no more in war in defence of their country or commonwealth, than they have already gained from the state by means of the social contract:

> . . . as a result of the contract . . . they have exchanged . . . the power to destroy others for the enjoyment of their own security . . . even when they risk their lives to defend the state, what more are they doing but giving back what they have received from the state? What are they doing that they would not do more often, and at greater peril, in the state of nature, where every man is inevitably at war and at the risk of his life . . . Assuredly, all must now fight in case of need for their country, but at least no one has any longer to fight for himself . . . when the prince says to him: 'It is expedient for the state that you should die', then he should die, because it is only on such terms that he has lived in security as long as he has and also because his life is no longer the bounty of nature but a gift he has received conditionally from the state.[103]

Soldiers have been rescued from the state of nature by means of the social contract and the commonwealth, and, through giving their lives while defending their country, they are giving no more than they have gained already from the state.

It is also interesting to note that this passage contains a Hobbesian, rather than a Lockean, depiction of the state of nature, in which 'every man is inevitably at war and at the risk of his life' and also contradicts Rousseau's earlier argument that war can only obtain between states and not between individuals in the state of nature. This Hobbesian position is used to support Rousseau's contention, here, that soldiers are better off even where they must risk their lives in war 'in case of need for their country', than they would be as individuals in the state of nature, where they must engage in perpetual combat for survival.

Both Locke and Rousseau characterise the state as a singular entity for the purposes of international relations, so that an attack on any citizen or subject of that state is an attack upon the state as a whole. According to Locke, 'a Commonwealth . . . in reference to the rest of Mankind, they make one Body . . . So that under this Consideration, the whole Community is one Body in the State of Nature, in respect of all other States or Persons out of its Community'.[104] States are treated as unified entities or discrete units in international relations, just as individuals within society would be, so that an injury against any citizen or part of the state 'engages the whole in the reparation of it'.[105]

This is also a point with which Rousseau agrees: 'in relation to foreign powers, the body politic is a simple entity, an individual . . . As soon as the multitude is united thus in a single body, no one can injure any one of the members without attacking the whole . . .'[106] Even so, for the purposes of self-defence, he distinguishes between soldiers and civilians, so that only active combatants can be targeted, although civilians are equally part, or members of, the state.

Locke distinguishes between three branches of government: legislative, executive and federative. The federative concerns international relations between states and 'contains the Power of War and Peace, Leagues and Alliances, and all the Transactions with all Persons and Communities without the Commonwealth' and has as its objective 'the management of the *security and interest of the publick without*'.[107] The executive branch of government concerns the implementation or enforcement of law domestically or 'the *Execution* of the Municipal Laws of the Society *within* its self'.[108] The legislative power, of course, concerns the making of legislation or law. The important point, for Locke, is that 'federative Power . . . is much less capable to be directed by antecedent, standing, positive Laws', reinforcing its status as a function of the state or commonwealth in the state of nature, rather than in civil society.[109]

The purpose or goal of both executive and federative types of state power are the same, however, according to Locke: 'all this for the preservation of the property of all the Members of that Society, as far as is possible'.[110] By property, in this context, Locke means the life and liberty, as well as the material possessions, of every individual. In other words, state violence, or 'the force of the Community', is to be employed '*only in the Execution of such Laws*, or abroad to prevent or redress Foreign Injuries, and secure the Community from Inroad and Invasion. And all this to be directed to no other *end*, but the *Peace, Safety*, and *publick good* of the People'.[111] Both aspects of state power – domestic and international – share a common objective, the public good, as well as a common means to achieve this objective – 'the force of the Society'.[112]

VIOLENCE AND SOCIAL TRANSFORMATION

There are also those who challenge social contract theory, and its justifications of the state and the rule of law, as merely a device for preserving an unequal and unjust social and political order, both domestically and internationally. Some recent proponents of political violence, for example, view it as a necessary mechanism for achieving essential political and social change and have been highly critical of peace as the central objective of human political activity, regarding it as pacification and a device for protecting the status quo. These include such unequivocal exponents of the value of revolutionary and anti-colonial political violence as Georges Sorel (*Reflections on Violence*) and Franz Fanon (*The Wretched of the Earth*). Sorel, for example, regarded 'social peace' as a 'chimera', pursued by 'a cowardly middle class', afraid of its encounter with proletarian, anti-capitalist violence.[113] Sorel refers to the value placed upon social peace as 'the *chatter* of the preachers of ethics and sociology', deflecting both middle class and proletariat from their true role as economic antagonists.[114] According to Sorel:

> Proletarian violence comes upon the scene just at the moment when the conception of social peace is being held up as a means of moderating disputes; proletarian violence confines employers to their rôle of producers, and tends to restore the separation of the classes, just when they seemed on the point of intermingling

in the democratic marsh . . . A growing and solidly organised working class can compel the capitalist class to remain firm in the industrial war; if a united and revolutionary proletariat confronts a rich middle class . . . capitalist society will have reached its historical perfection.[115]

Sorel presents an apolocalyptic view, according to which, proletarian violence is necessary to save civilisation from the barbarism of capitalism, by means of anarcho-syndicalism and the general strike, and efforts to achieve social peace merely divert the working class from its historical mission and responsibility.

Similarly, Fanon writes: 'At the decisive moment, the colonialist bourgeosie . . . introduces that new idea . . . non-violence' to persuade 'the intellectual and economic elite of the colonized country' that they share the same interest in opposing mass resistance to colonial rule.[116] Social peace and 'non-violence' become bywords for preserving the status quo for the benefit of existing elites.

Georges Sorel justifies violence as a mechanism for achieving social transformation, as distinct from preserving the social order (or the social contract). He compares 'social struggles' explicitly to war, about which he says 'quite contradictory things can be said',[117] depending upon whether it is used to preserve or challenge the status quo:

> War may be considered from its noble side . . . There is another aspect of war which does not possess this character of nobility, and on which the pacificists (sic) always dwell. The object of war is . . . to allow politicians to satisfy their ambitions: the foreigner must be conquered in order that they themselves may obtain great and immediate material advantages . . .[118]

This use of war internationally, for the purpose of 'conquest abroad', is used to augment the power of the state or the political elite domestically or through 'conquest at home'.[119]

The use of political violence in the context of the 'Syndicalist general strike',[120] on the other hand, is not associated with such conquest or the triumph of the state, both internationally and domestically:

> Pursuing no conquest . . . it counts on expelling the capitalists from the productive domain, and on taking their place in the workshop

created by capitalism. This conception of the general strike manifests in . . . its indifference to the material profits of conquest . . . The State has always been . . . the organiser of the war of conquest . . . the cost of which is borne by the general body of society . . .[121]

The political violence associated with the general strike performs an essential 'historical rôle', according to Sorel, resulting in the elimination of capitalism and, in this sense, corresponds to 'the noble side' of war.[122]

It is for this reason, Sorel distinguishes between violence and force: '. . . the term *violence* should be employed only for acts of revolt; we should say, therefore, that the object of force is to impose a certain social order in which the minority governs, while violence tends to the destruction of that order'.[123] Violence refers to the necessary action of destroying an unjust social order and is, therefore, benign or noble, whereas force refers to its preservation via the instruments or mechanisms of the state.

Such mechanisms for preserving the status quo – in this case, capitalism – can be best referred to as force, as distinct from overt violence, according to Sorel, because they are part of the ordinary functioning social order:

'In the ordinary run of things, the worker can be left to the action of the *natural laws of production*' . . . When we reach the last historical stage . . . the whole of society resembles an organised body, working automatically . . .[124]

There is no need for an economic or political elite to employ overt violence to maintain a social system that is working to their benefit, since the instruments of social order are contained within the smooth functioning of its ordinary, everyday operations: 'Whether force manifests itself under the aspect of historical acts of coercion, or of fiscal oppression . . . or whether it is wholly bound up with the economic system, it is always a middle-class force labouring with more or less skill to bring about the capitalist order of society'.[125]

This is why true revolutionaries must distinguish 'between the *force* that aims at authority, endeavouring to bring about an automatic obedience, and the *violence* that would smash that authority', according to Sorel.[126] The important point, for Sorel, is that revolutionary violence is a justified, and even necessary, response to the force that maintains an unjust social, political and economic status quo, epitomised by 'the State'.

It is a mistake for the proletariat to aim to seize state power to achieve the social transformation they desire or to assume (along with 'orthodox Marxians') that just because 'the State formerly played a most important part in the revolutions which abolished the old economic systems, so it must again be the State which should abolish capitalism'.[127] It is not the case that the 'workers should therefore sacrifice everything to one end alone – that of putting into power men who promise them solemnly to ruin capitalism for the benefit of the people'.[128] Instead, rather than imitating 'the middle class',[129] they need to abolish the old political instruments of class and capitalist oppression, by means of the general strike.[130] 'Socialist writers have often pointed out that the poorer classes have more than once allowed themselves to be massacred to no purpose, save to place power in the hands of new rulers'.[131]

> Syndicalists do not propose to reform the State . . . they want to destroy it, because they wish to realise this idea of Marx's that the Socialist revolution ought not to culminate in the replacement of one governing authority by another minority . . . there is an absolute opposition between revolutionary Syndicalism and the State . . .[132]

For Sorel, of course, the general strike must be viewed as an apocalyptic event, requiring violence, culminating in the end of one historical era, characterised by capitalist social relations, and ushering in a new era – proletarian socialism.

Franz Fanon also claims that for a colonised and oppressed people, violence leads to empowerment and even psychological liberation: 'When the people have taken violent part in the national liberation they will allow no one to set themselves up as "liberators"', such as politicians or a middle class elite: 'At the level of individuals, violence is a cleansing force. It frees the native from his inferiority complex and from his despair and inaction . . .'[133] This theme of the liberating power of violence was famously and bluntly reiterated by Jean-Paul Sartre in his 'Introduction' to *The Wretched of the Earth*: 'The rebel's weapon is the proof of his humanity . . . to shoot down a European is to kill two birds with one stone, to destroy an oppressor and the man he oppresses at the same time: there remain a dead man, and a free man . . .'[134]

CONCLUSION

Social contract theory, as developed in the writings of Hobbes, Locke and Rousseau, for example, provides perhaps the most compelling set of arguments in Western political theory for the state as a sovereign political institution, embodying and enforcing, in particular, the rule of law. The problems of peace, political violence and social order were central concerns of these writers, to which the social contract was supposed to provide some sort of solution. It is clear, however, that while these theorists sought to minimise or contain levels of violence within and between societies, they did not foresee or seek to achieve its elimination or replacement as a method of social control and guarantor of both individual and group security. Furthermore, while Locke, in particular, sought to define the limits of state authority in terms of popular sovereignty, there are still those who are suspicious of a coercive, centralised state, as, essentially, an instrument of elite domination or class oppression. This is represented in a somewhat extreme form, perhaps, by Sorel and Fanon, as supporters of political violence to challenge an unjust status quo, underpinned by the social contract and the state.

Proponents of nonviolent political action can be divided between those who accept, at least implicitly, conventional justifications of the state and its legitimacy, derived from the kinds of arguments associated with social contract theory, and those with a more transformative vision, who challenge some of the assumptions of social contract theory, on the basis of their interpretation of the requirements of nonviolence. They question, for example, whether freedom and security are best served by a state that depends upon highly centralised forms of power and authority and the threat or use of violence to enforce the rule of law and for self-defence.

Subsequent chapters will explore the response of differing interpretations of nonviolence and civil resistance to central themes and issues addressed by social contract theorists. The focus will be on the twin themes of power and violence, as epitomising the political and the ethical concerns of nonviolent political action.

Notes

1 Hobbes, *Leviathan,* pp. 185, 186, 188.
2 Ibid. p. 188.
3 Ibid. p. 189.
4 Ibid. p. 190 (italics in original).
5 Ibid. p. 190 (italics in original).
6 Ibid. p. 190 (italics in original).
7 Ibid. p. 190.
8 Locke, 'The second treatise of government', p. 311.
9 Ibid. p. 311 (italics in original).
10 Ibid. p. 311 (italics in original).
11 Ibid. p. 312 (italics in original).
12 Moseley, 'John Locke's morality of war', p. 127.
13 Locke, 'The second treatise of government', p. 321 (italics in original).
14 Ibid. p. 322 (italics in original).
15 Ibid. p. 322 (italics in original).
16 Laslett, 'Introduction', p. 112.
17 Ibid. pp. 112–13.
18 Locke, 'The second treatise of government', p. 323 (italics in original).
19 Laslett, 'Introduction', p. 131.
20 Moseley, 'John Locke's morality of war', p. 121.
21 Locke, 'The second treatise of government', p. 397 (italics in original).
22 Ibid. p. 397.
23 Hobbes, *Leviathan,* p. 225.
24 Ibid. p. 223.
25 Ibid. p. 224.
26 Rousseau, *The Social Contract,* pp. 80–1.
27 Macpherson, 'Introduction', p. 61.
28 Moseley, 'John Locke's morality of war', p. 121.
29 Ibid. p. 121.
30 Ibid. p. 121.
31 Rousseau, *The Social Contract,* p. 82.
32 See Rousseau, *The Social Contract,* pp. 75–6.
33 Rousseau, *The Social Contract,* p. 81.
34 Ibid. p. 64–5.
35 Hobbes, *Leviathan,* p. 227.
36 Ibid. pp. 227–8.
37 Ibid. p. 227.
38 Macpherson, 'Introduction', p. 44.
39 Hobbes, *Leviathan,* p. 232.
40 Ibid. p. 191.

41 Ibid. p. 271.
42 Macpherson, 'Introduction', p. 44.
43 Locke, 'The second treatise of government', pp. 316–17.
44 Rousseau, *The Social Contract*, p. 152. See, also, Hobbes, *Leviathan*, p. 268; and Locke, 'The second treatise of government', p. 374.
45 Rousseau, *The Social Contract*, p. 153.
46 Locke, 'The second treatise of government', p. 392 (italics in original).
47 Rousseau, *The Social Contract*, p. 153.
48 Locke, 'The second treatise of government', p. 401.
49 Ibid.p. 324 (italics in original).
50 Ibid. p. 324 (italics in original).
51 Ibid. p. 324 (italics in original).
52 Rousseau, *The Social Contract*, p. 60.
53 Rousseau, *The Social Contract*, p. 61.
54 Ibid. pp. 61–2.
55 Ibid. pp. 64–5 (italics in original).
56 Ibid. p. 72.
57 Ibid. p. 62.
58 Cranston, 'Introduction', p. 37.
59 Rousseau, *The Social Contract*, p. 64.
60 Hobbes, *Leviathan*, p. 272.
61 Ibid. p. 315
62 Ibid. p. 218 (italics in original).
63 Locke, 'The second treatise of government', pp. 402–3 (italics in original).
64 Ibid. p. 402.
65 Ibid. p. 402.
66 Moseley, 'John Locke's morality of war', p. 122.
67 Ibid. p. 120.
68 Laslett, 'Introduction', p. 125.
69 Locke, 'The second treatise of government', p. 348.
70 Ibid. p. 348.
71 Cranston, 'Introduction', p. 32.
72 Ibid. p. 41.
73 Rousseau, *The Social Contract*, p. 53.
74 Locke, 'The second treatise of government', p. 413 (italics in original).
75 Ibid. p. 448.
76 Ibid. p. 464 (italics in original).
77 Ibid. p. 449.
78 Ibid. p. 464.
79 Ibid. p. 465.
80 Ibid. p. 467.
81 See Locke, 'The second treatise of government', pp. 440–4.

82 Locke, 'The second treatise of government', p. 439 (italics in original).
83 Cranston, 'Introduction', p. 34.
84 Rousseau, *The Social Contract*, pp. 53–4.
85 Ibid. p. 58.
86 Laslett, 'Introduction', p. 131.
87 Hobbes, *Leviathan*, p. 186.
88 Ibid. pp. 185–6.
89 Ibid. p. 266.
90 Ibid. pp. 360–1.
91 Ibid. p. 394.
92 Locke, 'The second treatise of government', p. 317.
93 Ibid. p. 319 (italics in original).
94 Ibid. p. 319 (italics in original).
95 Ibid. p. 319.
96 Moseley, 'John Locke's morality of war', p. 125 (italics in original).
97 Ibid. p. 125.
98 Ibid. p. 125.
99 Locke, 'The second treatise of government', p. 320 (italics in original).
100 Rousseau, *The Social Contract*, pp. 55–6
101 Ibid. p. 56.
102 Ibid. p. 57.
103 Ibid. pp. 77–9.
104 Locke, 'The second treatise of government', pp. 410–11.
105 Ibid. p. 411.
106 Rousseau, *The Social Contract*, p. 63.
107 Locke, 'The second treatise of government', p. 411 (italics in original).
108 Ibid. p. 411 (italics in original).
109 Ibid. p. 411.
110 Ibid. p. 367.
111 Ibid. p. 399 (italics in original).
112 Ibid. p. 412.
113 Sorel, *Reflections on Violence*, p. 78.
114 Ibid. pp. 89–90 (italics in original).
115 Ibid. p. 92.
116 Fanon, *The Wretched of the Earth*, p. 61.
117 Sorel, *Reflections on Violence*, p. 166.
118 Ibid. pp. 166–7.
119 Ibid. p. 167.
120 Ibid. p. 167.
121 Ibid. p. 167.
122 Ibid. pp. 166–7.
123 Ibid. p. 171 (italics in original).

124 Ibid. p. 174 (italics in original).
125 Ibid. p. 175.
126 Ibid. p. 175 (italics in original).
127 Ibid. p. 176.
128 Ibid. p. 176.
129 Ibid. p. 176.
130 Ibid. pp. 175–7.
131 Ibid. p. 158.
132 Ibid. pp. 116–17.
133 Fanon, *The Wretched of the Earth*, p. 94.
134 Sartre, 'Preface', p. 22.

Chapter 3

NONVIOLENCE, THE STATE AND CIVIL RESISTANCE

INTRODUCTION

The role of the state is a central issue for any theory of nonviolent political action. In conventional Western political theory, a defining feature of the state is its monopoly over the legitimate use of violence. On the one hand, a central function of the state is to limit, control and contain the use of violence within (and between) societies. On the other hand, a central characteristic of the state, as a form of political organisation, is that it retains violence as its ultimate sanction or method of enforcement and security.

Thus, nonviolent political action maintains an ambivalent relationship with the state. Many examples of nonviolent political action operate within the constraints of the state, as a form of political organisation, seeking to make it more democratic, for example, or more respectful and protective of human rights. Some proponents of nonviolence, however, especially those with some sort of a structural analysis of the role of violence in maintaining social order or those with ethical objections to the use of violence, recognise a critical tension between nonviolence and the state as a form of political organisation, with its fundamental dependence upon violence as a mechanism for maintaining social order and ensuring security against internal and external threats.

Tolstoy's Christian pacifism, for example, led him to reject the centralised, hierarchical state as a form of political organisation. Gandhi's attitude towards the state was more ambivalent, perhaps, since he recognised its importance in maintaining the rule of law, while exploring smaller-scale, more direct forms of political organisation, relevant to the lives of rural Indians, for example. Sharp promotes nonviolent political action as an effective way of mobilising popular resistance to the centralised power of the state, dominated by self-serving elites. Many of the examples of civil resistance documented by Roberts and Ash in their edited volume, *Civil Resistance and Power Politics*, aim at establishing or restoring democratic governments within conventional state structures, however. As Roberts points out: 'When leaders of even the most determinedly non-violent movements have come to power in their countries, they have generally accepted the continued existence of armed forces and other more or less conventional security arrangements'.[1]

Tolstoy identifies three problems for the state (or 'Government'), as a form of political organisation. These are violence, freedom and inequality. Although these can be identified and analysed as distinct issues, they are also interconnected, for Tolstoy, in the sense, for example, that the violence of the state is a crucial mechanism for maintaining social inequality and also for restricting freedom. Thus, his opposition to violence and his commitment to nonviolence is connected to all aspects of his critique of the state as a form of political organisation. These three issues – violence, inequality and freedom – are useful categories for an initial discussion of the relationship between nonviolence and the state.

THE STATE AND VIOLENCE

The justification of the state's role in maintaining order and minimising violence within a society finds its most eloquent and persuasive expression in social contract theory. Tolstoy, in particular, challenges social contract theory, through arguing that the state merely replaces individual and spontaneous violence with institutionalised group-level violence between and within societies, thus intensifying the violence it is meant to eliminate or, at least, control. Tolstoy does suggest, however, that just as humanity made the transition from the state of nature to the nation-state and the rule of law (enforced by violence), so we must make the transition to 'the kingdom of God', in which human beings live without violence and according to conscience, which is, essentially, the law of God:

> There was a time when humanity lived like the wild beasts . . . Then came the time when men coalesced into societies, into kingdoms, and began to divide off into nations; defending themselves

from other nations. Men became less beastlike, but nevertheless they considered it not only possible, but even indispensable, to kill their enemies external and internal. But now the time is coming . . . when men, according to Christ's words, are entering into a new state of the brotherhood of all men, into that new state . . . when all men . . . should unlearn the art of war . . . and enter into the kingdom of God, the kingdom of unity and peace.[2]

The nation-state may have succeeded in containing the all-out violence of the state of nature, but only at the expense of centralising the capacity for violence in the state, which can use it against its own citizens and against the citizens of other countries: 'The organization, on principles of violence, of a society whose object was to insure the happiness of the individual and the family, and the social welfare of humanity, has brought men to such a pass that these benefits are practically annulled'.[3] Thus, according to Tolstoy, the state replicates and magnifies the violence of the state of nature it is meant to suppress: 'the evil of violence, passing into the hands of authority, must ever go on increasing, and soon becomes worse than the evil it is supposed to annihilate'.[4]

As a Christian pacifist, Tolstoy rejects the state as an 'organ of violence':[5] 'A Christian, as a Christian, cannot obey (and obeying thereby necessarily participate in) an authority which is entirely based on violence, maintained by violence, and unceasingly committing acts of violence the most contrary to the Christian law: soldiery, wars, prisons, executions . . .'[6] We cannot depend on governments to 'deliver men from the terrible and ever-increasing evils of armaments and war', via conferences and treaties, because government itself is essentially an instrument of violence, which it cannot, therefore, renounce.[7] Furthermore, 'a fresh kind of revolutionary or Socialist violence' cannot 'improve the position of society'.[8] Only a Christian commitment to nonviolence and the 'kingdom of God' can succeed in eliminating the institutionalised violence of the state.

War is the most obvious expression of the magnification of violence made possible by the state, resulting in increased threats to, rather than the increased protection of, human life:

Governments were expected to deliver men from the cruelty of individual discord and give them the guarantee of the inviolable regularity of State life. Instead of which they subject men to the necessity of the same strife, only transferring it from personal strife to warfare with the inhabitants of other lands, and there remains the same danger of destruction both to State and individual.[9]

The institutionalised violence of the state makes possible not only the destruction of human life (as one might find in the state of nature), but also the destruction of human communities. Rather than solving the problem of violence as a feature of social relationships, the state magnifies and intensifies it, according to Tolstoy.

Military conscription, for Tolstoy, is the epitome of the contradiction between social contract justifications of the state (that is, the 'social conception of life'), in terms of its protection of its citizens against unlawful and spontaneous violence and its dependence upon institutionalised violence for security and to maintain social order:

> General military service . . . is . . . the last expression of the internal contradiction of the social conception of life which arose as soon as violence was needed for its maintenance . . . Everyone is agreed that the significance of the social conception of life consist (sic) in this, that the individual, having realized the horror of man's strife against man, and the transitoriness of his own existence, transfers the meaning of his life to the community of human beings; whereas the result of general military conscription is that men, after having sacrificed all that was required of them to be delivered from individual strife and from the transitoriness of their personal lives, are, after all their privations, again called upon to suffer all the dangers they had hoped to have escaped.[10]

Any individual conscripted by a government to fight in a war is subject to the same dangers of death by violence that they would be in the state of nature, even though organised government and the rule of law are supposed to protect them from such dangers.

Tolstoy concedes that there may have been a time when governments or states were necessary to contain the violence of the state of nature, but their capacity to engage in war and internal repression now make them a greater danger than any hazards they may have been designed to reduce:

There may have been a time when such Governments were necessary, and when the evil of supporting a Government was less than
that of being defenceless against organized neighbours; but now
such governments have become unnecessary, and are a far greater
evil than all the dangers with which they frighten their subjects.[11]

It is now time to eliminate violence altogether through creating a cosmopolitan 'kingdom of God', in which men can govern their behaviour directly, in accordance with universal moral laws, undivided by
false allegiances to separate nation-states and different systems of
human-made laws. According to Tolstoy, 'the importance of annihilat-
ing violence is already recognized by men, and therefore this condition becomes as unavoidable as formerly after the wild state came the
monarchical state'.[12]

It is interesting that Peter Laslett also identifies 'anarchistic implications' in John Locke's 'doctrine of natural political virtue'.[13] The implication is that government is only made necessary by the incapacity of
some men to live according to natural virtue and that if they were able
to live entirely according to conscience in the 'kingdom of God', as
Tolstoy suggests, the state and its mechanisms of enforcement would
not be required. The crucial difference is that Tolstoy insists that such
a 'kingdom of God' is the only solution to the dangers of state violence
and also, of course, that it is within our grasp to realise this kingdom,
whereas Locke (and other social contract theorists) remain profoundly
sceptical that human beings can live in community, according to the
dictates of individual virtue (or the laws of God) alone.

Gene Sharp also expresses his mistrust of 'the institutionalized
capacity for political violence',[14] represented by the state, for example.
He claims that this capacity:

> once established for any purpose, can be shifted to other purposes
> . . . Hence, dictatorship, genocide, war, and systems of social
> oppression were viewed as closely interrelated, for they were four
> applications of institutionalized political violence; without that
> capacity they could not occur.[15]

According to Sharp:

> The combination of bureaucracy, police, prisons, and military
> forces, all under a single command, makes possible the turning

of that combined State power from serving the members of the society to control, repression, and on occasion, war, against its own population. In modern times, the State is always stronger than any other single institution of the society.[16]

The state may claim a monopoly over the legitimate use of violence for purposes of self-defence and law enforcement, but it is too easy for this institutionalised and centralised violence to be used for other, less benign purposes, once it has been acquired.

Unlike Tolstoy, Sharp does not argue along anarchist lines for the outright abolition of the state. He does suggest, however, that it is vital to empower social groups outside the state and the organisations of, what we now call, civil society to provide a counterweight to the state so that it cannot exercise its capacity for violence and oppression with impunity. Furthermore, these 'loci of power' can become a means for gradually reducing (and, perhaps, eventually replacing) the power of the centralised state, based ultimately on violence, by means of a process of progressive, functionalist substitution. According to Sharp:

> we need to do more than . . . to make changes to right particular wrongs. We must deliberately act in ways which strengthen the non-State institutions of our society . . . Institutional change is required . . . In order to reduce progressively the size of the existing central State apparatus, and thereby its dangers, it will be necessary to create or strengthen smaller-scale institutions (*loci* of power) . . . and then gradually to shift to them tasks now carried out by the State.[17]

In these passages, Sharp suggests that the longer-term goal of nonviolent political action is not only democratic reform within existing state structures, as important as this is, but structural change to the way society is organised, to reduce (and eventually eliminate) the dangers of institutionalised violence, resulting from a centralised, hierarchical state. He does not really explore or explain how these different *loci* of power or small-scale institutions are to coordinate their functions in the absence of the state, except to mention that they will need to cooperate 'where needed with others on projects of regional and national concern'.[18]

THE STATE AND INEQUALITY

Tolstoy equates the rule of law with violence, but also claims that the mechanisms of law enforcement enable those who control the state to engage in organised violence for their own purposes, against those they govern. In other words, the institutionalised violence that is a defining feature of the state, epitomised by law, becomes an instrument of class oppression and inequality. According to Tolstoy:

> laws are demands to obey certain rules . . . If there are laws, there must be the force that can compel people to obey them. There is only one force that can compel people to obey rules (to conform to the will of others), and that is violence . . . the organized violence used by people who have power, in order to compel others to obey the laws that they, the powerful, have made . . . The essence of legislature does not lie . . . in the idea of the dominion of the collective will of the people, or in other such indefinite and confused conditions, but lies in the fact that people who wield organized violence have power to compel others to obey them and do as they like. So the exact and irrefutable definition of legislation, intelligible to all, is that: *Laws are rules, made by people who govern by means of organized violence* . . . The same thing makes it possible to establish laws, as enforces obedience to them, namely, organized violence.[19]

Class or elite domination (and, hence, inequality) precedes the state, so that the instruments of the state (including the rule of law enforced by violence) become mechanisms for enforcing such domination and not for the expression of some mythical 'general will' or the public good.

Gene Sharp identifies some of the groups that may suffer from inequality perpetuated by the mechanisms of state power. He writes that: '. . . dominated groups may include exploited economic classes, harassed religious minorities, populations of attacked or occupied countries, victims of attempted genocide, people living under dictatorships, nations under foreign domination, or despised ethnic or racial groups'.[20]

According to Tolstoy, 'armies are only needed by governments in order to dominate their own working-classes', and the 'existence of armies' inevitably produces war.[21] Thus, Tolstoy inverts the conventional relationship between armies and war. Armies are not created by states or governments for the purposes of self-defence against external aggression; rather, states engage in aggressive wars, precisely because of the existence of armies. Eliminate armies and the capacity for such aggressive wars no longer exists. Furthermore, Tolstoy inverts the usual relationship between domestic and international politics in his discussion of war and armies. Armies were created primarily for purposes of domestic control (and to maintain class inequality), but then provide the means by which states or governments can engage in international conflict or war.

Elsewhere, Tolstoy claims that external aggression and internal repression are in a reciprocal, mutually reinforcing relationship, facilitated by the existence of armies:

> The despotism of Governments grows in proportion to their external success and the increase and strength of their armies; the aggressiveness of Governments grows in proportion to the increase of internal despotism.[22]

The strength of the armed forces increases with the success of military campaigns abroad and this can then be applied domestically, by the state or government. Similarly, a state that depends upon a strong army for internal security has a greater capacity or resources for external military action.

THE STATE AND FREEDOM

Tolstoy differed from the social contract theorists in identifying freedom as complete individual autonomy: 'freedom . . . consists in there being no power over man demanding from him actions contrary to his desires and advantages'.[23] According to the social contract theorists, however, this condition constituted the state of nature, rather than genuine freedom. Such complete individual autonomy was a source of conflict, competition and, ultimately, violence and needed to be regulated by the rule of law. It is the capacity to make law through self-government that constitutes true freedom, according to social contract theory. However, Tolstoy challenged this social contract view of freedom directly:

> In this non-comprehension of what constitutes freedom . . . lies a great and most pernicious error. This error is that men of our times

imagine that the servile subjection to violence in which they stand, in relation to the government, is a natural position and that the authorization by governmental power of certain actions defined by this power, is freedom.[24]

The view that the state and the rule of law are guarantors of the freedom of the citizens of a state is an egregious error, according to Tolstoy.

Tolstoy disagreed with the social contract view of the relationship between government, law and freedom, precisely because he claimed that government only reflected the will of a small elite, who used it for their own purposes to control the rest of the population and did not and could not express the general will:[25]

> According to science, legislation is the expression of the will of the whole people . . . But everyone knows that not only in despotic countries, but also in the countries nominally most free – the laws are made not by the will of all, but by the will of those who have power.[26]

He referred to the social contract view that 'in obeying the Government they [the people] obey themselves', as a 'deceit'.[27] The state and the rule of law do not provide the conditions of freedom for the people, instead, they deprive them of it.

Furthermore, this critique of the state held, no matter what form it took and no matter how democratic it claimed to be, because all states depended upon the coercion of the many by the few, according to Tolstoy: 'It is the same with any coercive State of whatever kind, a despotism, a constitutional monarchy, an oligarchy or a republic'.[28]

Tolstoy argued that only in 'the kingdom of God' could true freedom be realised. In other words, direct obedience to God's law must replace obedience to state or human law. Freedom, for human beings, consists in individual obedience to the laws of God and it is only on this basis that they can dispense with the human laws provided and enforced by the state: 'Deliverance from human law is only possible on condition that one acknowledge a divine law common to all men'.[29] The moral law of God and, in particular, the doctrine of love of one's neighbour must replace obedience to human authority, in the form of the state or government:

[I]f one is not to obey the Government, one has to obey God and live a righteous life. Only in that degree in which men live such a life can they cease to obey men and become free . . . It is possible not to obey men only when one obeys the higher law of God, common to all. One cannot be free whilst transgressing the higher universal law of mutual service.[30]

Tolstoy acknowledges that human beings cannot dispense with law and morality altogether if they are to live in a just and peaceful social order. They must obey the higher, universal laws of God if they are to engage in non-cooperation with, and moral resistance to, the laws and policies of particular states, countries and governments. Only obedience to God's law can ensure that individual autonomy from state control does not return human beings to the state of nature or 'the savage state of coarse violence to each other',[31] as suggested by social contract theory. Tolstoy is critical of conventional 'Anarchistic teaching', because 'holding an irreligious materialistic life conception', it 'does not possess this spiritual weapon'.[32] It wishes to dispense with the state, without providing an alternative method of maintaining social order based on the teachings of Christianity.

Gene Sharp, building upon his understanding of social power and following Hannah Arendt, suggested another view of freedom, as 'participation in public affairs'.[33] Furthermore, such participation must be direct and unmediated. The danger with 'representative government' and the centralised state is that it inhibits or curtails such ' participatory public freedom', because 'the individual withdrew from politics into his or her private domain'.[34] In contemporary capitalism, this domain is that of possessive and competitive individualism and consumerism. It is not so much that the state threatened individual autonomy, as that it restricted each individual's participation in public affairs, through making this the domain of a small, if, in some cases, ostensibly 'representative', elite.

SWARAJ, SOCIAL POWER AND THE STATE

Gandhi's attitude towards the state and the rule of law was more nuanced and perhaps ambivalent than Tolstoy's. This was, perhaps, partly because he had trained and worked as a lawyer (in England and South Africa), but also, of course, because one of his immediate political objectives was *swaraj* or political independence or a sovereign state for India. On the one hand, Gandhi shared Tolstoy's suspicion of the state as organised violence: 'The state represents violence in a concentrated and organized form' and 'it can never be weaned from violence to which it owes its very existence'.[35] Gandhi had his own vision of 'the kingdom of God' or the rule of complete and universal nonviolence (embodied in some of his discussions of full *swaraj*). Thus, he referred to 'political independence' as '*Ramaraj*, i.e. sovereignty of the people based on pure moral authority'.[36]

Furthermore, the principle of *swadeshi* directed Gandhi to look to local or village politics, rather than the politics of the nation-state, as most relevant to his vision of society: 'Swadeshi is that spirit in us which restricts us to the use and service of our immediate surroundings to the exclusion of the more remote'.[37] In the domain of politics, this involves relying upon indigenous, local forms of governance:[38]

> Following out the Swadeshi spirit, I observe the indigenous insti-
> tutions and the village panchayat hold me. India is really a repub-
> lican country . . . Princes and potentates whether they were Indian
> born or foreigners have hardly touched the vast masses except for
> collecting revenue.[39]

By 'republican', Gandhi means, presumably, a political dispensation in which direct rule of citizens over themselves through local political institutions (such as the village *panchayat*) has always had more impact on, and relevance for, the vast majority of its population, than the higher-level and more distant mechanisms of the state or government, which have been, at most, an inconvenience and an imposition.

At the same time, he recognised that the achievement of the imme-diate objectives of the Indian independence movement required a conventional, sovereign state that could take its place among the com-munity of similarly-defined states or countries. Thus, Gandhi could write, without apparent contradiction:

> I do not repent of my action in terms of *ahimsa*. For, under Swaraj
> too I would not hesitate to advise those who would bear arms to
> do so and fight for the country . . . Under Swaraj of my dream
> there is no necessity for arms at all. But I do not expect that dream
> to materialize in its fullness as a result of the present effort, first

because the effort is not directed to that end as an immediate goal, and secondly because I do not consider myself advanced enough to be able to prescribe a detailed course of conduct to the nation for such preparation . . . And therefore it is not possible for me to show the nation a present way to complete non-violence in practice.[40]

He acknowledged that the ethical or spiritual requirements of *ahimsa* (or 'non-harm', as the ethical basis of nonviolence) and the political requirements of *swaraj* (or an independent state) did not always coincide. Citizens were under an obligation to defend their country, 'even by participating in war' if they benefitted 'from the order which government provided',[41] if no alternative method of political organisation and self-defence existed.

Nonetheless, Gandhi believed even states could conduct their foreign policy on exclusively nonviolent lines, including their defence and security policies. He refers, for example, to a question concerning post-colonial India: 'would a strong and independent India rely on Satyagraha as a method of self-preservation, or would it lapse back to seeking refuge in the age-old institution of war, however defensive its character?'[42] Gandhi replied:

I believe that a State can be administered on a non-violent basis if the vast majority of the people are non-violent . . . Supposing, therefore, that India attained independence through pure non-violence, India could retain it too by the same means.[43]

In other words, the methods of nonviolent political action that could be used to remove an occupying or colonial power, such as Britain in India, could also be used to resist outside aggression.

Any apparent contradiction between the two was the result of an incapacity to suggest methods for governing international relations by nonviolent means, rather than any weakness of 'the doctrine of non-violence', as such. For the time being, at least, it was sufficient to restrict his 'preaching' to winning 'India's freedom with strictly non-violent means'.[44]

Gene Sharp (and others) have explored the possibilities of civilian-based defence, as a pragmatic substitute for defending the territory and the citizens of a state against external aggression:

The usual military superiority of aggressors and the desire to avoid immense casualties and vast destruction during a hopeless attempt at military resistance are well grounded reasons to explore seriously viable supplements or alternatives to military resistance and guerilla warfare in defense. The policy of 'civilian-based defense' has been developed to build on improvised experience with nonviolent struggle against aggression and occupations, such as in the Ruhr in Germany in 1923, Czechoslovakia in 1968–1969, and the Baltic countries in 1990–1991.[45]

The methods of nonviolent action and civil resistance that can be used so effectively against internal oppression can also be used against external aggression, according to Sharp. In the case of an occupying power, in fact, the two problems become synonymous (that is, external aggression becomes the source of internal oppression), so the methods of nonviolent action can be used directly to resist such an occupation. Anti-colonial struggles and campaigns for political independence against the domestic or internal instruments of foreign rule have furnished many examples of successful resistance to external aggression and occupation. This suggests that the methods of nonviolent political action can provide the basis for the security and defence policies of conventional states, with centralised governments and territorial boundaries to protect. In this sense, Tolstoy is wrong to argue that states are synonymous with armies and violence. Nonetheless, even civilian-based defence does not provide a substitute for any violence associated with enforcing the rule of law (either domestically or internationally), in the form of policing, the court system and prisons (for example).

Sharp does suggest, however, that the 'diffused power structure'[46] within a society that provides the basis for effective nonviolent political action, through facilitating the mobilisation of social groups and their withdrawal of consent from, or compliance with, oppressive structures and policies, will also contribute to the ability of a country to resist foreign occupation and invasion by nonviolent means. It is much more difficult for an occupying power to control a society with multiple or plural '*loci* of power' (to use Sharp's term), than to administer a territory through a centralised mechanism of control, such as the state, if it can seize control of this mechanism. This suggests that effective civilian-based defence may require forms of social and political organisation that are different from, or alternative to, a centralised, hierarchical state.

Robert Burrowes, for example, distinguishes between 'civilian-based defense . . . concerned with defense of the nation-state, its government and territory'[47] and 'social defense . . . as concerned with defense "at the community level"'.[48] According to this dichotomy:

> civilian-based defense . . . involves a nonviolent strategy working under the direction of a government. Like military defense, it would rely on centralized decision making and hierarchical organization for its implementation. In contrast, exponents of social defense seek its acceptance by the community at large . . . It would rely on cooperation and communication among community-based groups for its implementation.[49]

Thus, social defence corresponds to the sort of changes that would challenge or replace conventional state structures as a form of political and social organisation. According to Burrowes, 'advocates of social defense usually consider the problem of defense to be a part of the wider struggle for fundamental structural changes in society'.[50]

CIVIL DISOBEDIENCE

Civil disobedience involves the deliberate violation of the law for political purposes and, in this sense, involves a direct confrontation between political activists and the state. It is an obvious exemplification of nonviolence as a separate category of political activity, distinct from both conventional parliamentary politics and violent resistance. Civil disobedience has been employed both by prominent proponents of a principled or ethical approach to nonviolence, such as Gandhi and King, as well as by campaigns using nonviolent political action for more pragmatic or strategic reasons. Civil disobedience is one of the more controversial methods associated with nonviolent political action, precisely because it involves breaking the law and confrontation with state or government authorities in both democratic and non-democratic systems of government.

Civil disobedience is a common method of nonviolent political action or *satyagraha*, because such action often aims to resist and change unjust laws, according to Gandhi:

On the political field, the struggle on behalf of the people mostly consists in opposing error in the shape of unjust laws. When you have failed to bring the error home to the law-giver by way of petitions and the like, the only remedy open to you, if you do not wish to submit to error, is to compel him by physical force to yield to you or by suffering in your own person by inviting the penalty for the breach of the law. Hence *satyagraha* largely appears to the public as Civil Disobedience or Civil Resistance. It is civil in the sense that it is not criminal.[51]

Gandhi connected civil disobedience to the theme of voluntary self-suffering through a willingness to accept the penalty or punishment for breaking the law.

Furthermore, this willingness to accept punishment shows that such disobedience is civil, rather than criminal, because those who engage in it accept the penalty for breaking the law, in accordance with the rule of law in general. This also helps to demonstrate that its motive is political – for the general good – rather than personal or selfish and for private gain:

The law-breaker breaks the law surreptitiously and tries to avoid the penalty; not so the civil resister. He ever obeys the laws of the state to which he belongs, not out of fear of the sanctions, but because he considers them to be good for the welfare of the society.[52]

The purpose of civil disobedience is to draw public attention to an unjust law or policy, in order to get it changed, not to violate the law for personal benefit.

Civil disobedience consists of deliberately breaking the law, which involves a violation of political and, perhaps, moral obligation and could itself be seen as an immoral action. Gandhi justifies this under two conditions. Firstly, other lawful means of achieving change have been tried and have failed, such as conventional parliamentary politics, protest and negotiation. Gandhi regarded civil disobedience as a method of last resort, even if he used it himself on numerous occasions. In other words, civil disobedience could be used only if other, lawful methods of engaging with your opponent (such as negotiation and protest) had been tried and had failed. Hence, according to Gandhi, in a fully democratic society, civil disobedience could not be justified, because other, lawful means could be effective in achieving change: 'In a well-ordered democratic society there is no room, no occasion for lawlessness or strikes. In such a society there are ample lawful means for vindicating justice'.[53] In this sense, civil disobedience was a nonviolent alternative to violent resistance, where peaceful attempts to achieve change had not succeeded.

Secondly, civil disobedience is aimed at changing specific laws or policies that are themselves unjust or immoral, where we are otherwise in the habit of obeying the law: 'Civil Disobedience is civil breach of unmoral statutory enactments . . . Civil Disobedience presupposes the habit of willing obedience to laws'.[54] As Bharatan Kumarappa says: 'It is called "civil" because it is non-violent resistance by people who are ordinarily law-abiding citizens; also because the laws which they choose to disobey are not moral laws but only such as are harmful to the people'.[55]

A general habit of obedience to the law helps us to think in moral terms and therefore to identify those laws that are unjust or immoral and need changing:

> It is only when a person has . . . obeyed the laws of society scrupulously that he is in a position to judge as to which particular rules are good and just and which unjust and iniquitous. Only then does the right accrue to him of the civil disobedience of certain laws in well-defined circumstances.[56]

Civil disobedience was justifiable only in the context of a policy and pattern of general obedience to the law – to show that it was aimed at resisting or changing particular unjust laws – and not at challenging the rule of law or the legitimacy of the state as such.

Even so, as Kumarappa points out, under certain circumstances, it is appropriate to engage in civil disobedience towards an entire government or regime and not merely of specific laws or ordinances of that regime:

> But Satyagraha can also be on a nation-wide scale to resist an entire Government when that government is corrupt and demoralizes the people. It may then take the form of non-cooperation with the Government, as it did in Gandhiji's Civil Disobedience movements of 1920–22, 1930–34 and 1940–44 in India.[57]

The entire regime, or even system, of government is unjust and illegitimate and must be changed (in this case, British colonial rule in India), and this justifies a general policy or strategy of civil disobedience to all facets of regime control over the daily life of the people.

This points to a significant difference between the use of civil disobedience in a democracy and in an unrepresentative or autocratic regime. Civil disobedience can be used to challenge specific unjust or discriminatory laws in a democracy, where constitutional methods have failed or are unavailable for some reason, without challenging or undermining the system of government as a whole. In fact, such focused or targeted civil disobedience can strengthen or improve a democratic system, through ridding it of laws inimical to civil liberties or preventing equal representation and participation in the political life of the state. In a dictatorship or undemocratic regime, however, civil disobedience can be used to challenge an entire system of government, through a general policy of disobedience and non-cooperation with the regime, because the state as a whole lacks legitimacy.

Martin Luther King also distinguished between just and unjust laws and defended our right to disobey unjust laws, while acknowledging our obligation to obey just laws: 'Therefore the individuals who stand up on the basis of civil disobedience . . . are not anarchists. They believe that there are laws which must be followed; they do not seek to defy the law, they do not seek to evade the law'.[58]

King's famous 'Letter from Birmingham Jail' was written to defend the use of civil disobedience to achieve civil rights in the southern US, after one of his numerous arrests for participating in civil disobedience actions. In this letter, King distinguished between the two types of positive or human-made law, in explicitly natural law terms:

> A just law is a man-made code that squares with the moral law or the law of God. An unjust law is a code that is out of harmony with the moral law. To put it in the terms of Saint Thomas Aquinas, an unjust law is a human law that is not rooted in eternal and natural law.[59]

The laws of human legislation and government can be measured directly against a higher moral law, which he refers to as both 'the moral law of the universe' and 'the law of God'.[60]

Furthermore, and in terms directly relevant to segregation and discrimination in the southern US, the distinction between just and unjust laws can be made with reference to their impact on human dignity:

> Any law that uplifts human personality is just. Any law that degrades human personality is unjust . . . segregation . . . ends up relegating persons to the status of things. So segregation is not only politically, economically and sociologically unsound, but it is morally wrong and sinful.[61]

Legalised discrimination against African-Americans in the southern US was unjust, and these laws could be challenged and resisted directly, by means of civil disobedience.

It is interesting that both King and Tolstoy refer to 'the law of God' as an ethical standard against which to assess human behaviour and human institutions. King, however, felt that postive law, as enacted by government and the state, could be made to conform to the moral requirements of such divine or cosmopolitan or natural law. Tolstoy, on the other hand, argued that human-made law, encapsulated by the state, must be bypassed or superseded by direct, individual obedience to the moral commandments of God.

Gandhi asserted not only the right, but also the duty of every citizen to engage in civil disobedience in appropriate circumstances. It is the right of every citizen to assess the laws that apply to them within a state and, therefore, to engage in civil disobedience against those laws that are unjust or immoral, in order to change them where other methods (constitutional politics) have failed: 'civil disobedience is the inherent right of a citizen'.[62] Furthermore, it is our duty to disobey unjust laws, just as it is our duty to refuse to cooperate with any form of evil or injustice: 'Disobedience of the laws of an evil State is therefore a duty'.[63]

Gandhi's arguments for civil disobedience reflect his more general attitude towards the state and the rule of law. The laws of a legitimate, democratic state provide a just and fair mechanism for resolving social and political conflict. Justifications for civil disobedience, or the deliberate violation of specific laws, should not be confused with the quest for some sort of political order that transcends the limitations of the conventional state and conforms more closely to the full ethical requirements of nonviolence or *ahimsa*. The purpose of civil disobedience is to ensure that democratic states reach their full (if, nonetheless, still circumscribed) potential in supporting and protecting human dignity and social justice.

CIVIL RESISTANCE AND NONVIOLENT POLITICAL ACTION

We can now distinguish between two types of nonviolent political action – civil resistance and transformative nonviolence – based upon their attitude towards conventional state structures and their view of nonviolence as having either instrumental or ethical and structural significance as a form of political action. If we look at nonviolent political action not only as a method for achieving specific political objectives or even undermining and replacing a ruling regime, but also as a mechanism for releasing or liberating popular power, then perhaps we can see its transformative potential more clearly. In other words, rather than aiming only at regime change or regime improvement, perhaps it can aim at a more profound structural transformation of society, in which we create alternatives to conventional social and political structures (such as the state) that depend ultimately upon the suppression of popular power and the use of armed force or organised violence to maintain themselves. This transformative vision allows us to move beyond an instrumental assessment of nonviolent political action to an examination of its ultimate political and social objectives.

The purpose of civil resistance is, essentially, to defend the principles and institutions associated with liberal democracy, such as regular democratic elections and human rights or civil liberties. This can be done through protecting or promoting conventional state structures. Transformative nonviolence, on the other hand, seeks both to liberate popular power and to eliminate violence as a method of social control and political change. Rather than defending the liberal democratic state, this often involves challenging and even seeking to replace the state, as a form of social and political organisation.

Civil resistance is often identified as a third or separate category of political action, distinct from both conventional parliamentary or state-based political activity and various forms of violent or armed resistance against unjust, oppressive and authoritarian states or an aggressive, occupying power. Thus, civil resistance can be defined as collective action outside the formal institutions or procedures of the state that avoids the systematic or deliberate use of violence or armed force to achieve its political or social objectives.

Thus, Mary E. King views civil resistance, or 'nonviolent struggle', as a corrective when liberal democracy fails:

> protection of representative government when constitutional measures fail actually *demands* a corrective capability that can work without violence. If liberal democratic principles are threatened and institutionalised political systems fail, it is crucial for the populace to know that they have the option of turning to a technique of extra-parliamentary nonviolent sanctions . . . Collective nonviolent action is actually fundamental to democracy . . .[64]

Civil resistance can be justified as an extra-parliamentary technique aimed at restoring the principles and institutions of liberal democracy. In a fully functioning democratic polity, then, perhaps there would be no need for civil resistance.

The aim of civil resistance is to restore or establish liberal democracy and it can do so without resorting to violence:

> When combined with proper planning, it is possible for people, groups, and societies to use this repertoire of methods to protect liberty, achieve free elections, fight for human rights or reform, end totalitarian bureaucracies, and even dismantle despotic regimes, all without resort to violent measures, guerrilla warfare, or armed struggle.[65]

It is the capacity to achieve these objectives without using violence that characterises civil resistance as a form of nonviolent political action: 'The technique . . . does not seek to accomplish its goals through physical harm, injury, or killing'.[66]

Civil resistance does not employ violence, not out of any pacifist or moral conviction, but because violence is not necessary for its effectiveness. In fact, the use of violence can undermine its effectiveness, which depends upon the capacity for mass or popular political mobilisation: 'Injecting violence into a struggle destroys the potential for involving an entire people in self-reliant civil resistance'.[67] The significance of nonviolent popular mobilisation for the political effectiveness of civil resistance is often explained by means of the consent theory of power, according to which, 'political power rests ultimately on the cooperation of the ruled'.[68] The withdrawal of such cooperation, obedience or compliance is central to the methods of civil resistance or nonviolent political action.

Jonathan Schell suggests that it is fully consistent with the ideals of nonviolent political action to seek to replace authoritarian or undemocratic regimes with liberal democracies, because the explicit aim of 'liberal government', in accordance with social contract theory, is to restrain or tame violence.[69] He claims, for example, that:

> the spread of democracy . . . is an expansion of the zone in which the business of politics is conducted along mainly nonviolent lines. In this basic respect, the long march of liberal democracy is a 'peace movement' – possibly the most important and successful of them all.[70]

Protecting or establishing liberal democratic government is an appropriate objective of civil resistance or nonviolent political action, when other conventional and constitutional methods are unavailable or have failed.

Schell also extends the connection between liberal democracy as a peace movement from the domestic or internal sphere to the international sphere, through replacing what he calls 'the war system'[71] of international politics with the rule of law and 'liberal internationalism'.[72] He associates this, particularly, with the ideals of US President Woodrow Wilson, in the aftermath of World War I.[73]

Even if a central purpose of liberal democracy, epitomised by the rule of law, is to minimise violence as a feature of domestic and (perhaps also) international politics, because it takes the form of the sovereign, territorially-defined state, it can still facilitate or even require the use or threat of violence as a method of social control or self-defence. The price, as it were, of viewing liberal democracy as a peace movement, and the state as a mechanism for minimising or taming the levels of violence within (and between societies), is to concentrate the legitimate use of violence within the institutions of the state, such as the police force, the judicial system and the armed forces. Minimising the role of violence in human affairs requires its institutionalisation in the form of the state.

Although Schell identifies liberal democracy as a 'peace movement', he also acknowledges that the sovereign, indivisible state acts as a justification for, and is a requirement of, military force in the international sphere. According to Schell, the sovereign state 'should possess exclusive authority over *one* people residing in *one* territory'. Furthermore, such a state 'fits – and not by accident – the demands of military planning', because '[o]nly well-consolidated nations living in well-defined territories can have clear, defensible borders'.[74] The 'right of belligerency', or the right to kill in defence of the state, 'is one part (along with police powers and judicial powers) of what Max Weber called "the right of legitimate violence", the monopoly of which he took to be the defining characteristic of the modern state'.[75]

Civil resistance groups (non-governmental organisations or social movements) must restrict themselves to exclusively nonviolent forms of political action, because only states retain the right to the legitimate use of violence, both domestically (for law enforcement) and internationally (for self-defence), in accordance with conventional Western political theory. Civil resistance groups (as non-state actors) have an obligation to limit themselves to nonviolent forms of political action, in accordance with this view of state legitimacy (connected to social contract theory). They do not choose nonviolence out of a sense of morality that somehow makes them ethically superior to the state. Instead, they are morally obliged to pursue exclusively nonviolent forms of political activity, because the definition of state legitimacy includes its monopoly over the use of violence.

TRANSFORMATIVE NONVIOLENCE AND THE VIOLENCE OF THE STATE

Transformative nonviolence, on the other hand, challenges not only oppressive or authoritarian regimes, but also conventional state structures and forms of state power, whether they appear in the form of the liberal democratic state or not. It does so on the basis of forms of popular political power that do not revolve around hierarchical structures such as the state and also through its opposition to the systematic concentration of violence, legitimate or otherwise, in the institutions of the state. The critique of the state associated with transformative nonviolence is derived from both an alternative view of the nature of political power, as well as its opposition to the institutionalised or systematic violence associated with the state as a form of political organisation.

Thus, some proponents of nonviolent political action suggest that one of the central tasks of nonviolence is to provide an alternative to the violence of the state. In his chapter on 'Nonviolence and the state', for example, Richard Gregg claims that 'compulsion, intimidation and violence have been and still are a very large and perhaps predominating element in the state'.[76] This is true, both internationally – in the form of government expenditures on war and preparations for war – and domestically – through the criminal justice system and mechanisms of law enforcement, such as prisons. He points to 'state expenditures for prisons' and 'the administration of criminal law', as further evidence of the centrality of violence to the state.[77]

Barry Hindess returns to the theme of territory, as one of the defining characteristics of a state, which he associates with 'the threat of violence against those who do not belong'. Furthermore: 'Territory is associated with the threat of violence toward those who do belong, as much as those who do not',[78] as a way of regulating conduct. In other words, the threat of violence is an essential characteristic of the state, both internationally and domestically.[79] Furthermore, such violence (which he identifies with 'terrorism') is 'the ultimate source of peace and order within a territorial community', in accordance with Hobbes and conventional Western political thought:[80] 'In the Hobbesian story, then, their terrifying capacity for violent action enables states to pacify their own populations and to limit violent interaction between them'.[81] Both Western political theory and European political history (in the form of the Treaty of Westphalia) suggest 'the formation of the state and the concentration of terror in its hands as the constitutive moment in the formation of the modern world', according to Hindess.[82]

Thus, even though the concentration of the mechanisms of violence in the institutions of the state is justified or legitimated as a means to limit violence and maintain social order, as Lummis and others have pointed out, the greatest perpetrator of mass violence during the twentieth century – the century in which the state became the predominant form of political organisation worldwide – has been the state. 'In the twentieth century the state killed more than 200 million people', and 'most of the wars going on in the world are between states and some section of their own people',[83] certainly at the close of the century and the beginning of the current one.

This, according to Lummis, 'is the dark secret behind the state's claim to protect its citizens. The primal war of the state is the war the state fights against its people to found and to maintain itself'.[84] Western political theory may claim that the state is necessary to minimise violence within and between societies, but the historical evidence of the last century demonstrates the exact opposite. State power depends upon the threat and use of systematic, institutionalised and widespread violence, not only against the citizens of other countries, but against its own citizens.

According to Lummis, 'Gandhi believed . . . that the state is by nature a violent organization: "The state represents violence in a concentrated and organized form"'.[85] He suggests that Gandhi proposed a different type of polity or political structure for India, in the form of self-governing village republics. Such a polity would dispense with the possibility of military power, because it would preclude the type of centralised, sovereign political authority derived from the state.[86] The rhetorical pacifism of the Japanese constitution is hollow, precisely because it is attached to a conventional state. In Gandhi's 'proposed constitution' for a newly independent India, on the other hand, 'the tendency toward and the possibility of war are excluded from the polity by its very structure'.[87]

REBELLION VERSUS REVOLUTION

In *On Revolution*, Hannah Arendt distinguished between rebellion and the modern political phenomenon of revolution. Properly understood, according to Arendt, revolution aims at creating the conditions of public freedom. Such freedom consists of citizens acting together to achieve shared goals. Arendt suggests that 'the actual content of freedom . . . is participation in public affairs'.[88] Freedom as '"public happiness" . . . consisted in the citizen's right of access to the public realm, in his (sic) share in public power'.[89] She also suggests that 'power comes into being only if and when men (sic) join themselves together for the purpose of action'[90] and that such power rests on 'reciprocity and mutuality' or equality.[91] It does not depend upon violence, and, in fact, violence is the opposite of power, insofar as it undermines the conditions under which such cooperative action can occur. We can see that Arendt's discussion of revolution as political transformation responds directly to the three themes of Tolstoy's critique of the state: violence, freedom and equality. Arendt, however, challenges the role of violence in politics more because it undermines the conditions of public freedom and popular power and not necessarily because of some pacifist objection to the taking of human life, for instance.

Civil resistance, Arendt's views on revolution, and transformative nonviolence share an analysis of power as derived from consent or cooperation to achieve agreed objectives. Timothy Garton Ash goes so far as to suggest that nonviolent political action in the form of 'civil resistance has assisted at the birth of a new genre of revolution, qualitatively different from the Jacobin-Bolshevik model of 1789 and 1917',[92] precisely because it utilises the power of popular mobilisation, rather than aiming at the violent seizure of state power by a relatively small number of people who have access to the means of perpetrating political violence and who then employ the institutionalised violence of the state to hold on to power.

Civil resistance, however, utilises popular forms of nonviolent mass mobilisation to achieve tactical or strategic political objectives, such as civil rights, democratic elections or regime change, without challenging conventional state structures (including the state's monopoly over the legitimate use of violence). Mary E. King, for example, does suggest that 'collective nonviolent action . . . can shape the social, political, and economic institutions that evolve for governance as a result of a nonviolent struggle', because of the level of 'popular involvement' and 'cohesion and unity' required to carry it out effectively, but she also seems to limit these changes to 'the subsequent emergence and formation of democratic institutions', rather than a more radical challenge to the state.[93]

Mark R. Beissinger suggests, for example, that the struggle by the Baltic states for independence from the Soviet Union shows that this civil society strategy, as the basis for effective civil resistance, can have important consequences for the longer-term political impact of nonviolent struggle:

> [t]he success of Baltic civil resistance . . . lies as well in the important role played by civil resistance in precipitating and consolidating stable democratic outcomes . . . it activated civil societies, providing a basis for the emergence of civic life so crucial to democratic development. Thus, civil resistance in the Baltic left lasting legacies that helped to define the quality of democratic life in its aftermath.[94]

The use of nonviolent political action to achieve independence, based around popular mobilisation and civil resistance, strengthened the capacity of citizens to continue to engage in political life after new political structures had been put into place.

As Sharp points out, however, this process of popular empowerment, unleashed by civil resistance, is not irreversible or permanent. It is 'a tendency, and not a guaranteed process . . . The experience in popular power may be diminished . . . and largely lost as people fall back into their previous views and patterns of submission'.[95] This has happened in numerous recent instances of civil resistance, including some high profile examples, such as Eastern Europe in 1989, Serbia post-Milosevic and the 'colour revolutions' in Georgia and the Ukraine.

Arendt, on the other hand, builds on her conception of public freedom, as the outcome of revolution, to criticise and identify limits to conventional state-based party politics. In her final chapter on 'The revolutionary tradition and its lost treasure', Arendt suggests that 'the rise of the nation-state' and parliamentary or representative government 'crushed' the potential for a political system based on direct, popular power.[96] In this case, the antinomy or contradiction is between the conventional state structure and alienated political power, epitomised by representative government, and forms of popular power unleashed by revolution, including mass nonviolent political action.

Arendt uses the terms 'party system' and 'council system' to establish the distinction between these two forms of governance and power.[97] According to her analysis, 'the party . . . has been an institution to provide parliamentary government with the required support of the people' so that the government can rule.[98] It is not so much that the government represents the people, as that the people 'have surrendered their power to their representatives' so that they can be governed via the party system.[99]

According to Arendt:

Our whole tradition of political thought has concluded – that the essence of politics is rulership and that the dominant political passion is the passion to rule or to govern. This, I propose, is profoundly untrue.[100]

It is untrue, because, based on her analysis of revolution, the aim of political activity is establishing the realm of public freedom derived from popular power, which, in turn, depends upon reciprocity and equality. This objective has been betrayed by conventional state structures and conventional party politics: 'The relationship between a ruling élite and the people – between the few, who among themselves constitute a public space, and the many, who spend their lives outside it and in obscurity – has remained unchanged'.[101] In other words, the élite have colonised the realm of public freedom or political activity for themselves, via the institutions of the state, leaving the many in the realm of material necessity.

Jonathan Schell, in his 'Introduction' to *On Revolution*, suggests that 'the wave of democratic revolutions of the late twentieth century'[102] and, in particular, the events in Eastern Europe in 1989–90 conform to Arendt's views about revolution: 'All were largely nonviolent', and 'they repeatedly vindicated Arendt's new conception of power and its relationship to violence'.[103] Schell connects Arendt's analysis of power to 'the great essay by Václav Havel of 1978 The Power of the Powerless'.[104]

Havel's essay concludes with a somewhat startling (under the circumstances) critique of 'bourgeois democracy' that concurs with some of Arendt's themes, concerning the nature of political power. Almost as a coda to his novel and insightful analysis of the nature of power under communist regimes in Eastern Europe, Havel extends this critique to Western democracy:

> It would appear that the traditional parliamentary democracies can offer no fundamental opposition to the automatism of technological civilization and the industrial-consumer society . . . People are manipulated in ways that are infinitely more subtle and refined than the brutal methods used in the post-totalitarian societies.[105]

The contrast between 'living within the lie', based on the denial of fundamental human needs, and 'living within the truth',[106] which recognises and acknowledges those needs, that Havel identifies as the ideological basis of political power in post-totalitarian societies in Eastern Europe, applies equally, if perhaps more subtly, to Western democracies.

He goes on to say that 'to cling to the notion of traditional parliamentary democracy as one's political ideal . . . capable of guaranteeing human beings enduring dignity . . . would, in my opinion, be at the very least shortsighted'.[107] Instead, we need to focus on the needs of real people, as distinct from the requirements of the system or what he refers to as 'living within the truth', 'as something far more profound than merely returning to the everyday mechanisms of Western (or if you like bourgeois) democracy'.[108] He concludes by suggesting, in a move that parallels Arendt's discussion of 'councils' as distinct from state-based structures, that: 'There can and must be structures that are open, dynamic and small; beyond a certain point, human ties like personal trust and personal responsibility cannot work'.[109]

Civil resistance can be understood as rebellion, in Arendt's sense of the term, because 'the end of rebellion is liberation'[110] or regime change. Transformative nonviolence, on the other hand, can be understood as revolution in Arendt's sense, because it aims at a more profound transformation of social and political structures, by creating the conditions for public freedom and releasing popular power through cooperative action and through eliminating violence as a feature of political life. Both objectives of transformative nonviolence require us to challenge conventional state structures.

Transformative nonviolence moves beyond civil resistance to challenge state-based politics, because nonviolence is viewed not merely as an instrument or device to achieve specific political objectives within existing structures or as a means to an end, but as a characteristic of the society created by nonviolent political action or an end in itself. It can also benefit from the insights of Arendt's critical analysis of the nation-state, which suggests the full potential of nonviolent political action, through unleashing forms of popular power that transcend conventional state structures. In other words, transformative nonviolence challenges conventional state structures for at least two reasons: the ultimate dependence of the state upon the mechanisms of violence and its suppression of forms of popular power utilised by nonviolent political action and identified by Hannah Arendt, in her analysis of freedom and revolution.

CONCLUSION

Proponents of nonviolence, such as Tolstoy, identify three related problems for the state as a form of political and social organisation: violence, freedom and inequality. The three issues are related, because the institutionalised violence of the state can become a mechanism for maintaining and reinforcing social inequality and for controlling and suppressing autonomy and freedom. However, the response of

proponents of nonviolence to these problems with the state or government varies. Tolstoy proposes the elimination of the state, in favour of
individual autonomy through obedience to the moral laws of God and
purely voluntary and cooperative forms of social organisation. Gandhi's
attitude to the state is ambiguous, interpreting *swaraj* in terms of the
struggle for Indian political independence, but also connecting it to
swadeshi and the primacy of village-based forms of political and social
organisation. Sharp recognised the importance of independent *loci* of
power as sources of social power and political freedom (as distinct from
the centralised state), but argued for a gradual, functionalist approach
to replacing the state. Nonetheless, all three recognised the state or
the centralised, coercive apparatus of government as a central issue for
proponents of nonviolence, because of its continued dependence upon
violence as a method of social control and an instrument of security.

We can distinguish between two forms of nonviolent political action
– civil resistance and transformative nonviolence – at least partly on
the basis of their attitudes towards the state. Civil resistance aims to
defend the principles and institutions associated with the liberal democratic state, such as regular democratic elections and human rights or
civil liberties. Transformative nonviolence identifies specific limits to
civil resistance as a form of nonviolent political action, because of its
acceptance of, or allegiance to, the state. Such allegiance involves both
accepting the state's monopoly over the use of violence and the curtail-
ment or suppression of the public freedom or popular power derived
from nonviolent political action. Transformative nonviolence, on the
other hand, suggests that the ultimate aim of nonviolent political action
needs to be new forms of social and political organisation that do not
depend upon institionalised violence as a method of domination,
control and security and that liberate, rather than suppress, the popular
power central to its effectiveness as a mechanism of political change.

Notes

1 Roberts, 'Introduction', p. 20.
2 Tolstoy, 'Postscript to the "Life and Death of Drozhin"', p. 275.
3 Tolstoy, 'From *The Kingdom of God*', p. 259.
4 Tolstoy, 'The kingdom of God is within you, or Christianity not as a
   mystical doctrine but as a new conception of life', pp. 100–1.
5 Stephens, 'The non-violent anarchism of Leo Tolstoy', p. 7.

6 Tolstoy, 'The end of an age: An essay on the approaching revolution', p. 39.

7 Tolstoy, 'Patriotism and government', p. 86.

8 Tolstoy, 'The slavery of our times', p. 154.

9 Tolstoy, 'The kingdom of God is within you, or Christianity not as a mystical doctrine but as a new conception of life', p. 104.

10 Tolstoy, 'The kingdom of God is within you, or Christianity not as a mystical doctrine but as a new conception of life', p. 103.

11 Tolstoy, 'Patriotism and government', pp. 85–6.

12 Tolstoy, 'Postscript to the "Life and Death of Drozhin"', p. 276.

13 Laslett, 'Introduction', p. 131.

14 Sharp, *Social Power and Political Freedom*, p. 349.

15 Ibid. p. 349.

16 Ibid. p. 323.

17 Ibid. pp. 358–9.

18 Ibid. pp. 359.

19 Tolstoy 'The slavery of our times', pp. 139–40 (italics in original).

20 Sharp, *Waging Nonviolent Struggle: 20th Century Practice and 21st Century Potential*, p. 26.

21 Tolstoy, 'Letter to a non-commissioned officer', p. 121.

22 Tolstoy, 'The kingdom of God is within you, or Christianity not as a mystical doctrine but as a new conception of life', p. 103.

23 Tolstoy, 'The end of an age: An essay on the approaching revolution', p. 45.

24 Ibid. p. 45.

25 Ibid. p. 45.

26 Tolstoy, 'The slavery of our times', p. 138.

27 Tolstoy, 'The end of an age: An essay on the approaching revolution', p. 27.

28 Ibid. p. 48.

29 Tolstoy, *Government is Violence: Essays on Anarchism and Pacifism*, p. 178, footnote 27.

30 Tolstoy, 'The end of an age: An essay on the approaching revolution', p. 50.

31 Ibid. p. 59.

32 Ibid. p. 60.

33 Hannah Arendt, cited in Sharp, *Social Power and Political Freedom*, p. 144.

34 Sharp, *Social Power and Political Freedom*, p. 147.

35 Gandhi, *Selected Writings of Mahatma Gandhi*, p. 277.

36 Ibid. p. 280.

37 Ibid. pp. 135–7.

38 Ibid (paraphrased).

39 Ibid. p. 137.
40 Ibid. pp. 51–2.
41 Brown, 'Gandhi and civil resistance in India, 1917–47: Key issues', p. 49.
42 Gandhi, *Non-Violent Resistance (Satyagraha)*, p. 385.
43 Ibid. p. 386.
44 Gandhi, *Selected Writings of Mahatma Gandhi*, pp. 51–3.
45 Sharp, *Waging Nonviolent Struggle: 20th Century Practice and 21st Century Potential*, p. 515.
46 Sharp, *Social Power and Political Freedom*, p. 36.
47 Burrowes, *The Strategy of Nonviolent Defense: A Gandhian Approach*, p. 154.
48 Ibid. p. 155.
49 Ibid. p. 155.
50 Ibid. p. 155.
51 Gandhi, *Selected Writings of Mahatma Gandhi*, p. 65.
52 Ibid. pp. 65–6.
53 Ibid. p. 210.
54 Gandhi, *Non-Violent Resistance (Satyagraha)*, p. 3.
55 Kumarappa, 'Editor's note', p. iv.
56 Gandhi, *Non-Violent Resistance (Satyagraha)*, p. 75.
57 Kumarappa, 'Editor's note', p. iv.
58 King, 'Love, law, and civil disobedience', pp. 48–9.
59 King, 'Letter from Birmingham Jail', p. 293.
60 King, 'Love, law, and civil disobedience', p. 49.
61 King, 'Letter from Birmingham Jail', p. 293.
62 Gandhi, *Non-Violent Resistance (Satyagraha)*, p. 174.
63 Ibid. p. 238.
64 King, 'Nonviolent struggle in Africa: Essentials of knowledge and teaching', p. 38.
65 Ibid. p. 20.
66 Ibid. p. 23.
67 Ibid. p. 24.
68 Ibid. p. 23.
69 Schell, *The Unconquerable World: Power, Nonviolence, and the Will of the People*, pp. 236, 239.
70 Ibid. p. 240.
71 Ibid. pp. 270ff.
72 Ibid. p. 270ff.
73 Ibid. p. 270ff.
74 Ibid. p. 289.
75 Lummis, 'The smallest army imaginable', p. 318.
76 Gregg, *The Power of Nonviolence*, p. 103.
77 Ibid. p. 103.

78 Hindess, 'Terrortory', p. 244.
79 Ibid. p. 244.
80 Ibid. p. 247.
81 Ibid. p. 248.
82 Ibid. p. 249.
83 Lummis, 'The smallest army imaginable', p. 320.
84 Ibid. p. 320.
85 Ibid. p. 329–30.
86 Ibid. pp. 327–9.
87 Ibid. p. 330.
88 Arendt, *On Revolution*, p. 22.
89 Ibid. p. 118.
90 Ibid. p. 166.
91 Ibid. p. 173.
92 Ash, 'A century of civil resistance: Some lessons and questions', p. 377.
93 King, 'Nonviolent struggle in Africa', pp. 36–7.
94 Beissinger, 'The intersection of ethnic nationalism and people power tactics in the Baltic States, 1987–91', p. 246.
95 Sharp, *Waging Nonviolent Struggle*, p. 429.
96 Arendt, *On Revolution*, pp. 239–40.
97 Ibid. p. 239.
98 Ibid. p. 263.
99 Ibid. p. 240.
100 Ibid. p. 268.
101 Ibid. p. 269.
102 Schell, 'Introduction', p. xxi.
103 Ibid. p. xxii.
104 Ibid. p. xxii.
105 Havel, 'The power of the powerless', p. 116.
106 Ibid. p. 65.
107 Ibid. p. 117.
108 Ibid. p. 117.
109 Ibid. p. 118.
110 Arendt, *On Revolution*, p. 133.

Chapter 4

NONVIOLENCE AND POLITICAL POWER

INTRODUCTION

Power is a central theme of political theory (together with violence), because it concerns the capacity to achieve goals in a social context – individually, but also collectively – through social organisation and political institutions. The theme of power, then, is one of the most contentious issues affecting evaluations of nonviolent political action, but it also marks one of the most distinctive contributions of nonviolence to political theory.

Classic theories of power in Western political theory view it in terms of competition for scarce resources. Power, then, becomes intimately connected to issues of individual and collective security and survival and also to conflict and enmity. Explanations of the collective exercise of power through forms of political organisation, such as states or governments, are often derived from theories of human nature or individual psychology, interpreted as both acquisitive and competitive and, understandably, concerned with issues of self-preservation. According to social contract theorists, for example, the basic human condition is one of a 'state of nature', consisting of competition for resources and a struggle for survival. All forms of political and social organisation are designed as a remedy for this condition.

The first part of *Leviathan*, 'Of man', by Thomas Hobbes, for instance, consists of his analysis of human nature or human psychology, which he then uses as a platform for his political theory of the state (or 'commonwealth'). A central component of both his theory of human nature and his political theory concerns his analysis of power and its role in both human behaviour and political institutions. Hobbes roots the pre-emptive exercise of power over others in the search for security, because of the competition for scarce resources. He writes:

> . . . if any two men desire the same thing, which nevertheless they cannot both enjoy, they become enemies . . . And from this diffidence of one another, there is no way for any man to secure himselfe, so reasonable, as Anticipation; that is, by force, or wiles, to master the persons of all men he can, so long, till he see no other power great enough to endanger him: And this is no more than his own conservation requireth, and is generally allowed.[1]

The implication is that power over others is necessary for self-preservation, in the context of such competition. Thus, the quest for power over others is an essential and perpetual feature of human behaviour.

Furthermore, it is not sufficient to react defensively to specific threats, while attempting to avoid such competition. All human beings must engage actively in the constant pursuit of power over others, in order to ensure their own survival:

> Also because there be some, that taking pleasure in contemplating their own power in the acts of conquest, which they pursue farther than their security requires; if others, that otherwise would be glad to be at ease within modest bounds, should not by invasion increase their power, they would not be able, long time, by standing only on their defence, to subsist. And by consequence, such augmentation of dominion over men, being necessary to a mans conservation, it ought to be allowed him.[2]

Thus, the perpetual pursuit of power over others is derived from the requirements of individual survival and not necessarily from greed, ignorance or egotism (even though these factors may augment or reinforce this existential need for power).

Similarly, in another passage, Hobbes states:

> So that in the first place, I put for a generall inclination of all mankind, a perpetuall and restless desire of Power after power . . . because he cannot assure the power and means to live well, which he hath present, without the acquisiton of more.[3]

Thus, as C. B. Macpherson comments: 'Everyone, those with moderate as well as those with immoderate desires, is necessarily pulled into a constant competitive struggle for power over others, or at least to resist his powers being commanded by others'.[4] The ceaseless competition for power is prompted, in the first instance, by each individual's quest for basic survival, regardless of the moderateness (or not) of their own desires and appetites.

Hobbes interprets power in exclusively zero-sum terms, so that one person's power can be increased or augmented only at the expense of someone else's power. This drives not only the competition for the scarce resources necessary for basic survival, but also attempts to increase one's own power, through diminishing the power of others. As Macpherson writes, for Hobbes, 'every man's power resists and hinders the effects of other men's power . . . one man's power may be simply redefined as the excess of his over others'.[5]

It is this interpretation of power, in exclusively competitive, zero-sum, existential terms, that transforms 'man's need for power from a harmless to a harmful thing', according to Macpherson.[6] Power becomes inextricably linked to conflict and violence (most significantly, the infamous 'warre . . . of every man, against every man'[7] of the state of nature):

> So that in the nature of man, we find three principall causes of quarrell. First, Competition; Secondly, Diffidence; Thirdly, Glory. The first, maketh men invade for Gain; the second, for Safety; and the third, for Reputation.[8]

Thus, Hobbes' theory of power is intimately connected to explanations of violence and of the role of the state (or Leviathan) in maintaining social order, through controlling competition, conflict and violence.

Kenneth Boulding distinguishes between what he refers to as three 'faces' of power: threat power, economic power and integrative power. The first of these, 'threat power', corresponds most closely with conventional, coercive theories of power, such as those associated with the social contract theorists. 'I distinguish 'three faces' of power, though these categories are by no means unambiguous or complete: The first of these is threat power . . . The power of the law rests on rather specific threats',[9] involving the capacity to impose or inflict sanctions reinforced by violence. In addition to imposing the rule of law, such 'threat power' is used to defend a society against aggression, by means of military force. As Boulding points out, such a '. . . counterthreat . . . may lead to deterrence, that is abstention on the part of the original threatener from carrying out the threat'. It may also, however, 'lead to a breakdown, for instance, in war, if each tries to carry out the threat on the other'.[10]

> A second form of power is economic power . . . This sometimes emerges out of the successful use of threat power, as in the conquest of land. On the whole, however, economic power comes out of the skills of production and exchange . . . The third, and I argue the most important, source of power is what I have called 'integrative power'. This is the power of legitimacy, persuasion, loyalty, community, and so on.[11]

It is interesting that, for Boulding, integrative, or cooperative, power operates, in the first instance, at the level of ideas about political norms and social relationships.

This integrative, or cooperative, power involves the capacity of individuals and social groups to work together to achieve agreed or mutually beneficial goals and objectives. Power is not a function of violence or coercion, but 'instead comes from the mutual assistance and loyalty of people binding themselves together for some purpose'.[12] The eco-feminist Starhawk refers to this type of power as 'power-with', as distinct from more conventional views of 'power-over', which describes power 'in a way that reflects elite preoccupation with political, economic, and social control . . . Power-with is the influence we wield among equals – the ability to act as a channel to focus the will of the group'.[13]

This integrative view of power, or power-with, forms the basis of the so-called 'consent theory of power', associated with explanations of the effectiveness of nonviolent political action and civil resistance. Boulding argues, somewhat hesitantly, for the primacy of integrative over other forms of power:

> I have sometimes argued that if we are looking for any single element in the social system on which everything else depends – something which we should probably not do – the best candidate would be integrative power in the shape of legitimacy, for without

legitimacy neither threat power nor economic power is very effective.[14]

In other words, 'power is a gift to the powerful by those over whom the
power may be exercised, who recognize the power as legitimate',[15] so
that even elite power depends ultimately on the consent and cooperation of those they govern.

As Boulding points out, these three types of power are intimately
linked. They can reinforce each other, but they can also undermine or
challenge each other:

> Any actual exercise of power tends to involve all three 'faces' . . .
> Threat power is certainly dominant in the military, but unless it
> has a certain base in economic power, of course, the means of
> destruction and threat cannot be produced . . . economic power
> of property is supported by the threat power of the law, yet where
> ownership of property becomes illegitimate . . . no amount of
> threat power can preserve it.[16]

The dependence of so-called 'hard power', or institutionalised political
violence in the form of the military, for example, upon other types of
power is a central feature of the consent theory of power and of nonviolent political action.

Sharp also provides a slightly different definition of power from the
zero-sum, competitive view of power associated with Thomas Hobbes,
in particular. Sharp's definition of power brings out its cooperative, as
well as its competitive, aspect: '"Power" here means the capacity of
people to act in order to achieve objectives even in the face of opposition'.[17] He acknowledges that power can involve competition between
individuals and social groups to achieve their objectives. Nonetheless,
'the capacity of people to act in order to achieve their objectives'
can also involve cooperation between individuals and social groups,
depending upon whether or not these objectives are, or can be, shared.
Such cooperative power can involve two of Boulding's three faces of
power: economic power, or mechanisms of production and exchange,
and integrative power, derived from political norms and social relationships.

Furthermore, according to Sharp, the distribution of power throughout a society is crucial to its social and political health: 'All of our

grave social, economic, and political problems involve at some point a serious maldistribution of power'.[18] A 'maldistribution of power', for Sharp, refers to an unequal distribution of power within a society, 'because one group has the power to impose its will on a weak group'. 'Wherever one looks at a situation which one group or another regards as a "problem", one encounters an actual or a perceived inequitable distribution of power'.[19]

THE CONSENT THEORY OF POWER

The so-called 'consent theory of power' is at the core of explanations of the effectiveness of various forms of nonviolent political action or civil resistance. This theory of power is prevalent, or at least implicit, in many prominent proponents of nonviolence, from Tolstoy through Gandhi to Sharp, and it is also found in other political theorists, such as Hannah Arendt. According to this theory, the power of any ruling elite depends upon the consent, compliance and obedience of those they govern. This extends to sovereign or dominant political institutions, such as the state, which depends upon the compliance and obedience of citizens, subordinate social groups and those involved in the inter-mediate bodies constituting its apparatus of administrative and coercive control (such as the police, court system, military and civil service). This theory of power is also sometimes referred to as the pluralistic theory of power, because it claims that power ultimately flows upwards from the diverse social groups that make up the base of any social and political hierarchy, through this relationship of consent and compliance.

Gene Sharp contrasts this pluralistic or social view of power with more conventional views of political power, which he refers to as monolithic, because they focus on a single source of power – the ruling elites of any hierarchically-organised social or political institution (such as the state): 'When faced with such a strong State, power is seen to derive from the few who command the administrative system and the institutions capable of applying violence for political purposes'.[20]

According to Sharp, however: 'The views that power derives primarily from the capacity to wield violence and that the power of rulers is monolithic and relatively permanent are not correct'.[21] Instead, such power 'is always based upon an intricate and fragile structure of human and institutional relationships',[22] such as relationships of consent and cooperation. This is because:

power rises continually from many parts of the society. Political power is therefore fragile. Power always depends for its strength and existence upon a replenishment of its sources by the cooperation of numerous institutions and people – cooperation that does not have to continue.[23]

'The roots of political power, Sharp maintains, reach below the structure of the state into society itself . . . Power, then, Sharp and others contend, is not intrinsic to political elites'.[24] The power of the ruling elite is not monolithic, permanent and self-contained. Its relative fragility and mutability, despite appearances and conventional belief, and its dependence upon social power and the consent of the governed, makes it vulnerable to challenge by civil resistance and nonviolent political action.

This emphasis on the consent, compliance and obedience of the governed as the source of power within a society also implies an important distinction between violence and power, which are often treated as synonymous in conventional, 'realist' views of power. Even violent sanctions depend ultimately upon the willingness of those who implement them. Rather than violence producing power, it could be argued that social power provides the capacity to engage in, or utlise, violence. This is a theme explored by Hannah Arendt, amongst others.

Thus, Sharp contrasts a conventional, monolithic view of political power, located in hierarchical and centralised institutions such as the state, with a more pluralistic view of social power. Such social power is located in what he refers to as '*loci* of power', which include what might currently be referred to as organisations of civil society or social movements. According to Sharp:

> *loci* of power (or places in which power is located, converges, or is expressed) . . . are likely to include such social groups and institutions as families, social classes, religious groups, cultural and national groups, occupational groups, economic groups, villages, towns, cities, provinces and regions, smaller governmental bodies, voluntary organizations, and political parties.[25]

Such organisations and social groups provide autonomous and independent spaces of action, separate or distinct from such all-encompassing political institutions or structures such as the state. The policies and behaviour of these groups must align or comply with those of the state or the governing political apparatus of a society if it is to be able to maintain its control over those who live within that society. On the other hand, the power of the ruling elite 'is most likely to be subjected to controls and limits', to the extent that 'power is effectively diffused throughout the society among such *loci*'. Sharp associates such diffusion of power with 'political "freedom"'.[26]

The ruling elite would not be able to govern, and the state apparatus would not be able to function, without the compliance and obedience (or consent) of the vast majority of those they rule and whose cooperation and active involvement is essential for them to carry out and implement their decisions. As Gene Sharp points out: 'The persons who are at any point the rulers do not personally possess the power of control, administration, and repression that they wield'.[27] They do not personally have the capacity to implement decisions and to carry out these functions of control and administration, but depend upon the active involvement and cooperation of those working for state institutions, for instance, to do this, as well as the compliance or obedience of the population. For this reason, how much power rulers possess 'depends on how much power society will grant them', through cooperating with them and implementing their policies.[28]

Tolstoy uses the term 'public opinion' to refer to the sentiments of acquiescence, submission and consent that provide the basis for 'governmental power'. Furthermore, according to Tolstoy, there is a circular relationship between public opinion and governmental power, because government acquires the capacity to create, augment and strengthen the public opinion, facilitating its position of control within a society:

> The power of the government is maintained by public opinion, and with this power the government, by means of its organs – its officials, law-courts, schools, churches, even the press – can always maintain the public opinion which they need. Public opinion produces the power, and the power produces public opinion.[29]

Nonetheless, public opinion is the ultimate source of state power and because public opinion can change, it can also deprive a government of the basis of its power. Public opinion 'is that which produces governments and gives them power, or deprives them of it'.[30]

While Sharp (and other proponents of nonviolence) tend to focus on the consent theory of power as it operates in an explicitly political context and especially through the modern sovereign state as the focal point of political power and the all-ecompassing form of social organisation, he points out that it also functions in other hierarchically-organised institutions: 'Power relationships similar to those in political societies with State structures exist in other hierarchical institutions as well, which also derive their power from the cooperation of many persons and groups'.[31]

Thus, there are at least two main components to this theory of power – its pluralism and its emphasis on consent (rather than coercion or control) as a source of power. Its pluralism is derived from its focus on diverse sources of power, in the form of the multiple social groups that make up the base of society and to which the population as a whole have some affinity, connection, involvement or membership. The other dimension concerns the relationship of cooperation, obedience or, at least, compliance between the population and those in control of the ruling apparatus of any hierarchical social and political institution (including the state) and upon which they depend to implement their decisions and achieve their goals.

This theory of power is essential to explaining the effectiveness of nonviolent political action, because it shows that the power of ruling elites (and the state) can be challenged and undermined through social groups or sectors of the population removing their consent and ceasing their obedience:

> The extremely widespread practice of nonviolent struggle is possible because the operation of this technique is compatible with the nature of political power and the vulnerabilities of all hierarchical systems. These systems and all governments depend on the subordinated populations, groups, and institutions to supply them with their needed sources of power.[32]

This withdrawal of consent can be achieved nonviolently, through various forms of mass mobilisation and civil resistance. Sharp identifies three significant categories of nonviolent action, all indicating or involving the withdrawal of consent: protest, non-cooperation and nonviolent intervention.

Both principled and pragmatic proponents of nonviolence can acknowledge its effectiveness, on the basis of the consent or pluralistic theory of power. According to Christina Fink:

Aung San Suu Kyi has also insisted on non-violence for moral rather than tactical reasons. As a practising Buddhist who has also been deeply inspired by Gandhi, she has argued that 'united action by a people armed merely with the principles of justice and non-violence can achieve far greater results than the vast institutions of a state that is not upheld by the consent of the populace'.[33]

A commitment to justice and nonviolence can replace an ideology or a culture of compliance and obedience and can provide the impetus required for a sustained or prolonged struggle, involving non-cooperation and the withdrawal of consent.

Sections of the general population can withdraw their consent or compliance, but so can those who might otherwise administer the institutions of the state or systems of repression and violence on behalf of the ruling elite against the rest of the population. 'Organizations and institutions . . . which supply the necessary sources of power to the opponent group, are called "pillars of support"', according to Sharp.[34] And, as he says: 'Without their support, the oppressive system disintegrates'.[35]

MULTIPLE SOURCES OF POWER WITHIN SOCIETY

Theorists or proponents of nonviolent political action who promote or utilise this theory of power (such as Sharp) sometimes seem to imply or suggest that this relationship of consent is the only or, at least, the ultimate source of power in society. This challenges more conventional views that hard, coercive power – in the form of the military (or other forms of institutionalised violence) – or material power, such as economic wealth in the form of money and natural resources, are the ultimate or, perhaps, the only forms of power. And yet, the consent theory of power can also be pluralistic, in the sense that it recognises these other types of power within or between societies. It is sufficient for proponents of nonviolent political action to identify and utilise this relationship of consent as the basis of their own political action, to demonstrate the reasons for its effectiveness and its capacity to challenge other forms of political and economic power. This also conforms to Kenneth Boulding's pluralistic view of power, in which he recognises its three 'faces', while emphasising the significance of integrative power (which shares central features of the consent theory of power).[36]

Sharp identifies six specific sources of power of ruling or dominant groups within society, including, but not restricted or limited to, those in control of the state or government. These are: authority, human resources, skills and knowledge, 'intangible factors', material resources and sanctions. All of these sources of power depend upon, or are supported by, the consent and cooperation of the population, at least to some extent. According to Sharp:

> In order to control the power of rulers, those sources of power that are provided by the society's groups and institutions must first be identified. Then the population will be able, when needed, to restrict or sever the supply of those sources.[37]

Identifying these specific sources of power of the ruling group allows the population to challenge them through nonviolent political action.

The first of these sources of power, *authority*, 'may also be called legitimacy', according to Sharp. 'It is the quality that leads people to accept a right of persons or groups to lead, command, direct, and be heard or obeyed by others'.[38] It is both voluntary and normative, because it involves the acceptance of this right to command and to be obeyed.

Tolstoy points out that one source of government authority is the sentiment of loyalty to one's community or country, translated into feelings of patriotism and the principle of self-defence. Tolstoy claims that 'all government authority is founded upon patriotism, that is, upon the readiness of people to subordinate themselves to authority in order to defend their nation, country, or state'.[39] Thus, war and violence in the name of self-defence and loyalty to one's country is intimately connected to the legitimacy and authority granted to a state or government by the population it governs. One cannot underestimate the power of an ideology, such as patriotism, in maintaining a social structure, where it conveys this sense of the legitimacy and, even, normalcy that supports the authority of a regime and the acceptance of this authority, or its right to rule or govern, by the rest of the population. This ideology, or sense of legitimacy, can be held by even the most repressive regime.

Human resources and *skills and knowledge* concern the number of persons who cooperate with and assist the rulers, as well as their abilities or skills.[40] By *intangible factors*, Sharp seems to mean socially conditioned beliefs or norms ('psychological and ideological factors') about forms of social and political organisation and 'habits and attitudes toward obedience and submission'.[41] These can include culturally or historically created attitudes towards individual autonomy and authority, for example, framed by religious beliefs or social traditions. They can also include the extent to which ruling and subordinate groups share a common ideology or belief system about forms of social organisation, embedded in attitudes towards social stratification and, even, cosmological order.

The final two sources of power are not uniquely dependent upon cooperation and consent, although they can be affected (strengthened or weakened) by it. *Material resources*, or the 'degree to which the rulers control property, natural resources, financial resources, the economic system',[42] correspond to what Boulding refers to as 'economic power'.[43] *Sanctions* correspond to Boulding's 'threat power'[44] and 'have been described as "an enforcement of obedience" . . . Sanctions are used by rulers to supplement voluntary acceptance of their authority'.[45] Sanctions involve the use of hard or coercive power by ruling groups and can be either violent or nonviolent.[46] Even so, as Sharp points out, the enforcement of sanctions depends upon the active cooperation of at least some sectors of the population employed in institutions of state control (such as the police or the legal system).[47]

The important point, for Sharp, is that each of these six sources of power 'is in turn closely related to, or directly dependent upon, the degree of cooperation, submission, obedience, and assistance that the ruler is able to obtain from his subjects. These include both the general population' and those who carry out the instructions or policies of the governing institutions or elites.[48]

Following Boulding, Burrowes and Sharp, we can suggest three types of power within a society: 'power over', 'power with' and consent. The pyramid in Figure 4.1 represents the hierarchical structures within a society, with the government or ruling elite of the society in the top level (single triangle). The intermediate level (three triangles) represents the governing mechanisms of the state, including army, police and civil servants, or what Sharp refers to as a government's 'pillars of support'.[49] The bottom level represents those who are governed (five triangles), in the form of the different social groups constituting the vast majority of the population.

The arrows represent the three types of power and the directions in which they flow within a society. Thus, 'power over' flows downwards

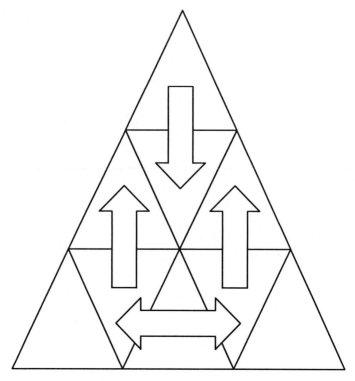

Figure 4.1 Three types of power[50]

from the government or ruling elite within a society and represents the power of domination and control. Crucially, this power is exercised against the social groups at the bottom of the social pyramid, by means of the intervening, governing mechanisms of the state.

The horizontal arrows represent 'power with' or the power that results when social groups (or individuals) cooperate to achieve agreed goals. Finally, the arrows pointing upwards represent the power of consent, compliance and obedience, on the part of subordinate social groups, in maintaining both elites and the intermediate institutions of the state in power, in accordance with the consent theory of power. Taken together, these three forms of power represent a pluralistic understanding of the sources or types of power within a society, even if proponents of nonviolent political action argue for the primacy of the third type – consent – in maintaining the whole structure (including the other two types of power).

Tolstoy identifies three core problems in society that must be addressed by struggles for social justice: 1) violence; 2) freedom; and 3) inequality. All three problems are crystallised into the power of domination and control epitomised by the state or government, represented by the upper tier in the pyramid and the first type of power – 'power over'.

> The Government, in the widest sense, including capitalists and the Press, is nothing else than an organization which places the greater part of the people in the power of a smaller part, who dominate them . . . So that all this organization resembles a cone, of which all the parts are completely in the power of those people or of that one person, who happen to be at the apex.[51]

The multi-levelled character of the pyramid or cone illustrates the inequality (3) inherent in any hierarchical social structure. Violence and mechanisms of enforcement (1) are use to maintain order, or the status quo, in the form of this hierarchy. Both violence and inequality severely curtail or restrict the freedom and autonomy (2) of those at the bottom of the hierarchy.

The three levels of this hierarchical social structure illustrates the significance of what Gene Sharp refers to as 'pillars of support',[52] for the functioning and survival of any regime and any hierarchical social order. The 'pillars of support' refer to the mechanisms of the state available to a government or ruling regime. This includes the ongoing administration of state rule, by means of the civil service, for example, as well as the mechanisms of coercion and enforcement, especially the legal or court system, the police and the military. These 'pillars of support' are represented by the middle level of the pyramid and arbitrate or mediate between the ruling regime or government and the mass of the population. The allegiance of these state institutions can be crucial to the success of any campaign of civil resistance or nonviolent political action. The youth movement Otpor and opposition political parties in Serbia were able to remove Milošević from power eventually, at least partly, because some of those pillars of support ceased to obey him:

> An essential element of the success of the movement was to be found within the structures of the state. After the 1996–7 events,

and in particular after the 1999 NATO intervention, a number of middle- and higher-ranking police and army officers . . . made secret pacts with the democratic opposition and helped the movement forward.[53]

The events of 1996–7 refer to sustained three-month protests that followed Milošević's falsification of municipal election results in November 1996.

This can be contrasted with Christina Fink's assessment of the failure of protests against the military regime in Burma in 2007, led by Buddhist monks:

> To use the language of Gene Sharp, the 2007 movement was not able to remove all or even most of the 'pillars of support' for the regime . . . the State Monastic Council . . . and most leading abbots did not publicly endorse the ABMA [All Burma Monks Alliance] . . . Only a small number of civil servants participated. Thus, the normal functioning of the state was not paralysed.[54]

Fink points out that these pillars of support are unlikely to switch their allegiance, unless they sense that the tide is turning against the regime or, in some cases, because they develop their own grievances against the regime: '. . . it is not easy to persuade the civil service and members of the military to demonstrate their support before it is clear that an opposition movement will win'.[55] This occurred in Serbia in the 1990s, but not in Burma in 2007.

THREE TYPES OF NONVIOLENT ACTION

Non-cooperation is one of three categories of nonviolent political action identified by Sharp. The other two categories are nonviolent protest and persuasion and nonviolent intervention. Nonetheless, Sharp claims: 'Noncooperation is the second and largest class of the methods of nonviolent action. Overwhelmingly, the methods of nonviolent action involve noncooperation with the opponents'.[56]

Protest and persuasion involve the communication of dissent and dissatisfaction by means of 'symbolic actions', such as demonstrations or marches, and may or may not escalate into forms of non-cooperation. Both non-cooperation and intervention involve a progressive intensification of levels of confrontation between the grievance group and the oppressor or dominant group. The methods of nonviolent non-cooperation involve the active withdrawal of consent or obedience to the policies and procedures of the ruling regime, in the form of boy-cotts, strikes and some forms of civil disobedience, for example. The methods of nonviolent intervention move beyond non-cooperation and the withdrawal of consent to 'actively disrupt the normal opera-tion of policies or the system by deliberate interference. Among the large number of methods in this class are . . . nonviolent occupation . . . alternative social institutions . . . nonviolent land seizures . . . alternative economic institutions . . . and parallel government'.[57]

Such disruptive forms of nonviolent intervention can be comple-mented by, what are sometimes referred to as, the creative class of such methods, through which the grievance group begins to build alterna-tive political institutions and forms of social organisation to replace those of the old, oppressive society. Gandhi, for example, put consider-able time and energy into his 'constructive programme' or the pursuit of specific social reforms within Indian society, complementary to the struggle for political independence from British colonialism.

Both non-cooperation and nonviolent intervention directly chal-lenge the opponents' sources of power, in the form of consent and compliance with existing social relations and institutions, in a way that the methods of protest and persuasion (which focus on communica-tion) do not. Furthermore: 'Demonstrations of protest and persuasion may precede or accompany acts of noncooperation or nonviolent inter-vention, or may be practiced in their absence'.[58]

Nonetheless, the significance of communicating mass dissent through nonviolent protest should not be underestimated, especially in repressive regimes, where such protests may be illegal (in which case, they can also be seen as forms of non-cooperation). Charles S. Maier refers to the impact of the ongoing peaceful street protests in East Germany (and elsewhere in Eastern Europe), for example:

> If repressive regimes cannot control public space, they are shown to possess neither efficacy nor legitimacy. If day after day protest-ers claim the streets with impunity, no regime can survive intact.[59]

More recently, the inability of the repressive regimes of Mubarak in Egypt and Ben Ali in Tunisia to contain mass protests in public spaces, such as Tahrir Square in Cairo, involved a direct challenge to their capacity to control the population and, ultimately, to their ability to retain state power. In particular, through communicating dissent, mass protests challenge the authority and legitimacy of a regime as a source of its power or its claim to be ruling on behalf of, or in the interests of, its citizens.

Sharp identifies the methods of non-cooperation as the most significant and most commonly used forms of nonviolent political action, precisely because of their direct connection to the basic source of the opponents' sources of power, in the form of the ongoing, daily compliance and obedience of the population:

> By applying methods of this class, the resisters often can use their usual roles in the society as means of resistance. For example, consumers refuse to purchase, laborers refuse to work, citizens disobey orders or practice civil disobedience . . . Noncooperation on a large scale or at crucial points produces a slowing or halting of normal operations of the relevant unit, institution, government, or society. In very extreme applications of widespread determined noncooperation, even a highly oppressive regime can simply fall to pieces.[60]

Non-cooperation involves a direct reversal of the usual relationship between the grievance group and the opponent group, in the form of an oppressive regime or an unjust employer, for example, and, thus, becomes an obvious and accessible form of action on the part of the grievance group.

Nonviolent non-cooperation was a vital component of the final phase of the campaign against apartheid in South Africa, led by the United Democratic Front (UDF):

> Repetitive national stay-away strikes – stoppages by millions of workers that closed down whole cities – became the most obvious form of protest after the declaration of the 1986 emergency. Boycotts were also a key tactic . . . when the UDF called upon African city-dwellers to withhold rents and service charges, denying the authorities a substantial source of local revenue.[61]

Methods such as strikes and boycotts were available to the vast majority of black South Africans and facilitated the transition of the domestic anti-apartheid campaign into a mass movement. As Tom Lodge says, 'it was the sheer scale of the rebellion by the UDF that made it unprecedented, and this scale was most evident in protests that were essentially non-violent'.[62]

Gene Sharp emphasises the importance of the number of those involved in non-cooperation, in terms of its impact on the power dynamics of a conflict situation:

> The impact of the various forms of noncooperation hinges heavily on the number of people participating in the use of these methods and the degree to which the opponents are dependent on the persons and groups that are refusing cooperation.[63]

Numbers also increase the confidence of those engaged in non-cooperation and their ability to persist in the face of oppression and violence.

Such large-scale mobilisation suggests that nonviolent resistance is best organised through 'social groups and institutions', which Sharp refers to as '*loci* (or places of power)'.[64] Such *loci* of power include, what we now call, civil society organisations and social movements. This, in turn, implies the need for a structural, and not merely a behavioural, analysis of power, in order to understand the relationship between these *loci* of power, the centralised, hierarchical state and other actors, such as transnational corporations.

Figure 4.2 shows how the grievance group can be one of the social groups that forms the base of the social and political hierarchy within a society. This grievance group may be marginalised for a variety of reasons, often to do with social identity (race, gender, ethnicity, nationality, language, religion), economic status (class) or some combination of these factors. The arrow shows how the orginal grievance group can form an alliance with other social groups, in order to engage in civil resistance or nonviolent political action. Furthermore, the resistance group (represented by the solid diamond) is often a relatively small group of committed activists, who manage to mobilise wider sectors of this social group and also help build alliances with other social groups.

It is important to acknowledge, however, that many social conflicts consist of horizontal conflicts (in terms of the social hierarchy represented by this pyramid) between social groups competing for scarce resources or around issues of social and cultural identity. In this case,

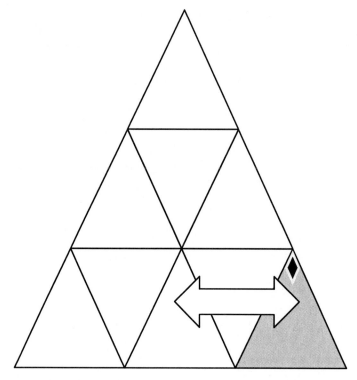

Figure 4.2 Grievance group and resistance group

the resources of the state, inluding its law enforcement mechanisms, but also any machinery of dispute resolution it has at its disposal, will be directed at containing and perhaps alleviating these social conflicts, both to minimise their destructive impact, but also to maintain social order.

Furthermore, in many complex and protracted political conflicts, some social groups – which can include, in some cases, a significant proportion of the population – can remain allied with dominant groups against grievance groups. Carlos Huneeus points out, for instance, that the Pinochet regime retained the support of 'a significant part of the population which had opposed the socialist and communist Popular Unity government of Allende'.[65]

Even though the methods of non-cooperation might be relatively accessible to the grievance group, this does not mean they are without cost and that they do not require a high level of commitment: 'Refusal of consent requires self-confidence, motivation to resist . . . and often involves considerable inconvenience and suffering'.[66] As Sharp points out:

> Participating in a nonviolent struggle does not make an individual immune from imprisonment, injury, suffering, or death. As in violent conflicts, the participants often suffer harsh penalities for their defiance and noncooperation.[67]

The consequences of non-cooperation can also include the serious economic and personal costs resulting from participation in consumer boycotts and labour strikes. The difficulties associated with the withdrawal of consent or non-cooperation may also explain the importance of the principle of voluntary self-suffering for many proponents of nonviolence. Nonetheless, Sharp claims that 'commonly the casualties in nonviolent struggles are significantly fewer than those in comparable violent struggles for similar objectives'.[68]

Sharp identifies civil disobedience, or the deliberate violation of specific laws or ordinances of a regime, as a form of political non-cooperation,[69] although he acknowledges that under certain circumstances, other types of political action (such as nonviolent protest) can also involve civil disobedience:

> There are political circumstances in which some of the forms of nonviolent protest, such as marches, are illegal. Under such circumstances, these methods would merge with civil disobedience and possibly other forms of noncooperation.[70]

Similarly, many of the methods of nonviolent intervention, such as blockades or occupations, also involve the violation of laws concerning trespass or public order, for instance, so it seems as though civil disobedience, or nonviolent direct action, is a broader category of nonviolent political action that crosses the boundaries between Sharp's own categories.

The counterpart of this is that specific examples of civil disobedience often fit into more than one of Sharp's three basic categories of nonviolent political action, because they contain elements of protest or communication, non-cooperation through deliberately violating specific laws, and intervention involving direct confrontation with state authorities (for instance). The Pitstop Ploughshares action at Shannon airport in Ireland in March 2003, prior to the US-led invasion and occupation of Iraq, illustrates this point. This action included communication or protest through the use of relevant symbols, such as religious artefacts and photos of Iraqi children affected by UN-imposed sanctions. It also involved the deliberate violation of laws and security regulations involving the airport, although, significantly, the five activists were eventually acquitted of all charges (including charges of criminal damage) following three trials and more than three years after the action. Finally, it could be argued that the action involved disruptive nonviolent intervention, because the activists remained in the aircraft hangar until they were arrested by the police.

Sharp considered nonviolent non-cooperation, and nonviolent action more generally, not only as a mechanism for dealing effectively with specific grievances, but also as a more general method for counteracting (and perhaps even replacing) the power of a centralised, hierarchical state or government. This is important, because a 'free society needs strong social groups and institutions capable of independent action and able to wield power in their own right in order to control an established government'.[71]

Thus, nonviolent action releases the power potential implicit in social groups, through facilitating cooperative forms of political action both within, and between, them:

> The technique of nonviolent action produces changes in the participants . . . power becomes more widely diffused in the society . . . Even more important than the changes produced by the nonviolent struggle on the opponents is the strengthening of the former subordinates who have learned to use this technique.[72]

Nonviolent political action contributes to the capacity of these social groups to achieve their own objectives, while strengthening their ability to respond to externally-imposed oppression and injustice.

As Sharp says, such empowerment is the constructive counterpart 'of noncooperation with the opponent'.[73]

> Effective nonviolent sanctions are likely to strengthen the group using them . . . Internal cooperation is needed to apply the nonviolent sanctions effectively, and also to provide those needs

formerly met by the opponent with whom cooperation has been withdrawn.[74]

If power is understood as the capacity to meet the goals of action, and this depends on cooperation between individuals and social groups, then the power of resistance groups is augmented and strengthened through the requirements of successful nonviolent political action.

One could argue that the objective of non-cooperation is primarily negative, because it involves undermining the sources of power of the opponent through withdrawing consent, compliance and cooperation. The empowerment of social groups engaging in non-cooperation is, in a sense, a byproduct of this primary objective. On the other hand, the third and final category of nonviolent action, especially creative nonviolent intervention, aims deliberately at releasing social power or integrative power to achieve specific, positive objectives. These include creating new institutions and forms of interaction to replace the old, in the form of alternative health and educational provision, for example, or even alternative forms of government. Gandhi's constructive programme, which focused on issues such as village hygiene and local government, could be seen as a form of creative nonviolent intervention, since it aimed at building the practices and institutions of the new society (or *hind swaraj*) within the shell of the old. As Jonathan Schell points out: 'Whereas noncooperation drained power away from the oppressors, the constructive programme generated it in the hands of the resisters'.[75]

MECHANISMS OF POLITICAL CHANGE

Gene Sharp identifies three (or perhaps four) mechanisms of political change that help explain the political effectiveness of nonviolent political action. These are conversion, accommodation and coercion. In the case of conversion, the opponent groups become convinced of the justice of the grievance group's demands and concede, or agree, to most or all of them. In the case of accommodation, the grievance group exerts sufficient power that the opponent group realises that they cannot be defeated, and they come to some sort of negotiated settlement, perhaps by means of mediation or conflict resolution. In the case of coercion, the grievance group exerts sufficient power so that they are able to defeat or severely weaken the opponent group and extract most of their demands from them. In these conflicts:

the numbers of resisters have become so large, and the parts of the social and political order they influence or control are so essential, that the noncooperation and defiance (sic) have taken control of the conflict situation . . . The opponents can no longer wield power contrary to the wishes of the nonviolent struggle group. This is nonviolent coercion . . . In more extreme situations, the nonco-operation and defiance are so vast and strong that the previous regime simply falls apart.[76]

In the case of disintegration, which Sharp sometimes refers to as a fourth mechanism of political change, the exercise of coercive power has increased to such an extent that the opponent group or regime falls apart as an effective political entity.

Accommodation and coercion both involve the use of threat power, to use Boulding's terminology, or the capacity to achieve one's objectives against the resistance of the opponent group. Accommodation depends upon a rough symmetry of power between conflicting groups, so that a negotiated settlement becomes the best approach for all protagonists. Coercion can, of course, take the form of violence, but it need not do so, according to Sharp.[77] This is important, because it opens up the possibility of achieving political change nonviolently, even where the other mechanisms (conversion and accommodation) have failed. Nonviolent coercion involves exerting coercive power against your opponent, without intending them physical or psychological harm. The three categories of nonviolent political action (protest, non-cooperation and intervention) can all involve some element of coercion, or forcing an opponent to do something against their will, to varying degrees.

Even though both accommodation and coercion, as mechanisms of political change, involve the use of threat or coercive power, when these are used nonviolently, they depend ultimately upon integrative power or social power. This is because when threat power is used non-violently, it is exercised through the withdrawal of consent, obedience or cooperation – all of which are forms of integrative power.

Principled proponents of nonviolence, such as Gandhi and King, tend to emphasise mechanisms of conversion or of persuading your opponent of the justness of your cause, even where this is preceded by some element of coercion to rectify power imbalances between conflicting groups or to convince one's opponent of your capacity to exercise coercive power. Sharp, as a pragmatic proponent of nonviolence, with his almost 'realist' emphasis on the centrality of power to nonviolent conflict, was sceptical of conversion as a mechanism of change:

> Rarely, the opponents have a change of view; that is a conversion takes place . . . A much more common mechanism is called accommodation. This essentially means that both sides compromise on issues . . . One must remember that these settlements are highly influenced by how much power each side can wield in waging the conflict.[78]

The important point, for Sharp, is that he has identified nonviolent methods of exercising 'hard' or coercive power, especially through the consent theory of power, that do not depend upon 'soft' power, persuasion or the conversion of one's opponent to your point of view or position.

Sharp's analysis of these mechanisms allows him to identify a specific process of political change that helps explain the effectiveness of nonviolent political action against a violent or repressive opponent. He refers to this metaphorically as 'political ju-jitsu',[79] because, just as in the martial art, the repressive force or violence of the opponent returns against them to undermine their power or their capacity to achieve their objectives:

> In this process, brutal repression against disciplined nonviolent resisters does not strengthen the opponents and weaken the resisters, but does the opposite. Widespread revulsion against the opponents for their brutality operates in some cases to shift power to the resisters . . . Third parties may change their opinions and activities to favor the resisters . . . Even members of the opponents' usual supporters may become unreliable . . . The use of the opponents' supposedly coercive violence has then been turned to undermine their own power capacity.[80]

The disproportionate and violent repression of peaceful protestors or nonviolent activists can create sympathy or support among those who had been neutral or indifferent to their cause and even among some of those who had been active or passive supporters of the regime or the dominant group.

Similarly, however, and by means of this process of 'political jiu-jitsu', the use of violence by protestors and activists can alienate potential supporters of a grievance group. The other point about this violence is that it attacks individuals or material property, without challenging the social relationships and structures (in the form of consent and compliance, for example) that form the basis of the power of the opponent group.

Sharp suggests that political ju-jitsu works precisely because of the asymmetry between the opponents' use of violence and the nonviolence of the grievance group. In other words, this process is available only where nonviolent resistance meets violent repression. It widens the constituency of support for the grievance group and, hence, strengthens its capacity to act and to achieve its political objectives.

Violent repression can rebound against those who use it and augument the power of those against whom it is employed, 'because it "deepens the injustice" and "reveals the true nature of the opponents"', according to Sharp.[81] The specific grievance of the resistance group expands to become a universal human rights issue of concern to a much wider range of social groups. It also adds to the orginal injustices characterising the relationship between dominant and marginalised groups within society and brings these original injustices to the attention of a much larger audience or constitutency: 'Repression against nonviolent resisters may at times attract wide public and even international attention to the struggle'.[82]

Carlos Huneeus, for example, refers to the, ultimately, counterproductive use of repression by Pinochet's regime in Chile:

> In the short term, repression worked to his [Pinochet's] advantage, but it was detrimental in the medium term because the atrocities committed by military personnel and the police were rejected by the population at large, including some sectors of his support, and because it caused conflict between the CNI [National Centre for Intelligence] and the police.[83]

According to Huneeus, 'the autonomy acquired by the repressive organizations resulted in acts that harmed the regime',[84] through alienating public support and creating conflict between state institutions: 'In other words, coercion ended up damaging the regime because it failed to stop the opposition while having a negative effect on the regime's image in the eyes of the population at large'.[85] The change in public opinion towards the Pinochet regime, because of its use of repressive measures against peaceful protestors and nonviolent political opponents, was especially important, because, as Huneeus points out, an important feature of the regime was that 'it was supported by a significant part of the population which had opposed the socialist and communist Popular Unity government of Allende'.[86]

SABOTAGE, MATERIAL POWER AND VIOLENCE

Sharp is opposed to acts of sabotage, even where they deliberately avoid direct harm to human beings (or other living beings), not so much because they could be interpreted as acts of violence through the destruction of property, but because they do not use the consent theory of power to achieve political change.

> Sabotage – defined for this discussion as 'acts of demolition and destruction of property' – is *not* compatible with nonviolent struggle. The dynamics and mechanisms of sabotage are different from those of nonviolent struggle. Sabotage:
>
> - requires only a few persons to implement plans and hence reduces the number of effective resisters; . . .
> - is a physical-material action, not a human-social action; . . .
> - attempts to undermine the opponents by destroying their property, not by withdrawal of consent by the population.[87]

Sabotage, according to Sharp, does not aim at breaking the relationship of consent and compliance that forms the power base of the rulers and, in this sense, is not the sort of 'human-social action' that is at the core of nonviolence and civil resistance. It attacks material or economic power, in the form of physical property, without mobilising the social or integrative power that forms the basis of the effectiveness of nonviolent political action.

Sharp claims, for example, that such acts of sabotage are sometimes seen as an alternative to mass mobilisation, that can operate independently of it to achieve social and political change:

> Acts of sabotage . . . are not generally applied in combination with mass popular resistance, and may contribute to a reduction of

such resistance as confidence is placed in the acts of demolition and destruction.[88]

Sabotage also succumbs to, what is sometimes referred to as, the fallacy of misplaced concreteness, by directing action against the material weapons of war, rather than against the social structures and power relationships that support militarism and other forms of injustice and oppression. There is also a danger that sabotage can undermine, rather than reinforce, public support for a cause, through deflecting public attention towards perceived acts of violence (even if these are small-scale and directed at property, rather than people) and away from the issue itself.

Even so, some forms of nonviolent civil disobedience involve the deliberate, if largely symbolic, destruction of state property, in particular. These include the Ploughshares actions, pioneered by the Berrigan brothers during the US war in Vietnam. These continue, to the present day, as anti-war actions and have been used to protest against nuclear weapons, the Indonesian occupation of East Timor and the invasion and occupation of Iraq, for example.[89] Such actions involve inflicting damage against draft files, computer equipment, military aircraft and even missiles, as well as symbolic gestures, involving religious items and photographs. The actions themselves, by their nature, are carried out by a small group of people (a half dozen or less), often independently of larger peace groups or peace movements. Even though they involve the deliberate destruction of property, these actions are largely symbolic, in the sense that their primary aim is to communicate dissent against, or disagreement with, government policy and practice, in order to increase public awareness of an issue and encourage widespread opposition.

The issue of sabotage once again directs our attention to the complex relationship between violence and nonviolence as forms of political action. Violence and nonviolence are sometimes viewed as opposites, with a clear dichotomy or division between them. In the context of political action, however, they may instead form ends of a spectrum, with sabotage occupying some sort of ambiguous or ambivalent middle ground between them. Acts of sabotage can both undermine efforts to achieve social change nonviolently, through alienating public opinion, for instance, but also support them through reinforcing a commitment to struggle and a sense of empowerment.

The campaign against apartheid in South Africa, led by the African National Congress (ANC), provides one example of this complex mixture of violence and nonviolence in a successful example of resistance and political change. According to Tom Lodge, following the Sharpeville massacre of 1960:

> ANC leaders and communists agreed to sponsor an armed wing, Umkhonto we Sizwe . . . Large-scale non-violent protest seemed impossible. Umkhonto was intended to lead a sabotage campaign. The saboteurs attempted to avoid bloodshed.[90]

Umkhonto's military commanders may have 'understood sabotage as simply a preparatory state for guerrilla warfare,'[91] but, in fact, it turned out to be a prelude to the mass civil resistance campaigns of the United Democratic Front in the 1980s.

As Lodge points out, however, Umkhonto's military activity was 'essentially symbolic' – a form of 'armed propaganda' that played a secondary role to the broader political struggle:

> the warfare was essentially symbolic . . . Command structures remained external and there were never more than 500 Umkhonto soldiers deployed inside South Africa . . . cadres were warned of the dangers of 'militarism', the isolation of military from political activity.[92]

The role of Umkhonto was 'to enhance the ANC's popular status and win for it a loose mass following'.[93] Umkhonto's military activity, although it never posed a serious military challenge to the South African government, was important, even during the phase of mass civil resistance, because, for example, 'the political culture that motivated and sustained the UDF's young African following was nurtured by the ANC's guerrilla warfare'.[94] The armed struggle was not seen as an alternative to, or a replacement for, political activity (under the control of the ANC and the UDF) and could therefore support and complement, rather than undermine and supplant, organised mass nonviolent civil resistance. It was a mechanism for communicating dissent and demonstrating a capacity for sustained resistance, rather than for achieving specific military objectives.

CONCLUSION

The effectiveness of nonviolence as a form of political action depends upon a distinctive analysis of the nature of social and political power, according to its proponents. This view of power is referred to as the consent theory of power or sometimes as the pluralistic theory of power. It is an important contribution to political theory more generally, because it emphasises the dependence of those in control of institutions such as the state upon the support or, at least, compliance or obedience of those they rule or govern. If this consent, compliance and support are withdrawn, then the ruling regime can no longer function. Furthermore, the methods of nonviolent political action, as outlined by Gene Sharp, in particular, are most effective in mobilising mass withdrawal of consent and obedience, because these methods are available to all who live in a society or under a particular regime and not merely to those who have access to weapons or the instruments of 'hard', material power.

Notes

1 Hobbes, *Leviathan*, p. 184.
2 Ibid. pp. 184–5.
3 Ibid. p. 161.
4 Macpherson, 'Introduction', p. 37.
5 Ibid. p. 35.
6 Ibid. p. 36.
7 Hobbes, *Leviathan*, p. 185.
8 Ibid. p. 185.
9 Boulding, 'Nonviolence and power in the twentieth century', p. 10.
10 Ibid. pp. 10–11.
11 Ibid. p. 11.
12 Sharp, *Social Power and Political Freedom*, p. 148. Here, Sharp is referring to Hannah Arendt's analysis of the relationship between power and violence.
13 Burrowes, *The Strategy of Nonviolent Defense: A Gandhian Approach*, pp. 83–4.
14 Boulding, 'Nonviolence and power in the twentieth century', p. 15.
15 Ibid. p. 11.
16 Ibid. p. 12.
17 Sharp, *Social Power and Political Freedom*, p. 312.
18 Ibid. p. 312.
19 Ibid. pp. 312–13.

20 Sharp, *Waging Nonviolent Struggle: 20th Century Practice and 21st Century Potential*, p. 26.

21 Ibid. p. 27.

22 Sharp, *Social Power and Political Freedom*, p. 24.

23 Sharp, *Waging Nonviolent Struggle: 20th Century Practice and 21st Century Potential*, p. 28.

24 Burrowes, *The Strategy of Nonviolent Defense: A Gandhian Approach*, p. 85.

25 Sharp, *Waging Nonviolent Struggle: 20th Century Practice and 21st Century Potential*, pp. 27–8.

26 Sharp, *Social Power and Political Freedom*, p. 28. The inverted commas around 'freedom' are Sharp's.

27 Sharp, *Waging Nonviolent Struggle: 20th Century Practice and 21st Century Potential*, p. 29.

28 Ibid. p. 29.

29 Tolstoy, 'On patriotism', p. 85.

30 Ibid. p. 85.

31 Sharp, *Waging Nonviolent Struggle: 20th Century Practice and 21st Century Potential*, p. 30.

32 Ibid. p. 23.

33 Fink, 'The moment of the monks: Burma, 2007', p. 367.

34 Sharp, *Waging Nonviolent Struggle: 20th Century Practice and 21st Century Potential*, p. 35.

35 Ibid. p. 33.

36 See Kenneth E. Boulding, 'Nonviolence and power in the twentieth century', in Stephen Zunes, Lester R. Kurtz and Sarah Beth Asher (eds), *Nonviolent Social Movements: A Geographical Perspective* (Oxford: Blackwell Publishing, 1999). See, also, Kenneth E. Boulding, *Three Faces of Power* (London: Sage Publications, 1990).

37 Sharp, *Waging Nonviolent Struggle: 20th Century Practice and 21st Century Potential*, p. 29.

38 Ibid. p. 29.

39 Tolstoy, 'On patriotism', p. 80.

40 Sharp, *Waging Nonviolent Struggle: 20th Century Practice and 21st Century Potential*, p. 29.

41 Ibid. p. 29.

42 Ibid. p. 29.

43 Boulding, 'Nonviolence and power in the twentieth century', p. 11.

44 Ibid. p. 10.

45 Sharp, *Waging Nonviolent Struggle: 20th Century Practice and 21st Century Potential*, p. 29–30.

46 Ibid. p. 30.

47 Ibid. p. 31.

48 Sharp, *Social Power and Political Freedom*, p. 23.
49 For an explanation of what Sharp means by 'pillars of support', see, for example: Sharp, *Waging Nonviolent Struggle: 20th Century Practice and 21st Century Potential*, p. 451.
50 See Burrowes, *The Strategy of Nonviolent Defense: A Gandhian Approach*, pp. 85–9, for a similar use of triangles to illustrate aspects of the consent theory of power.
51 Tolstoy, 'Patriotism and government', p. 86.
52 Sharp, *Waging Nonviolent Struggle: 20th Century Practice and 21st Century Potential*, p. 451.
53 Vejvoda, 'Civil society versus Slobodan Milošević: Serbia, 1991–2000', p. 311.
54 Fink, 'The moment of the monks: Burma, 2007', p. 261.
55 Ibid. p. 361.
56 Sharp, *Waging Nonviolent Struggle: 20th Century Practice and 21st Century Potential*, p. 399.
57 Ibid. pp. 41–3.
58 Ibid. p. 399.
59 Maier, 'Civil resistance and civil society: Lessons from the collapse of the German Democratic Republic in 1989', p. 274.
60 Sharp, *Waging Nonviolent Struggle: 20th Century Practice and 21st Century Potential*, p. 400.
61 Lodge, 'The interplay of non-violent and violent action in the movement against apartheid in South Africa, 1983–94', p. 228.
62 Ibid. p. 228.
63 Sharp, *Waging Nonviolent Struggle: 20th Century Practice and 21st Century Potential*, p. 54.
64 Sharp, *Social Power and Political Freedom*, pp. 26–7.
65 Huneeus, 'Political mass mobilization against authoritarian rule: Pinochet's Chile, 1983–88', p. 201.
66 Sharp, *Waging Nonviolent Struggle: 20th Century Practice and 21st Century Potential*, p. 35.
67 Ibid. p. 43.
68 Ibid. p. 43.
69 Ibid. p. 42.
70 Ibid. p. 399.
71 Ibid. p. 427.
72 Ibid. p. 424.
73 Sharp, *Social Power and Political Freedom*, p. 346.
74 Ibid. p. 345.
75 Schell, *The Unconquerable World: Power, Nonviolence, and the Will of the People*, p. 141.

76 Sharp, *Waging Nonviolent Struggle: 20th Century Practice and 21st Century Potential*, p. 46.
77 Ibid. p. 418–19.
78 Ibid. p. 46.
79 Ibid. p. 47.
80 Ibid. p. 47.
81 Ibid. p. 408.
82 Ibid. p. 410.
83 Huneeus, 'Political mass mobilization against authoritarian rule: Pinochet's Chile, 1983–88', p. 210.
84 Ibid. p. 206.
85 Ibid. p. 206.
86 Ibid. p. 201.
87 Sharp, *Waging Nonviolent Struggle: 20th Century Practice and 21st Century Potential*, p. 390.
88 Ibid. p. 390.
89 See, for example, Laffin (ed.), *Swords into Plowshares: A Chronology of Plowshares Disarmament Actions 1980–2003*.
90 Lodge, 'The interplay of non-violent and violent action in the movement against apartheid in South Africa, 1983–94', p. 214.
91 Ibid. p. 214.
92 Ibid. p. 215.
93 Ibid. p. 215.
94 Ibid. p. 228.

Chapter 5

STRUCTURE, AGENCY AND NONVIOLENT POLITICAL ACTION

INTRODUCTION

Critics of the consent theory of power have suggested at least three limits to both its analytical accuracy and its explanation of, and contribution to, the effectiveness of nonviolent political action. These criticisms focus on the role of external influences, material capacity and social and political structures in understanding and explaining power relations.[1]

Robert Burrowes suggests the first criticism of the consent theory of power. He argues that elites do not always depend on the consent of the governed. Sometimes they depend more on the support of other elites. The military regime in Burma, for example, depends on other state or corporate elites, rather than on the people of Burma, for its support.[2] The consent theory of power, in other words, can underestimate the importance of external influences, or sources of power, to the survival of a particular regime.

The eventual success of the independence struggle in East Timor, on the other hand, was due to its ability to gain widespread international support for its cause, in order to undermine external connivance or collaboration with Indonesian rule. Similarly, a weakness of nonviolent resistance to Serbian repression in Kosovo was its inability to gain such support, despite its mobilisation of the Kosovar-Albanian population.

A second criticism might be that the consent theory of power is reductionist. Even if we concede the importance of consent or compliance as sources of power, we should not underestimate the significance of more conventional forms of hard or coercive power, based on material capacity or access to material resources. Such power corresponds to the conventional 'Weberian' meaning of power as 'the imposition of our will on the other, in spite of the other's resistance'.[3] The suggestion that this is a distinct category of power, of course, directly contradicts Sharp's position that all relations of power, even those involving sanctions or the coercive use of physical violence, depend ultimately on an act of volition or consent on the part of those at its receiving end.

The important point is that these two types of power co-exist in the world of politics and identifying and accepting the significance of the consent theory of power does not imply the elimination of rival forms of power. 'Hard power', or material capacity and coercion, cannot be reduced to 'soft power', or consent, and the two compete in the realms of politics and society.[4]

As Jonathan Schell writes:

> The power that flows upward from the consent, support, and nonviolent activity of the people is not the same as the power that flows downward from the state by virtue of its command of the instruments of force, and yet the two kinds of power contend in the same world for the upper hand.[5]

To use Schell's terminology, cooperative and coercive power 'are antithetical. To the extent that one exists, the other is ruled out'.[6] Neither can be fully reduced to the other type of power.

The third criticism concerns the emphasis on human agency and choice, as distinct from social, political and economic structures, on the part of some proponents of the consent theory of power. This ignores the problem of structural limits to human agency or choice, however.

Sharp is quite explicit, for example, in his emphasis on the willing obedience or consent of the individual subject or citizen as the basis of any relationship of power between rulers and ruled. This extends even to the sanctions available to the governing authority to enforce obedience, involving, ultimately, the threat or use of coercive force or violence. According to Sharp, such sanctions can only operate or be effective 'through the volition, or will, of the subject',[7] because the subject can still ultimately decide whether or not to incur the costs of disobedience:

> In reviewing the reasons for obedience we find that although they are highly influenced by various social forces, each reason must operate through the will or the opinion of the individual subject to

be effective . . . the subject's evaluation of the reasons for obedience will even include sanctions. There is thus an important sense
in which the obedience of subjects is essentially the result of an act
of volition.[8]

Sharp's conclusion is that 'if choice and volition are present even where
obedience is largely produced by sanctions – where one could least
expect an act of will', then choice and consent must be determining
factors affecting all other reasons for obedience to the commands of the
ruling authority.[9]

Kate McGuinness, on the other hand, provides an interesting critique
of the consent theory of power from a gender perspective. McGuinness
is particularly concerned with patriarchy as one source of structural
limits to individual and collective choice.[10] Other relevant structures
might be those associated with capitalism (from a Marxist perspective)
and the state (from an anarchist perspective).

Robert Burrowes refers to social structures and systems as by-
products of entrenched and regular social interactions.[11] In the case of
patriarchy, such structures or systems can include the gender division
of labour, the economic dependence of women resulting from rules
governing property ownership and inheritance, the legal inferiority
of women, the socialisation associated with gender roles, the lack of
access to political institutions and so on.

The crucial point is that such structures or systems 'limit the capacity
for individual decision-making'[12] and, hence, the role of consent in any
given power relationship. The consent theory of power is 'individualistic and voluntaristic' and overlooks such structural factors.[13]

EXTERNAL SUPPORT AND INTERNAL CONSENT

One criticism that has been made of the consent theory of power is
that 'there are situations in which elites do not depend on the cooperation of the people they dominate'.[14] In some cases, for instance,
elites or occupying powers are interested in land or resources, but
not in governing the people who live on that land. Burrowes refers to
Andrew Rigby's analysis of the failure of Palestinian nonviolent resistance to Israeli occupation, during the first intifada in the late 1980s.
According to Rigby, 'Israel wants to rule over the *land* of Palestine,
it does not want the *people*'.[15] In such circumstances, withdrawal of

cooperation or compliance by the Palestinians is irrelevant to Israeli occupation.

There are also situations, as Gene Sharp acknowledges, in which the governing elite or occupying power do not depend upon a population and also seek quite actively to displace or even exterminate them. This includes situations of ethnic cleansing or genocide.[16] Howard Clark refers to the difficulties confronting the sustained nonviolent campaign for independence from Serbia, led by Ibrahim Rugova and the LDK in Kosovo, for example:

> Kosovo Albanians had little hope of undermining Milošević: far from depending on them, he wanted them to leave and was even willing to abandon Kosovo's industry. This was a profound weakness for civil resistance.[17]

Milošević was interested in controlling the territory of Kosovo, but not the population of Kosovar Albanians. He did not seek their compliance or obedience, but, rather, their removal or elimination from the territory.

Similarly, there are situations in which the ability of elites to dominate and control a population depends upon the support of other elites, such as other governments, but also, in some cases, transnational corporations, through investment, financial assistance and the provision of military hardware. Burrowes claims, for example, that 'some elites (such as the military junta in Burma) are principally dependent on other state and corporate elites rather than their own people'.[18] Christina Fink points out that: 'China has provided the Tatmadaw [the military regime in Burma] with over a billion dollars worth of military equipment, and India has also supplied arms in recent years'.[19] Furthermore, China's permanent position on the UN Security Council makes it difficult for the UN to take action against human rights abuses in Burma.[20]

One of the reasons the Burmese generals do not depend upon their relationship with the population or the citizens of Burma is because their sense of authority or legitimacy (as a source of power) is connected directly to their control of, and perceived protection of, the institution of the state itself. The Burmese military identify themselves with the interests and the survival of the state and justify their repression of opposition groups and disobedient citizens, including peaceful protests, on this basis. According to Christina Fink:

... the top military leaders seem genuinely to believe that it is their
duty and right to govern. Since the late 1950s, the military leader-
ship has regarded the military as the one truly patriotic institution
which can safeguard the interests of the state. In conjunction with
this ... the generals consider Burmese citizens as 'objects of dis-
trust and potential enemies' ... in a country where obedience to
superiors is the norm ... Than Shwe, the top general and decision-
maker, treated the peaceful marches as insubordination.[21]

Obedience to the state is required and expected, and it does not depend
on any relationship of consent between the governed and the government for its authority and legitimacy.

According to Burrowes, this suggests that 'if an elite does not necessarily depend on the cooperation of the people it dominates, then if its
power is to be systematically undermined, it is necessary to organize
corporate resistance by those constituencies on which the elite does
depend'.[22] International solidarity groups have successfully mobilised
campaigns to place pressure on Western governments to withdraw
their support and complicity with undemocratic regimes or occupying powers, in the case of the Indonesian occupation of East Timor,
for example, or apartheid in South Africa. This can be done directly,
through appealing to commitments to human rights on the part of
these governments, but also indirectly, through mobilising the citizens
of complicit governments against the unjust or undemocratic elements
of their foreign policies.

Mark R. Beissinger makes an important point, in his analysis of the
successful nonviolent struggle for independence by the Baltic states
against the Soviet Union in 1990–1, when he states that 'for many
movements, the locus of protest and the locus for resolving issues
diverge'. He points out that the 'issue of Baltic independence could not
have been resolved in the Baltic alone: ultimately it could be settled
only in Moscow'.[23] This is because the old Communist regimes in the
Baltic states depended for their survival much more on support from
the centre (i.e. the Soviet Union), than on the support of their own
citizens. When the political dispensation altered in Moscow with the
arrival of Gorbachev, those promoting change in the status of the Baltic
states could look to Russia for support. According to Beissinger, then:
'perhaps the most important external allies for the Baltic fronts were
Russian liberals in Moscow ... Russian sovereignty justified Baltic

independence'.[24] The significant point is that the locus of grievance (sometimes, but not necessarily, including the locus of protest) can differ from the locus of resolution, where dependence upon external support is crucial for the survival of a regime.

CONSENT AND COERCION

A second criticism is that proponents of nonviolence place too much emphasis on soft power or consent, while ignoring the significance of hard power, in the form of armed force and political violence. Furthermore, the threat or use of violence by the state may provide the ultimate guarantee of political effectiveness and security for civil resistance groups. Adam Roberts, in his 'Introduction' to *Civil Resistance and Power Politics*, provides an interesting examination of the relationship between civil resistance and the use of force, by which he seems to mean coercive political violence. Roberts argues that 'while civil resistance can be an alternative to the use of force, the two can also have a subtle and complex relationship'.[25] He points out that the use of non-violent political methods at one level (local or community) can sometimes depend on the threat, availability or use of force at another level (national or federal) in the political system. He claims, for example, that 'the US civil rights movement in the 1960s generally welcomed the use of federal forces to protect civil rights campaigners from the wrath of police forces in the Deep South'.[26] In other words, the ability of civil society groups or social movements to utilise the methods of nonviolent political action effectively depended upon the capacity of the state to enforce the rule of law.

Similarly, the use of nonviolence by civil resistance groups at the national level, against an authoritarian regime, for example, sometimes depends on the support of outside powers or states, which have at their disposal the use of armed or military force. He refers to the 'long struggles in central and eastern Europe up to 1989',[27] which occurred in the context of the military stalemate between the two superpowers during the Cold War: 'Often, as in this case, the military force of an outside power is important to resisters largely because it provides a defended space which their oppressors cannot control'.[28] The dissidents were able to persist with nonviolent resistance to communist regimes in central and eastern Europe, precisely because the ability of the Soviet Union and the Warsaw Pact to employ their armed forces was limited or constrained by their military stalemate with the US and NATO. He concludes from this that 'the classic view of civil resistance as a form of action counterposed to the use of force' shows 'only one aspect of civil resistance'.[29]

Japan's post-World War II 'peace constitution' provides another example, perhaps, of the complex relationship between nonviolence and conventional power politics. Article 9 of the Constitution of Japan says that the Japanese 'government does not have the power to make war, threaten war, or make preparations for war'.[30] This is often identified as a somewhat idiosyncratic and inneffectual pacifist clause in a post-war 'peace constitution'. Furthermore, this pacifist clause was imposed to enforce the demilitarisation of Japan by a victorious occupying power, the United States, not as part of some new, peaceful international order. Japanese state pacifism was only made possible under the protection of the extensive US military presence in the region and globally, including, of course, America's arsenal of nuclear weapons. 'So the experiment proposed in the constitution, that Japan abandon the method of protecting national security with military force and instead seek to protect itself with peace diplomacy, has never been attempted', according to Lummis.[31]

Thus, Roberts seems to question both the pacifist view that nonviolent political action or civil resistance provide a morally superior alternative to the use of armed force; and the pragmatist view that they can supply a complete, if not immediate, functional replacement for the use of state-sanctioned violence, through a process of 'progressive substitution'.[32] Civil resistance operates as one method or technique among many within the framework of conventional state structures and power politics, at both domestic and international levels. He states that he 'increasingly questioned the tradition of seeing civil resistance as being a complete substitute for force, viewing it more as a special option for special circumstances'.[33]

In other words, Roberts seems to belong among those who see civil resistance and nonviolent political action as being, at most, supplementary to and, in many cases, highly dependent upon conventional forms of political activity, all of which function within a framework in which violence and the threat of violence provide a fundamental source of political and social power. Civil resistance organisations can be the main source of struggle against unjust or repressive uses of state power, but this is not necessarily extended to a rejection of conventional state

structures as such. This is in sharp contrast with traditions of transformative nonviolence that seek to challenge and change such conventional notions of political power precisely because of their connection
to state-sanctioned violence.

However, pragmatic proponents of nonviolent political action, following Gene Sharp, in particular, make an important distinction
between coercion and violence as forms of hard power. They acknowledge that in many situations of political struggle, hard coercive power
plays an important and sometimes dominant or determining role,
but distinguish between coercion as a mechanism of political change
and violence. One's opponent can be forced to change a policy or
practice, and regimes can even be removed from control of a government, country or state, through using the methods of nonviolent
non-cooperation and intervention, as outlined by Sharp, for example.[34]
Also, as Sharp and Randle have pointed out, even the exercise of
violent state repression or aggression depends ultimately on the cooperation or consent of those in the state security apparatus, for instance,
and this allegiance is often challenged in examples of successful nonviolent resistance.

INDIVIDUAL DISSENT AND RESISTANCE TO EVIL

According to Tolstoy, a fundamental requirement of social and political
change is a change in public opinion, especially to mistaken feelings of
patriotism or support for a particular state that are the ultimate source
of government authority: 'No feats of heroism are needed to achieve the
greatest and most important changes in the existence of humanity . . .
but a change in public opinion'.[35] Tolstoy's 'public opinion' resembles
the attitudes of compliance and obedience to authority at the heart of
the consent theory of power, reinforced by the ideology of patriotism.

Tolstoy understood this consent or compliance primarily in individual or behavioural, rather than structural, terms. Social change
began at the personal level, through changing the attitudes and behaviour of each individual and, especially, patterns of obedience to unjust
authority:

> For Tolstoy, the State could only survive with the consent of
> the governed; a revolution to overthrow it had to take a per-
> sonal rather than a political form. The German anarchist Gustav

Landauer developed this point further . . . 'The State is not something that can be destroyed by a revolution, but is a condition, a certain relationship between human beings; we destroy it by contracting other relationships, by behaving differently'.[36]

Behavioural change by individuals, through non-cooperation with evil, is the key to dissolving relationships of unjust authority and developing new forms of social interaction based on equality and mutual respect. The withdrawal of the consent and compliance that is at the basis of governmental power and authority begins with each individual and their refusal to subscribe to the lie of patriotism that provides the basis of such authority. As Tolstoy says, 'strength is not in force but in truth'.[37]

This unbending moral commitment to 'living within the truth',[38] to use Havel's phrase, becomes the basis of non-cooperation with evil and nonviolent resistance to injustice and oppression, for Tolstoy. According to George Woodcock: 'The refusal to obey . . . is Tolstoy's "great weapon"'.[39] Methods of non-cooperation, or moral resistance through disobedience to authority, complements other, more directly confrontational categories of nonviolent political action identified by Sharp, such as protest and nonviolent intervention. Such non-cooperation 'is as valid a means of struggle as is revolutionary action in the form of strikes and, above all, the General Strike'.[40]

One implication of social contract theory is that the power of organised society has its source ultimately in the power each individual possesses in the state of nature. As Alexander Mosely frames it, in his commentary upon John Locke:

political power is derived from and conditional upon the power that every man in the state of nature possesses, but which is given over to the society that they form: i.e. to the government set up, by a majority, to create an established and known set of laws, to arbitrate in disputes, and to preserve the life and property of its members.[41]

Power is delegated to the state to facilitate the self-preservation of its members or citizens, through enforcing an agreed and equitable set of laws and other forms of dispute resolution, to which all have equal access.

Tolstoy's views on non-cooperation and moral resistance to authority were a central influence on Gandhi's approach to nonviolent political action: 'It was from Tolstoy's ideas of non-compliance, refusal of taxes and non-violent resistance to Authority that Gandhi developed his theory of *satyagraha*'.[42]

Martin Luther King, in particular, emphasised non-cooperation with evil as a moral imperative and also as the basis for his own approach to nonviolent political action. Reflecting upon the Montgomery bus boycott, he began to see its underlying morality, in terms of non-cooperation with evil:

> As I thought further I came to see that what we were really doing was withdrawing our cooperation from an evil system, rather than merely withdrawing our economic support from the bus company. The bus company, being an external expression of the system, would naturally suffer, but the basic aim was to refuse to cooperate with evil.[43]

Although the bus boycott began as a struggle to change a specific policy of discrimination against African-Americans on public transport in Montgomery, it very quickly became part of the wider struggle against the evil system of racial segregation in the southern United States, according to King.

King argued that non-cooperation with evil is a moral imperative, because even passive acceptance of wrong-doing was the moral equivalent of actively cooperating with it:

> Something began to say to me, 'He who passively accepts evil is as much involved in it as he who helps to perpetrate it. He who accepts evil without protesting against it is really cooperating with it'. When oppressed people willingly accept their oppression they only serve to give the oppressor a convenient justification for his acts. Often the oppressor goes along unaware of the evil involved in his oppression so long as the oppressed accepts it. So in order to be true to one's conscience and true to God, a righteous man has no alternative but to refuse to cooperate with an evil system. This I felt was the nature of our action. From this moment on I conceived of our movement as an act of massive noncooperation. From then on I rarely used the word 'boycott'.[44]

King's point that the passive acceptance of oppression can be taken as a justification for their actions by the oppressor, and that active non-cooperation is required to make them conscious or aware of their wrong-doing, is an important one. Such passive acceptance or obedience can be conveniently interpreted as consent towards an unjust system and both facilitates and legitimates the behaviour of the oppressor.

Gandhi emphasised non-cooperation with the legal and educational systems of the state as being especially important, because 'it is through Courts that a Government establishes its authority and it is through schools that it manufactures clerks and other employees'.[45] The legal and educational systems are vital intermediate state institutions, through which it exercises its control over the rest of the population, so interrupting or undermining these institutions can be vital to the success of nonviolent political action and civil resistance. Gandhi wrote, for example: 'Perhaps no one co-operates with a Government more than lawyers through its Law Courts. Lawyers interpret laws to the people and thus support authority'.[46] In India, such non-cooperation took the form of a 'boycott of Law Courts by lawyers and of Government schools and colleges by parents or scholars'.[47]

Gene Sharp also views consent as the result of a deliberate and voluntary choice. Consent is a conscious act of each individual: 'Each reason for obedience, whether it is free consent or fear of sanctions (intimidated consent), must operate through the will or volition of the individual person to produce obedience . . . Obedience remains essentially voluntary'.[48]As Robert Burrowes phrases it, 'obedience and cooperation are not inevitable. Despite incentives and the threat of sanctions, cooperation is essentially voluntary'.[49]

At the same time, Sharp acknowledges that such choices or decisions occur in the context of social structures and political institutions, which mediate the relationship between the individual and the governing elite. The social formation with which Sharp is particularly concerned is 'the State' and the degree to which 'effective power capacity . . . is centralized in the State, or decentralized among the independent institutions of the society'. This 'structural condition of the society affects the capacity of the society to control the power of rulers'.[50] According to Sharp: '"State" here refers to a particular form of government which possesses, among other elements, a permanent bureaucracy, a permanent military system, and a permanent police force utilizing violent means of control, backed by a prison system'.[51] A discussion of other social structures or formations (such as capitalism or patriarchy, for instance) would deepen this structural analysis of power, although it would not contradict it.

This suggests that social relationships (such as consent and cooperation) and social structures are more important than formal political structures, and constitutional or legal arrangements, to understanding the functioning of power in a society:

> The formal institutional framework and procedures of government remain important . . . but the underlying structural condition is in the long run dominant over the formal political arrangements. *It is the distribution of power throughout the society's structure as a whole which determines the de facto power of the ruler, regardless of the principles which are avowed for the system or its institutional forms.*[52]

Furthermore, according to Sharp: 'Not even a democratic constitution, which sets limits on the legitimated powers of the government, which establishes regular procedures for the conduct of government and for the choice of ruler, and which guarantees certain liberties and rights to the subjects, is sufficient to reverse this tendency'.[53] Controlling or limiting political or institutional power requires 'a technique of struggle', such as nonviolent action or civil resistance, based on the social power expressed through organised popular action, but it also needs 'a structural condition of the society which sets effective boundaries on the power potential of rulers', which they exercise through political institutions, such as the centralised, sovereign state.[54] This 'structural condition' involves recognising and utilising the social power embodied in the capacity for political action, by the plurality and diversity of citizens and social groups in a formal and systematic way.

GRAMSCI, HEGEMONY AND CONSENT

Antonio Gramsci's theory of hegemony and Michel Foucault's views on the pervasiveness and polymorphism of power may contribute to a more sophisticated understanding of the nature and role of the consent at the centre of the consent theory of power. At one end of the scale, Gramsci may provide us with a better understanding of some of the global structures within which such consent operates (and is constrained), while at a much more local (and diffuse) level, Foucault offers insight into forms of consent that can evade the charges of individualism and voluntarism.

Gramsci explained consent as a primary form of political power, by means of his theory of 'hegemony', according to which, certain social institutions (educational, religious, etc.) function to manufacture and maintain the consent of non-dominant groups. He refers to 'social hegemony', for example, as the '"spontaneous" consent given by the great masses of the population to the general direction imposed on social life by the dominant fundamental group'.[55] According to Brian Martin: 'Hegemony refers to the processes by which a given way of organizing social life, in which one class dominates another, becomes accepted as inevitable and desirable by most people'.[56] In other words, Gramsci incorporated the significance of beliefs about the legitimacy or inevitability of social systems or ways of life into more conventional Marxist concerns about class structures of inequality and exploitation.

Hegemony simply refers to the prevalence of 'a close identity between people and their political and social institutions'[57], as the basis for embedded systems of power: 'To the extent that the consensual aspect of power is in the forefront, hegemony prevails'.[58]

Thus, 'a group maintains its supremacy not simply through the direct domination of the coercive state apparatus but also through the organized consent of the governed in civil society'.[59] The coercive power of the state remains available, but is not the most prominent or pervasive form of power:

> Coercion is always latent but is only applied in marginal, deviant cases. Hegemony is enough to ensure conformity of behaviour in most people most of the time.[60]

Gramsci refers to the 'apparatus of state coercive power which "legally" enforces discipline on those groups who do not "consent" either actively or passively'.[61] This apparatus needs to be utilised, however, only 'when spontaneous consent has failed'.[62] In other words, as Joan Cocks points out, political power 'exhibits itself in normal times through the spontaneous consent rather than the coerced obedience of a whole population'.[63]

Hegemony emphasises the importance of ideas in shaping and controlling behaviour, including compliance and consent, while not ignoring completely the significance of hard, coercive power supported by material resources and capabilities. Thus, in Gramsci's version of historical materialism, 'ideas and material conditions are always bound together, mutually influencing one another, but not reducible one to the other'.[64] He refers to 'the State', for example, as 'political society + civil society, in other words hegemony protected by the armour of coercion'.[65] In this way, Gramsci avoids the reductionism associated with some interpretations of the consent theory, by acknowledging that such consent operates in tandem with the repressive potential of the state, without fully replacing it.

The role of civil society as a vehicle for hegemony is of particular significance for Gramsci's theory:

> What we can do, for the moment, is to fix two major superstructural 'levels': the one that can be called 'civil society', that is the ensemble of organisms commonly called 'private', and that of 'political society' or 'the State'. These two levels correspond on the one hand to the function of 'hegemony' which the dominant group exercises throughout society and on the other hand to that of 'direct domination' or command exercised through the State and 'juridical' government.[66]

As such, civil society plays an ambiguous role, concerning possibilities for social change. On the one hand, the ideas and norms transmitted and maintained by civil society help sustain status quo political and economic structures. On the other hand, civil society provides an arena for autonomous and independent group action that can form the basis of social and political change: 'Civil society is both . . . an agent of stabilization and reproduction, and a potential agent of transformation'.[67]

Thus, there are two intersecting tensions in Gramsci's theory of hegemony, concerning the conservative versus emancipatory functions of civil society and the relationship between consent (in the form of civil society) and coercion (in the form of the state) as fundamental expressions of political and social power. The flip side of hegemony (or consent) as a crucial and conservative form of political power is the liberating power of ideas embodied through autonomous civil society organisation and action.

It also follows from Gramsci's version of historical materialism that he is concerned with the way in which hegemony operates in the

context of large-scale, even global, social, economic and political structures, reinforced by material resources and capabilities. In other words,
he is interested in analysing the way in which consent or hegemony
contributes to and perpetuates sustained social interactions or structures and not merely as a psychological disposition on the part of individuals towards those who rule or govern them.

FOUCAULT AND THE 'MICRO-PHYSICS' OF POWER

Whereas Gramsci analyses the interplay between ideas and material forces, in the form of his theory of hegemony in the context of
large-scale national, international and even global structures, Michel
Foucault dissects and examines specific social relations, including relationships of power, in the sphere of everyday life. For Foucault, power
is both ubiquitous, and plural or polymorphous. He is not interested
in providing a general theory of power, but in documenting or chronicling its pervasive manifestations at multiple levels of social existence
and interaction. Suspicious of the assumptions implicit in theory, he
claims to study, instead, the micro-physics or 'micropractices'[68] of
power.

Foucault emphasises the ubiquity and plurality of power, rather than
its embodiment or reification in large-scale structures. Power operates primarily at this micro-level of everyday existence, rather than at
the level of some essential dichotomy between elites and oppressed
or rulers and ruled, that then permeates smaller-scale social relations.
'Power comes from below', from 'the manifold relationships of force
that take shape and come into play in the machinery of production, in
families, limited groups, and institutions'. There is 'no binary and all-
encompassing opposition between rulers and ruled at the root of power
relations, and serving as a general matrix'.[69]

He does not begin his analysis of power, in other words, with large,
homogeneous, impermeable blocs, such as the state or social structures. According to Lois McNay:

> Partly in explicit counterposition to a Marxist perspective,
> Foucault's interest was not directed at the expression of power
> in its most central and institutionalised forms such as state appa-
> ratuses or class relations. Rather, he was concerned to examine
> how power relations of inequality and oppression are created and

maintained in more subtle and diffuse ways through ostensibly humane and freely adopted social practices.[70]

For Foucault, 'social control is not always achieved through a monotonous logic of domination' involving groups arranged hierarchically in a relatively fixed or stable social or economic order, 'but is often realized indirectly through a convergence of different social practices'.[71] Thus, 'neither the caste which governs, nor the groups which control the state apparatus, nor those who make the most important economic decisions direct the entire network of power that functions in a society'.[72]

It follows from this that repression, domination or exploitation, as examples of negative power, are not the state's only, or even its primary, manifestations: 'Repression . . . is only one in a multiplicity of positive and negative effects generated through the interplay of power relations'.[73] The state, for example, may 'rely on juridical conceptions of power as a negative or repressive' or coercive force, but these are rooted in, or are merely a magnification or codification of, the pervasive power relations operating at the level of everyday social practice.[74] Thus, according to Foucault, 'the sovereignty of the state, the form of the law' must be understood as 'only the terminal forms that power takes'.[75]

For Foucault, power must be analysed 'in its most diverse and specific manifestations rather than focusing on its most centralized forms such as its concentration in the hands of a coercive elite or a ruling class'. He refers to this as 'a *microphysics* rather than a macrophysics of power'.[76]

Furthermore, power is not a commodity or entity to be seized or owned or controlled. Thus, Foucault writes: 'Power is not something that is acquired, seized, or shared, something that one holds on to or allows to slip away'. 'Relations of power' are not exterior to, but, rather, immanent within, 'other types of relationships' (economic, epistemological, sexual).[77] The implication is that power is not a discrete and separate quality or characteristic applicable to these multiple relationships, but, rather, something generated only by them.

Foucault is particularly famous, of course, for his discussion of the intersection between knowledge and power, which are joined together through discourse.[78] Dreyfus and Rabinow suggest that this depiction of the mutual, or correlative (rather than causal), relationship between knowledge and power 'is one of Foucault's major contributions'.[79] For Foucault, 'knowledge is one of the defining components for the operation of power in the modern world'.[80] He argues that 'power and knowledge directly imply one another', because 'there is no power relation without the correlative constitution of a field of knowledge, nor any knowledge that does not presuppose and constitute at the same time power relations'.[81]

The purpose of discursive analysis is not to arrive at some objective, underlying truth, discoverable through the correct combination of theory and empirical research. Its purpose, instead, is to examine 'the particular way power-knowledge complexes operate at a microsocial level in order to produce regimes of truth'.[82] Such 'regimes of truth' illustrate the way in which such microsocial practices, including the micropractices of power, intersect to form larger, but constantly fluctuating, fields of social interaction, sometimes mistaken for, or reified as, 'structure'.

Thus, for Foucault, 'power underlies all social relations from the institutional to the intersubjective'[83] or interpersonal. Furthermore, one implication of Foucault's analysis of power as a pervasive social practice combined with his discussion of discourse – or the way in which knowledge and power intersect – is that power is also a significant feature of the construction of the knowing subject, including an individual's sense of self-identity. Foucault links subjectivity to forms of subjection, subjugation or submission. The social construction of the knowing subject 'ties the individual' to particular conceptions of him or herself:[84]

> This form of power applies itself to immediate everyday life which categorizes the individual . . . attaches him to his own identity . . .
> It is a form of power which makes individuals subjects.[85]

Foucault himself suggests that it is the subject, rather than power as such, 'which is the general theme of my research'.[86]

This dissection of the 'knowing subject' has important implications for any analysis of consent that emphasises its voluntary or voluntaristic characteristics. As Mark Bevir points out, Foucault 'opposed . . . the idea of the autonomous individual. The subject is not a rational agent thinking and acting under its own self-imposed and self-created commands'.[87] Instead, the subject is a product of diverse social forces and social practices, especially the intersection of knowledge and power through discourse.[88] Furthermore, 'what renders the modern state

so powerful is its successful annexation of . . . techniques of subjec-
tivization', expressed through its concern with individual salvation
in the form of each citizen's health, standard of living and security,
for example.[89] In this sense, as McNay points out, the success of the
modern state rests upon its capacity to be 'simultaneously individual-
izing and totalising'.[90]

DISCIPLINARY POWER AND CONSENT

This concern with the microphysics of power expressed through
everyday social practices, the intersection of knowledge with power in
discourse and the construction of the knowing subject are combined
in Foucault's discussion of 'disciplinary' (or 'bio') power. Such disciplinary power involves subtle and pervasive forms of social control
applied to specific individuals in diverse social institutions, such as 'fac-
tories, schools, barracks, hospitals . . . prisons'.[91] Foucault uses Jeremy
Bentham's plan for a Panopticon – a prison based on utilitarian criteria,
such as efficiency and comprehensiveness – to exemplify a disciplinary
power and technology applied through processes of surveillance and
normalisation, rather than overt repression.[92] These daily 'modalities'
of disciplinary power operate at a much lower and humbler level than
'the majestic rituals of sovereignty or the great apparatuses of the state',
according to Foucault.[93]

The subject or citizen can identify very closely with a system that, in
some ways, oppresses or constrains them or denies them some fundamental aspect of human dignity, at least partly, because of the impact
of disciplinary power upon them. Thus, the individual or the knowing
subject can collaborate with their own oppression at multiple levels,
from the intrasubjective, to the pragmatic social relations of daily life,
to the institutional, in a manner that is far more complex and polymorphous than the term 'consent' might ordinarily imply.

Some of these points coincide with Václav Havel's discussion of
repression in the former Soviet bloc, which he referred to as a 'post-
totalitarian system'.[94] Havel described the Soviet bloc countries, in
their later years, as post-totalitarian, precisely because they depended
more on the tacit collaboration and involvement of their citizens with
the system, than on forms of overt repression or suppression. They
identified with the system 'as though it were something natural and
inevitable'[95] and behaved accordingly: 'What we understand by the

system is not, therefore, a social order imposed by one group upon another, but rather something which permeates an entire society'.[96] According to Havel, participants in a social or political system, such as post-totalitarianism, 'create through their involvement a general norm' forming the basis of the normalising processes central to its disciplinary power.[97]

Furthermore, 'only a very generalized view . . . permits us to divide society into the ruler and the ruled'. Instead, 'this line runs *de facto* through each person, for everyone in his or her own way is both a victim and a supporter of the system'.[98] Thus, the self-identity of each citizen or subject was constituted, to some extent, through their willing and active participation in the system, and the system maintained and sustained itself through the mundane, daily activities of those caught up in it. Similarly, Joan Cocks quotes Foucault's emphasis on 'cleavages in a society . . . furrowing across individuals themselves' as being more significant than '"massive binary divisions" cutting a society in two',[99] between ruler and ruled, for example.

There are certain similarities between Foucault's discussion of power and consent theory, in that they both emphasise power's ubiquity and plurality. The crucial difference concerns Foucault's focus on the micro-practices of the social interactions of daily life, down to the level of the constitution of the knowing subject, rather than on the hierarchies or structures of power within society as a whole.

Foucault's detailed dissection of power as an element of social practice has crucial implications for the contribution of consent theory to the possibilities for nonviolent social and political change. Power is a much more complex and multifarious phenomenon than the relatively transparent social contract between the rulers and the ruled suggested by consent theory. As Roland Bleiker suggests, 'consistent with an already widespread Foucauldian position that views power as working in a diffused and stratified way', consent theory's 'model of power relations' may be too parsimonious.[100]

Instead, identifying and challenging these social practices, and even the self-understanding of the knowing subject, may be a vital part of adjusting power balances within a society. This resembles Havel's discussion of 'living in truth' as a central form of resistance in post-totalitarian society, according to which, resistance 'shifts to the area of the existential and the prepolitical', although it must be conceded that Havel's notion of truth is much more conventional and humanistic than

Foucault's.[101] Thus, Havel simply identifies 'living within the truth' with 'the real aims of life', as distinct from 'the aims of the system'.[102]

In other words, 'consent' may consist in tacitly participating in the social practices and routines of daily life and not merely in conforming to the requirements of larger social and political structures and institutions (such as the state or government), as suggested by more conventional interpretations of consent theory. Foucault certainly remained sceptical, or critical, of consent or consensus as merely a vehicle for the processes of normalisation and the 'regimes of truth' central to the disciplinary power maintaining and sustaining modern society.

Thus, according to Foucault, 'one can perfectly well conceive of revolutions' involving a change of government or regime, for example, that do not confront these more fundamental and ubiquitous levels, or layers, of power and, hence, 'leave essentially untouched the power relations which form the basis for the functioning of the state'[103] in its conventional format. Also, one set of power relations (such as patriarchy) can survive a challenge to another set (such as state or government power), partly because such systems resemble 'discursively embedded' and polymorphous networks, more than discrete, homogeneous social structures or power blocs.[104]

One implication of Foucault's emphasis on social practices, rather than social structures, as the embodiment of power, as well as the plurality and ubiquity of power, as Cocks points out, is that 'several major systems of power can be operating simultaneously in one society, with any individual implicated in power and resistance in a multiplicity of different ways at once'.[105] Thus, one could be a trade unionist and a male chauvinist, for example, or an anti-militarist and homophobic.

Foucault himself distinguishes power quite clearly from both consent and violence. Thus, he writes that 'power is not a function of consent', where consent is understood as 'a renunciation of freedom'[106] or 'voluntary servitude'.[107] 'Power is exercised only over free subjects' capable of making decisions or choices about their conduct.[108]

For similar reasons, power must be separated from violence, as the coercive and destructive use of force. Thus, both consent and violence may be instruments of power, but they are not synonymous with it, because power precedes them both.[109]

Furthermore, for Foucault, this link between power and freedom implies the permanent potential of resistance.[110] In addition, the plurality of power also implies 'a plurality of resistances'[111] at all levels: 'Where there is power, there is resistance . . . These points of resistance are present everywhere in the power network'.[112] Thus, a 'revolution' can consist of a congruence of many different types of resistance, at many levels of power, in its multifarious manifestations.[113] This is particularly true of efforts at social change or social transformation that rely exclusively on the multiple methods of nonviolent political action.

Finally, Foucault's emphasis on practice, rather than structure, as the basic feature of forms of social life, especially power, comes through in his assertion that liberty and freedom are social practices that cannot be 'assured by the institutions and laws that are intended to guarantee them', because 'it can never be inherent in the structure of things to guarantee the exercise of freedom'.[114] Freedom appears in the daily social practice of human beings, rather than being crystallised in a particular type of political institution or legal system, for example, that supposedly functions to protect or guarantee it.

CONCLUSION

Although not fully complementary, by any means, the ideas of both Gramsci and Foucault provide resources for developing a more sophisticated and comprehensive version of the consent theory of power, relevant to explaining and ensuring the effectiveness of nonviolent political action. Both Gramsci and Foucault provide expositions of power that cannot be reduced to 'the monopolization of the means of physical violence'[115] epitomised by the state, for example.

Gramsci provides perhaps the most direct response to the three criticisms of the consent theory of power mentioned earlier. He answers the reductionist criticism through linking the power of ideas (including consent) to material capacity in the context of his theory of hegemony. This theory also forms a vital part of his analysis of the structures of international capitalism and state power that provide the context and limits for individual and group political action. Finally, his discussion of such large-scale structures suggests the significance of external constraints for any direct social contract, or relationship of consent, between rulers and ruled.

Foucault, on the other hand, rejects or at least bypasses, such an explicit structural analysis, in favour of his careful documentation of the micro-physics of power. This indicates that relationships of power within any society are both more pervasive and more multifarious than those identified by the consent theory of power.

However, the contribution of Foucault's views to a more sophisticated explanation of the effectiveness of nonviolent political action, through providing a more nuanced view of the nature of consent and obedience, in particular, is ambiguous. There are at least two important limits to, or criticisms of, the usefulness of Foucault's views for nonviolent political activists, arising from his dissection of the autonomous knowing subject, in particular. The first is that his critique of the subject undermines the possibilities derived from human agency for large-scale social and political change. If the knowing subject is the result of, rather than the instigator of, regimes of power, it is difficult to see how he or she can be an innovative and autonomous agent of social and political change.[116] It must be acknowledged, however, that this is not a criticism that would particularly trouble Foucault, since he is interested in understanding social processes, rather than inspiring them.

A related criticism, however, is that Foucault's 'rejection of an objectivist epistemology'[117] and his suspicion of the disciplinary and normalising elements of any social order make it difficult for him to be optimistic about the liberating potential of any large-scale political or social change. We can see this in his comment that liberty and freedom are practices that can be exercised, but not guaranteed by any particular set of political institutions. Again, while Foucault may provide a detailed delineation of the complex networks of power running through society, he is not particularly interested in proposing alternative visions of social order or strategies to achieve specific social and political changes.

On the other hand, Foucault's detailed depiction of the microphysics of power is particularly useful in providing a more sophisticated understanding of the nature of the obedience and compliance at the heart of the consent theory of power that helps transcend a simple voluntarism. Such voluntarism suggests a straightforward and transparent contract between rulers and ruled that can be abrogated and strategically re-negotiated. Foucault, however, suggests that there are multiple, fluid networks of power running through any society, at many different levels. This also suggests that there are, correspondingly, multiple points of resistance – from the personal to the explicitly political

– available to those who wish to challenge and change any aspect of these networks of power. The success of such resistance 'does not, then, obey the law of all or nothing'.[118] Furthermore, and even more optimistically, 'no matter how terrifying a given system may be, there always remain the possibilities of resistance, disobedience, and opposi-tional groupings'[119], in some form and at some level.

Notes

1 See Schock, *Unarmed Insurrections: People Power Movements in Nondemocracies*, pp. 44–6, for a discussion of similar criticisms of the consent theory of power.
2 Burrowes, *The Strategy of Nonviolent Defense: A Gandhian Approach*, pp. 88–9.
3 Bharadwaj, 'Principled versus pragmatic nonviolence', p. 80.
4 Joseph Nye uses these two terms in, for example, *Soft Power: The Means to Success in World Politics* (New York, NY: Public Affairs, 2004). He is widely credited with introducing these terms to describe these different dimen-sions of power.
5 Schell, *The Unconquerable World: Power, Nonviolence, and the Will of the People*, p. 231.
6 Ibid. p. 227.
7 Sharp, *The Politics of Nonviolent Political Action: Part One: Power and Struggle*, p. 26.
8 Ibid. p. 26.
9 Ibid. p. 28.
10 McGuinness, 'Gene Sharp's theory of power: A feminist critique of consent', pp. 101–15.
11 Burrowes, *The Strategy of Nonviolent Defense: A Gandhian Approach*, p. 91.
12 Ibid. p. 91.
13 Ibid. p. 90. See, also, Martin, 'Gene Sharp's theory of power', p. 219. Martin also refers to Sharp's theory as 'essentially voluntarist' (p. 219).
14 Burrowes, *The Strategy of Nonviolent Defense: A Gandhian Approach*, p. 87.
15 Ibid. p. 87.
16 Sharp, *Waging Nonviolent Struggle: 20th Century Practice and 21st Century Potential*, p. 521.
17 Clark, 'The limits of prudence: Civil resistance in Kosovo, 1990–98', p. 290.
18 Burrowes, *The Strategy of Nonviolent Defense: A Gandhian Approach*, p. 88.
19 Fink, 'The moment of the monks: Burma, 2007', p. 363.
20 Ibid. p. 363.

21 Ibid. pp. 361–2.
22 Burrowes, *The Strategy of Nonviolent Defense: A Gandhian Approach*, pp. 90–1.
23 Beissinger, 'The intersection of ethnic nationalism and people power tactics in the Baltic States, 1987–91', p. 245.
24 Ibid. p. 245.
25 Roberts, 'Introduction', p. 2.
26 Ibid. p. 14.
27 Ibid. p. 15.
28 Ibid. p. 16.
29 Ibid. p. 19.
30 Lummis, 'The smallest army imaginable', pp. 314–15.
31 Ibid. p. 316.
32 Roberts, 'Introduction', pp. 7–10.
33 Ibid. p. 12.
34 Sharp discusses these two categories of methods of nonviolent action (non-cooperation and intervention) extensively in *The Politics of Nonviolent Political Action, Part Two: The Methods of Nonviolent Action* (Boston, MA: Porter Sargent Publishers, 1973).
35 Tolstoy, 'On patriotism', p. 88.
36 Stephens, 'The non-violent anarchism of Leo Tolstoy', p. 18.
37 Tolstoy, 'On patriotism', pp. 88–9.
38 Havel, 'The power of the powerless', pp. 36–122 (cf. p. 56, for example).
39 Cited in Stephens, 'The non-violent anarchism of Leo Tolstoy', p. 18.
40 Max Nettlau, cited in Stephens, 'The non-violent anarchism of Leo Tolstoy', p. 17.
41 Moseley, 'John Locke's morality of war', p. 121.
42 Stephens, 'The non-violent anarchism of Leo Tolstoy', p. 18.
43 King, 'Stride toward freedom', p. 429.
44 Ibid. p. 429.
45 Gandhi, *Non-Violent Resistance (Satyagraha)*, p. 188.
46 Ibid. p. 188.
47 Ibid. p. 142.
48 Sharp, *Waging Nonviolent Struggle* pp. 33–4.
49 Burrowes, *The Strategy of Nonviolent Defense: A Gandhian Approach*, p. 86.
50 Sharp, *Social Power and Political Freedom*, p. 24.
51 Ibid. p. 25.
52 Ibid. p. 32 (italics in original).
53 Ibid. p. 47.
54 Ibid. p. 25.
55 Gramsci, *Selections from the Prison Notebooks of Antonio Gramsci*, p. 12.
56 Martin, 'Gene Sharp's theory of power', p. 215.

57 Cox, 'Civil society at the turn of the millennium: Prospects for an alternative world order', p. 104.
58 Cox, 'Gramsci, hegemony and international relations: An essay in method', p. 37.
59 Durst, 'Hegel's conception of the ethical and Gramsci's notion of hegemony', p. 175.
60 Cox, 'Gramsci, hegemony and international relations: An essay in method', p. 37.
61 Gramsci, *Selections from the Prison Notebooks*, p. 12.
62 Ibid. p. 12.
63 Cocks, *The Oppositional Imagination: Feminism, Critique, and Political Theory*, p. 41.
64 Cox, 'Gramsci, hegemony and international relations: An essay in method', p. 40.
65 Gramsci, *Selections from the Prison Notebooks*, p. 263.
66 Ibid. p. 12.
67 Cox, 'Civil society at the turn of the millennium: Prospects for an alternative world order', p. 104.
68 Dreyfus and Rabinow, *Michel Foucault: Beyond Structuralism and Hermeneutics*, pp. 184–5.
69 Foucault, 'Method', p. 87.
70 McNay, *Foucault: A Critical Introduction*, p. 2.
71 Ibid. pp. 124–5.
72 Foucault, 'Method', p. 87.
73 McNay, *Foucault: A Critical Introduction*, p. 91.
74 Ibid. p. 117.
75 Foucault, 'Method', p. 86
76 McNay, *Foucault: A Critical Introduction*, p. 3.
77 Foucault, 'Method', p. 87.
78 Ibid. p. 90.
79 Dreyfus and Rabinow, *Michel Foucault: Beyond Structuralism and Hermeneutics*, p. 203.
80 Ibid. p. 203.
81 Foucault, 'The body of the condemned', p. 175.
82 McNay, *Foucault: A Critical Introduction*, p. 108.
83 Ibid. p. 3.
84 Dreyfus and Rabinow, *Michel Foucault: Beyond Structuralism and Hermeneutics*, p. 212.
85 Foucault, 'Afterword: The subject and power', p. 212.
86 Ibid. p. 209.
87 Bevir, 'Foucault, Power, and Institutions', p. 347.
88 Ibid. p. 349.

89 Dreyfus and Rabinow, *Michel Foucault: Beyond Structuralism and Hermeneutics*, p. 215.

90 McNay, *Foucault: A Critical Introduction*, p. 121.

91 Ibid. p. 93.

92 See McNay, *Foucault: A Critical Introduction*, pp. 93–5; and Dreyfus and Rabinow, *Michel Foucault: Beyond Structuralism and Hermeneutics*, pp. 192–3, for example.

93 Foucault, 'The means of correct training', p. 188.

94 Havel, 'The power of the powerless', p. 52.

95 Ibid. p. 52.

96 Ibid. p. 53.

97 Ibid. p. 52.

98 Ibid. p. 53.

99 Cocks, *The Oppositional Imagination: Feminism, Critique, and Political Theory*, p. 79.

100 Bleiker, 'Writing human agency after the death of God', p. 95.

101 Havel, 'The power of the powerless', p. 61.

102 Havel, 'The power of the powerless', p. 79.

103 Foucault, 'Truth and power', p. 64.

104 Cf. Bleiker's discussion of the survival of patriarchy through the East German revolution in 'Writing human agency after the death of God', p. 96.

105 Cocks, *The Oppositional Imagination: Feminism, Critique, and Political Theory*, p. 80.

106 Foucault, 'Afterword: The subject and power', pp. 219–20.

107 Ibid. p. 221.

108 Ibid. p. 221.

109 Ibid. p. 220.

110 Ibid. pp. 225–6.

111 Foucault, 'Method', p. 88.

112 Ibid. pp. 87–8.

113 Ibid. pp. 87–8.

114 Foucault, 'Space, knowledge and power', p. 245.

115 Cocks, *The Oppositional Imagination: Feminism, Critique, and Political Theory*, p. 39.

116 See Bevir, 'Foucault, power, and institutions', pp. 354, 357–8.

117 Ibid. p. 347.

118 Foucault, 'The body of the condemned', p. 174.

119 Foucault, 'Space, knowledge and power', p. 245.

Chapter 6

PACIFISM AND NONVIOLENCE

INTRODUCTION

Pacifism and nonviolence are sometimes seen to be synonymous, because they both oppose the use of violence to achieve particular political ends. They are, however, logically distinct, if sometimes complementary and even overlapping, moral and political positions.

Pacifism objects to the institutionalised or organised use of violence, in the form of war and armed conflict, for ethical reasons. It involves the refusal to participate in political violence, because of the loss of human life and the scale of destruction it entails.

A pacifist position can be adopted at the level of individuals or social groups, with particular religious or ethical beliefs concerning the taking of human life, for instance. This takes the form of conscientious objection to military conscription, for example, or what is sometimes referred to as 'vocational pacifism'.[1] Even more controversially, pacifism can apply at the level of states or governments, through objections to the use of armed force, as an instrument of foreign and security policy, and to war, as a feature of international relations.

Pacifism can provide a vital moral impetus for the search for nonviolent alternatives to war and armed conflict as mechanisms of political and social change. In particular, pacifist objections to violence encapsulate many of the moral argument in favour of a principled commitment to nonviolence. At the same time, nonviolent political action, or civil resistance, provides pacifists with a practical alternative to the use of violence to deal with domestic or internal oppression or external aggression.

Thus, Adam Roberts identifies pacifism as one of 'three traditions of thought' contributing to civil resistance or nonviolent political action (the other two traditions are '"progressive substitution", and defence by civil resistance').[2] He acknowledges the contribution of pacifist 'individuals and organizations . . . to many civil resistance campaigns', without reducing civil resistance or nonviolent political action to pacifism or conflating the two positions, because 'actual experience suggests that it [civil resistance] is a broader phenomenon that does not easily fit into a preconceived ideological pigeon-hole'.[3] As Sharp suggests, many groups use nonviolence because of the perceived effectiveness of its methods, rather than because of any ideological or ethical opposition to the use of armed force, for example. Nonetheless, many pacifists find civil resistance or nonviolent political action appealing, precisely because it is seen as providing 'a substitute for armed force', even though the two positions are logically distinct.[4]

Tolstoy, with his strong moral and religious objections to the use of violence under any circumstances, embodied a commitment to both principled nonviolence, more generally, and a pacifist rejection of war and political violence, more specifically. In the case of Tolstoy, his principled or philosophical support of nonviolence and his pacifism were synonymous.

However, as we have seen, neither pragmatic nor principled proponents of nonviolence need to be pacifists. Pragmatic proponents of nonviolence, such as Gene Sharp and those involved in the many recent examples of nonviolent civil resistance, can support and utilise the methods of nonviolent political action for purely practical reasons, because they are the most effective way of achieving political and social change under the circumstances. This has more to do with the nature of political power, than with ethical or moral arguments against violence. Nonetheless, there is a sort of residual pacifism attached, even to pragmatic nonviolence, that supports a 'moral preference', in favour of nonviolent forms of political action.[5] It is difficult to understand the thorough-going commitment to the nonviolent features of civil resistance characteristic of strategists and theorists of nonviolent political action, such as Sharp, in purely power-political terms and in the absence of the moral impetus towards nonviolence provided by pacifism.

Gandhi, on the other hand, is a prominent example of someone with a principled commitment towards the philosophy and practice of nonviolence, who was not a pacifist. Gandhi accepted the use of armed force by states or governments under certain circumstances –

for self-defence against aggression, for instance, or to enforce the rule of law. The main difference between Gandhi and Tolstoy, concerning pacifism (as distinct from nonviolence), revolves around political theory and, more particularly, the role and status of the state as a form of political and social organisation. Tolstoy regarded the state as a form of institutionalised violence, and all manifestations of this violence (including war and the used of armed force) must be rejected.

Gandhi, however, accepted that states or governments were necessary to maintain social order and the rule of law under certain circumstances (in accordance with social contract theory) and had the right to employ legitimate violence to do so, if necessary. Furthermore, citizens were required to comply with such state violence if they benefitted from the social order it helped to maintain, via the rule of law, for instance. At the same time, Gandhi had a vision of a fully peaceful or nonviolent society (*ramaraj*) that accorded with his philosophy of *ahimsa* or nonviolence and that could be achieved through expanding the practice of nonviolence into all spheres of political and social life. In this sense, Gandhi's position was one of 'progressive substitution' (to use Adam Roberts' term)[6] of nonviolence for violence, until this peaceful or nonviolent society was achieved (sometimes also referred to, somewhat awkwardly, as 'pacificism'), rather than the absolute or immediate pacifism of Tolstoy.

Thus, both pragmatic and principled proponents of nonviolent political action may insist that its use is appropriate for civil society organisations or social movements seeking political change, without rejecting the claim of the state to a monopoly of the legitimate use of violence for purposes of law enforcement and self-defence. In other words, those engaging in efforts to achieve domestic political reform or even more profound structural change, by means of these organisations or popular movements, must restrict themselves to nonviolent political action. This does not prevent a representative and legitimate state from relying upon its security forces for self-defence or law enforcement, however, in accordance with the strictures of domestic or international law. In this sense, even a principled commitment to nonviolent political action does not necessarily entail pacifism, because such a philosophy of nonviolence may involve a longer-term vision of a nonviolent society that does not require an immediate pacifist rejection of all forms of state violence. It is only when this transformative nonviolent vision is combined with a more immediate and unrelenting critique of state violence (as in Tolstoy) that it coincides with, or requires, a fully pacifist position.

Pacifism and principled nonviolence may share a long-term vision of a peaceful or nonviolent society, but they differ in terms of their immediate political analysis of the role of the state and its use of violence. The difficult issue for pacifists is how to contain all forms of violence (oppression and aggression) in the current or immediate absence of fully developed or comprehensively effective nonviolent methods of resistance to such violence. The difficult issue for proponents of 'progressive substitution', on the other hand, is to ensure that their acceptance of some supposedly temporary mechanisms of state violence or enforcement does not prevent the realisation of a fully peaceful or nonviolent society.

NONVIOLENCE, PACIFISM AND WAR

Gandhi referred to war as 'wrong' and as 'an unmitigated evil. I know too that it has got to go'.[7] He appealed to 'every Briton'[8] to use 'non-violent non-co-operation (sic)',[9] as pioneered in India, rather than armed force to resist Nazism, for example, because of the horrors being perpetrated against civilians by all sides during World War II:

> This war . . . is brutalizing man on a scale hitherto unknown. All distinctions between combatants and non-combatants have been abolished . . . No cause, however just, can warrant the indiscriminate slaughter that is going on minute by minute.[10]

The scale and destructive capacity of the violence resulting from modern, large-scale warfare, even on behalf of an ostensibly just cause, appalled Gandhi.[11]

And yet, he also acknowledged that there were other evils as great or greater than violence or war. He famously supported the use of violence where the only other choice appeared to be cowardice, for example: 'I do believe that, where there is only a choice between cowardice and violence, I would advise violence'.[12] For those unable to commit themselves to nonviolence, it was better to use violence, than not to engage in self-defence: '. . . he who cannot protect himself or his nearest and dearest or their honour by non-violently facing death, may and ought to do so by violently dealing with the oppressor'.[13]

I would rather have India resort to arms in order to defend her honour than that she should, in a cowardly manner, become or remain a helpless witness to her own dishonour.[14]

Similarly, he defended his role in recruiting Indians to the British Army during 'the Boer War, the so-called Zulu Rebellion' and World War I, because it represented 'a choice between cowardice and violence'.[15]

Nonetheless, this inability to respond to evil nonviolently indicated a weakness or an incapacity on the part of the protagonist, rather than a failing of the doctrine of nonviolence as such. Gandhi remained committed to the search for exclusively nonviolent methods of dealing with conflict and social evil, as part of his experiments with truth, because 'experience convinces me that permanent good can never be the outcome of untruth and violence'.[16]

Martin Luther King also made the connection between the use of nonviolence to achieve internal or domestic change and anti-war pacifism in the sphere of international relations: 'We have experimented with the meaning of nonviolence in our struggle for racial justice in the United States, but now the time has come for man to experiment with nonviolence in all areas of human conflict, and that means nonviolence on an international scale'.[17] He acknowledged, however, that such pacifism was not an easy or straightforward moral choice:

> During recent months I have come to see more and more the need for the method of nonviolence in international relations. While I was convinced during my student days of the power of nonviolence in group conflicts within nations, I was not yet convinced of its efficacy in conflicts between nations. I felt that while war could never be a positive or absolute good, it could serve as a negative good in the sense of preventing the spread and growth of an evil force . . . But more and more I have come to the conclusion that the potential destructiveness of modern weapons of war totally rules out the possibility of war ever serving again as a negative good. The choice today is no longer between violence and nonviolence. It is either nonviolence or nonexistence. I am no doctrinaire pacifist. I have tried to embrace a realistic pacifism. Moreover, I see the pacifist position not as sinless but as the lesser evil in the circumstances. Therefore I do not claim to be free from the moral dilemmas that the Christian nonpacifist confronts.[18]

The pacifist must confront the moral dilemma of avoiding violence, while resisting other evils, such as military aggression and the threats to freedom, human rights and human life that it entails.

Both Tolstoy and Gandhi connected pacifism – at the level of individual conscience and behaviour – to war, as an instrument of state policy and practice. Tolstoy located the source of a commitment to truth and nonviolence in individual conscience, which becomes the basis for resisting unjust policies that require its violation. Thus, he viewed conscientious objection, or 'the refusals of individuals to take military service', as 'the key to the solution of the question' of war and other forms of violence.[19] The solution to the problem of war, in particular, rests with each individual and their behaviour, in accordance with conscience: 'The way to do away with war is for those who do not want war, who regard participation in it as a sin, to refrain from fighting'.[20] Ending war originated in the conscientious action of each individual, not at the political level, with conferences and tribunals and international law: 'the easiest and surest way to universal disarmament is by individuals refusing to take part in military service'.[21]

Such refusal is a particular instance of obedience to God and non-cooperation with evil: '. . . no action is more opposed to the will of God than that of killing men. And therefore you *cannot* obey men if they order you to kill'.[22] According to Tolstoy, 'a Christian cannot be a murderer and therefore cannot be a soldier'.[23]

Gandhi supported the importance of conscientious objection in ending war, but argued that military refusal did not go far enough:

> I would say that merely to refuse military service is not enough. To refuse to render military service when the particular time arrives is to do the thing after all the time for combating the evil is practically gone. Military service is only a symptom of the disease which is deeper . . . He or she who supports a State organized in the military way – whether directly or indirectly – participates in the sin . . . Therefore, all those who want to stop military service can do so by withdrawing all co-operation. Refusal of military service is much more superficial than non-co-operation with the whole system which supports the State.[24]

If the purpose of conscientious objection is to end war and not merely to express individual dissent, then it must extend to non-cooperation, with all aspects of a state system that facilitates, organises and depends upon militarisation or the systematic and institutionalised use of violence to maintain unjust and inequitable social structures. This could include boycotting taxes, for example, or a refusal to hold public or state office. Non-cooperation with the state, for Gandhi, also requires constructing or establishing alternative forms of social and political organisation that do not depend upon the systematic use of violence.

Pacifism is conventionally defined in somewhat negative terms, as the refusal to participate in war or preparations for war, most often for moral reasons of one sort or another. Furthermore, pacifism is often depicted in absolutist terms, as the view, for instance, that 'it is always wrong to go to war'[25] or that 'participation in and support for war is always impermissible'.[26]

There is also, however, a positive dimension to pacifism that complements this outright opposition to war and the use of armed force. This concerns the pacifist commitment to peacebuilding and to finding alternatives to war and violence, as responses to social and political conflict. On this view, pacifism seeks the abolition of war through the use of exclusively nonviolent methods to deal with social and political conflict, whether internally, within states, or internationally, between states. In other words, pacifism has a positive objective – replacing armed conflict with peaceful methods of conflict resolution – that complements its strict anti-war position.

Thus, there are two components to pacifism as a moral and political position. The first concerns the pacifist refusal to participate in war and political violence more generally. The second concerns the pacifist commitment to replacing war with exclusively nonviolent methods of dealing with social and political conflict.

Even if all pacifists share this outright opposition to war and a commitment to replacing it with exclusively peaceful methods of conflict resolution, they do not always do so for precisely the same reasons. We can identify conscientious pacifists, for instance, whose reasons for opposing war tend to be strongly ethical or even theological. Such pacifists often derive their opposition to war from a more general or fundamental prohibition against the taking of human life under any circumstances, of which war is simply the most egregious example.

Anti-war pacifists, or war resisters, on the other hand, are concerned primarily with the negative and destructive consequences of war as such, which includes, but is not limited to, the taking of human life on a widespread and sometimes massive scale. While these varieties of pacifism share many features in common, such as their suspicion of the state as a form of organised violence, their analysis of the problem of war and their reasons for refusing to participate in it do not always coincide.

An exploration of these different types of pacifism and their limits reveals a dilemma for pacifists, concerning the need to use some form of institutionalised violence or armed force (in the form of policing or law enforcement, peacekeeping or peacemaking and so on), in order to prevent or eliminate war as a feature of international relations. There seems to be a contradiction between the anti-war objectives of pacifism and its objections to the use of violence if some state violence is required to enforce the rule of law and resist aggression. In other words, there is a tension between the moral strictures of conscientious or absolute pacifism and the political outcomes anticipated by anti-war pacifism. This mirrors the tension between some forms of principled nonviolence that accept a role for the state in maintaining social order (such as Gandhi, for example) and the anti-state pacifism of Tolstoy.

CONSCIENTIOUS OR ABSOLUTE PACIFISM

Both conscientious pacifism and anti-war pacifism involve the refusal to participate in all war, even if their diagnosis of the problem of war and their proposed solutions are not identical. Richard Norman, for example, suggests that the more general moral principle that underlies the pacifist prohibition against participation in war is the wrongness of killing human beings: 'Pacifism . . . is a principled position, and the relevant principle to which it appeals is the principle of not taking human life'.[27] Furthermore, Norman argues that this principle provides a vital distinction between pacifism and just war theory.[28] In other words, pacifism rejects the principle of discrimination, according to which, some human beings (such as combatants) become legitimate targets during war and armed conflict, in favour of a much stronger prohibition against the taking of human life under any circumstances.

Adin Ballou provides a classic nineteenth-century statement of the conscientious pacifist position, which he characterises as 'Christian non-resistance'[29]: 'The term non-resistance . . . signifies total abstinence from all resistance of injury with injury'.[30] He further identifies seven types of behaviour from which a 'Christian non-resistant' must abstain. The very first of these prohibitions is this: 'He cannot kill, maim or otherwise absolutely injure any human being, in personal self-defence, or for the sake of his family, or any thing he holds dear'.[31]

Furthermore, Ballou makes the connection between 'the infliction of . . . absolute personal injury' and various social evils to which he is opposed, including war, but also slavery and capital punishment.[32] Thus, Ballou's conscientious, Christian pacifism or 'non-resistance' is based on his opposition not merely to killing, but even to injuring other human beings, under any circumstances. This, in turn, is the source for his oppositon not only to war, but also to other social evils.

William Lloyd Garrison, a contemporary and compatriot of Ballou, made the connection between Christian non-resistance and opposition to war and the use of armed force quite explicit. He wrote this 'Declaration of principles' for the New England Non-Resistance Society, of which Adin Ballou was also a member:

> We register our testimony, not only against all wars, whether offensive or defensive, but all preparations of war . . . against the militia system and a standing army . . . against all appropriations for the defence of a nation by force and arms, on the part of any legislative body; against every edict of government requiring of its subjects military service. Hence, we deem it unlawful to bear arms, or to hold a military office.[33]

Christian non-resistance requires 'the forgiveness instead of the punishment of enemies . . . in all cases whatsoever', because 'evil can be exterminated from the earth only by goodness'.[34] War and the use of military force, whether offensively, defensively or for any purpose whatsoever, violate this central message of the Christian Gospel. Therefore, according to Garrison: 'all who manufacture, sell, or wield those deadly weapons, do thus array themselves against the peaceful dominion of the SON OF GOD (sic) on earth'.[35]

Garrison's opposition to war and its instruments is unequivocal, although, at least in this statement, he does not derive this explicitly from an absolute prohibition against the taking of human life. Nonetheless, its origins in the principle of non-resistance and its reference to forgiveness, instead of punishment, provide a clear connection to conscientious pacifism, with its prohibition against killing or even harming other human beings, no matter what harm they may have committed themselves.

Such pacifists also often emphasise the importance of individual conscience and individual action as the locus of resistance to war and political violence. Peter Mayer, in the introduction to his seminal and wide-ranging anthology of pacifist writing – *The Pacifist Conscience* – identifies 'absolute pacifism' as 'that aspect of peace activity . . . which relied on a personal testimony against violence – individual *acts* of conscience'.[36] According the the well-known American pacifist of the twentieth century, A. J. Muste, 'for the individual to pit himself in Holy Disobedience against the war-making and conscripting state . . . is now the beginning and the core of any realistic and practical movement against war'.[37]

Tolstoy is perhaps the most influential and uncompromising proponent of this theologically-based conscientious pacifist position. He brings together and crystallises the central themes of this position in his essays on war and peace. He writes, for example:

> A Christian, whose doctrine enjoins upon him humility, nonresistance to evil, love to all (even to the most malicious), cannot be a soldier; that is, he cannot join a class of men whose business is to kill their fellow-men.[38]

Furthermore, like Muste and many others, Tolstoy emphasises the importance of individual conscientious objection or 'the refusals (sic) of individuals to take military service . . . as the key to the solution of the question'.[39]

Like Adin Ballou and other Christian pacifists, Tolstoy bases his opposition to war on a particular interpretation of the Christian message as prohibiting not merely killing, but all forms of violence. For Tolstoy, for example, pacifism or nonresistance 'was a personal obligation from which there was no exemption', which, furthermore, 'formed the core of the Gospels'.[40] The Sermon on the Mount, in particular, (as well as the Decalogue) 'forbade killing a being created in the image of God', thus reiterating 'the sanctity of human life'.[41]

> The essential thing, however, is that the law given to us by God . . . distinctly forbids, not killing only, but also every kind of violence.

Therefore we cannot, and will not, take part in your preparations for murder, we will give no money for the purpose.[42]

Tolstoy is concerned with war as a specific social and political problem, but also as representative of much broader theological and ethical issues, epitomising human sin and disobedience to God's will in the form of violence and the deliberate taking of human life.

Another distinguishing characteristic of conscientious pacifism is that it often coincides most closely with an absolute or unqualified pacifist position, involving a complete prohibition against specific (and related) types of behaviour, such as the taking of human life or participation in war. This may be partly due to its emphasis upon the requirements of individual conscience and behaviour, since it may seem easier to both insist upon and to implement such an absolute prohibition at this level, than at the level of larger groups or political entities or communities.

Furthermore, such conscientious pacifism, with its unqualified prohibitions against certain types of behaviour, is often based in a deontological, rather than a consequentialist, approach to establishing ethical principles. In other words, conscientious pacifism is often based upon an assessment of the intrinsic moral quality of certain types of action in themselves (such as killing or the taking of human life), rather than the consequences of these actions. Such a deontological appraisal of action lends itself more easily to establishing clear-cut or unqualified prohibitions against certain categories of action, than does a consequentialist approach.

Finally, those who base their pacifism in a deontological, rather than a consequentialist, approach to ethics, do so in the context of a much wider set of philosophical, religious or ideological commitments, from which they derive their explicitly pacifist principles. As Martin Ceadel points out:

> Most deontologists do not simply assert on their own authority that the use of force, killing, or participation in war is intrinsically wrong. They insist that the latter is the correct inference to be drawn from a particular religious, political, philosophical, or humanitarian doctrine.[43]

In other words, the pacifist evaluation of a particular type of action (such as killing) as intrinsically wrong, in deontological terms, is derived from a much broader set of beliefs relevant to moral judgements about human behaviour. In the case of Ballou, Garrison and Tolstoy, as we have already seen, the absolute prohibition against killing or the use of violence against human beings that provides the basis of their pacifism is derived from a particular interpretation of the Christian message. Although these examples have been selected from the Christian tradition, such pacifism is not unique to Christianity, but also finds its counterparts in other religious or faith traditions. Furthermore, such pacifism can also find support within broadly humanist or even cosmopolitan perspectives.[44]

It must be acknowledged that such conscientious or absolute anti-killing pacifism has more often than not been a minority view, even within these religious or philosophical traditions. As Joseph J. Fahey points out, 'pacifism was abandoned as the dominant model' within Christianity quite early in its history, 'first with the shift to the just war in the fifth century and later in the shift to the total war model in the eleventh century during the Crusades'. Even so, 'pacifism has always existed as a personal witness throughout Christian history'.[45] It has also appeared as a characteristic of smaller Christian sects or groups, such as the historic peace churches (Quakers, Mennonites and Brethren), especially in the post-Reformation era.

ANTI-WAR PACIFISM

The distinguishing characteristic of anti-war pacifism is its focus on war and the use of military force, as distinct from the taking of human life as such, as the central problem or issue for pacifists. There are those, for instance, who oppose modern war, in particular, because of the destructiveness associated with the technology of modern warfare. In other words, it is the scale of destruction and even annihilation associated with modern warfare, especially in the form of nuclear weapons, that requires us to adopt an anti-war pacifist position. War may have been conceivable or excusable as an instrument of foreign policy for previous generations, but this is no longer the case.

Bertrand Russell was a well-known twentieth-century proponent of such 'modern war' pacifism, which he distinguished from a Tolstoyan or absolute pacifist position. He argued, for instance, that 'war cannot still be used as an instrument of policy', even if it could have been justified under certain circumstances in the past, precisely because of the destructiveness of the weapons of modern warfare, including nuclear weapons.[46] Thus, according to Martin Ceadel: 'Russell was explicit that his pacifism was a contingent objection on consequential-ist grounds to modern war'.[47] Russell derived his anti-war pacifism from an assessment of the destructive capabilities of the technology of modern war, rather than from a prohibition against the taking of human life as such.

Such 'modern war' pacifist views reveal another significant differ-ence between the anti-war pacifist position more generally and the conscientious pacifist position, in terms of the types of arguments or principles each position advances in its own support. As discussed earlier, conscientious pacifism tends to be deontological, or derived from moral rules or norms established independently of the conse-quences of human actions, such as a general prohibition against the taking of human life or the use of violence. Anti-war pacifism, on the other hand, tends to be consequentialist and derives its opposition to war from an assessment of its negative consequences.

Thus, Russell's assessment of the widespread destruction result-ing from the technology of modern warfare is an example of such consequentialist moral reasoning. Other consequentialist anti-war arguments include a utilitarian assessment of 'the enormous cost and wastefulness of modern war'.[48] The suggestion here is that the resources expended on war and preparations for war could achieve far more to satisfy the basic needs or promote the well-being of humanity if used in some other way. Similar consequentialist arguments against war concern its use to promote elite interests, through the arms trade or the capture of valuable natural resources, for example, in a way that does little to meet the needs of the mass of humankind and, in fact, can be directly inimical to meeting those needs.

Thus, such anti-war pacifism also tends to take a broader, political view of war, focusing on the social and economic structures giving rise to armed conflict, as distinct from its sources in the moral qualities of individual behaviour. In addition to the moral or theological impetus for conscientious pacifism, came efforts to derive pacifism from a criti-cal social and political analysis. As the Protestant theologian Reinhold Neibuhr pointed out, for example:

> Gradually the effort to present a Christian testimony against war
> forced an increasingly large number of F.O.R. [Fellowship of

Reconciliation] members to oppose the capitalistic social system as a breeder of war and injustice.[49]

Pacifists began to complement their commitment to individual conscientious objection to war with a need to understand and rectify its social and political causes.

Tolstoy also connected war to the existence of armies and armies to the need for governments to control their citizens: 'In reality, war is an inevitable result of the existence of armies; and armies are only needed by governments in order to dominate their own working-classes'.[50] Similarly, Albert Einstein, in his famous exchange of letters with Sigmund Freud prior to World War II, linked war to the economic interests of the ruling class: 'the governing class in every nation . . . regard warfare, the manufacture and sale of arms, simply as an occasion to advance their personal interests'.[51] War is challenged as a vehicle for pursuing elite economic interests. In other words, we must challenge the connection between the economic order and war, in the form of vested corporate or state interests in arms production and the arms trade, for example. We need to address such structural inequalities if we want to eliminate war as a feature of international relations and not merely modify individual behaviour.

One reason for this is an awareness of the limits of pacifism, based in individual or small group conscience, as a basis for effective war resistance. Conscientious or anti-killing pacifism is often presented in individualistic or sectarian terms. In other words, the choice to refuse participation in all wars under any circumstances is a matter for an individual's conscience, sometimes justified by their membership in a particular religious (or political) sect or group. It is for this reason that pacifism is often associated with conscientious objection to military service on the part of individuals or members of specific groups. Similarly, Fahey points out that even though 'pacifism ceased to be the dominant position of Christians on warfare after the fourth century',[52] it 'was still required of monks and clergy after laity were allowed to participate in war'.[53] In this way, pacifism becomes a way of life or vocation, binding only on those who choose it, perhaps through membership in a particular group or organisation, such as the clergy or the historic peace churches (Mennonites, Quakers and Brethren), within Christianity.

A central problem with such individual or sectarian pacifism is that it can co-exist with the continued use of armed force, providing those individuals or groups who so desire are not required or compelled to participate. According to John Rawls, such vocational pacifism 'no more challenges the state's authority [to engage in war] than the celibacy of priests challenges the sanctity of marriage'.[54]

In other words, pacifism becomes a matter of choice for some, but not a universal obligation. It expresses individual or group dissent, without engaging in processes of political and social change to eliminate war and armed conflict.[55] It addresses the moral problem of individual participation in war, but not that of the phenomenon of war itself.[56] Conscientious objection to participation in war, expressed in this way: 'can encourage mere escapism rather than efforts to prevent war'[57] or a withdrawal from political life, rather than an engagement with the structures that facilitate or require war, in order to change them. Thus: 'Without tackling the roots of war in a faulty economic system, moral protest remained an empty gesture'.[58]

Neibuhr associated himself with such a socialist or 'Marxian' critique of war as a social and economic system. This social and political critique of the war system, with capitalism as its basis, led him away from conscientious pacifism, although he retained his anti-war stance. In other words, he retained his outright opposition to war and the use of armed force in international relations, while recognising the need for radical social change if the causes of war were to be eliminated:

> I am forced to associate myself with 20 per cent of the Fellowship who are pacifists only in the sense that they will refuse to participate in an international armed conflict. Perhaps it would clear the issue if we admitted that we were not pacifists at all . . . We expect no basic economic justice without a destruction of the present disproportion of power and we do not expect the latter without a social struggle.[59]

Neibuhr recognises the divergence between his own anti-war stance and a pacifist position, based upon the conscientious objection to the use of violence or the taking of human life. He acknowledges the division between such conscientious pacifism and an anti-war position, based in a radical social and political critique of the status quo. He accepts that the latter may not be a conventionally pacifist position, even if it aims to achieve social change, in order to eliminate the conditions of international armed conflict. Neibuhr's anti-war position is contingent upon the need to use force to achieve such social and political change.

The dilemma presented by this tension between an anti-war position, based in a radical social and political critique of the status quo, and conscientious pacifism may not be as stringent as Neibuhr presents it, however. One can accept the necessity of 'social struggle' against those with vested economic and political interests in the war system, for instance, without accepting the necessity of violence or the use of armed force. The campaigns led by Gandhi and other twentieth century proponents of nonviolent political action, such as Martin Luther King, provide inspiring examples of the possibility of achieving social and political change, without resorting to violence or armed struggle.

Neibuhr, who was a contemporary of Gandhi, almost wilfully misunderstood *satyagraha*, or mass nonviolent civil disobedience, as a form of passivity or 'passive resistance'. Gandhi, in particular, however, provides an important link between the moral impetus associated with a moral or theological commitment to nonviolence and the possibilities of mass nonviolent political resistance to social and political oppression. As Peter Mayer says: 'The example of Mohandas K. Gandhi . . . more than any other enlarged the perspectives of the pacifist tradition in the twentieth century'.[60]

ANTI-WAR INTERNATIONALISM

Nonetheless, the dilemma for both conscientious and anti-war pacifists is that some form of armed force, or threat of the use of armed force, may be required to achieve the conditions necessary for peace, or the absence of war, in international relations. In other words, the conditions for peaceful international relations can only be achieved through the rule of law, and law always requires some mechanism of enforcement, up to, and including, the use of coercive physical violence, in order to be effective. Kant's scheme of 'Perpetual Peace' is one such mechanism for eliminating war as a feature of international relations, through establishing the rule of law at multiple levels: 'Thus the state of peace must be established', and this 'can only be done in a state of society regulated by law'.[61]

Kant, for instance, opposed standing armies ('*miles perpetuus*') as inimical to international peace: 'For they are always threatening other states with war by appearing to be in constant readiness to fight'.[62]

Nor did he accept a voluntary professional army as an alternative to such standing armies obtained by conscription: 'To which we must add that the practice of hiring men to kill or to be killed seems to imply a use of them as mere machines and instruments in the hand of another (namely the state) which cannot be reconciled with the right of humanity in our own person'.[63]

Kant did, however, support the use of military force in response to violent or aggressive incursions against state sovereignty, as a violation of a central principle of international law. Kant's fifth preliminary article of perpetual peace, for example, prohibits any state from violently interfering 'with the constitution and administration of another'.[64] Thus, the limited circumstances for the legitimate use of armed force involved the 'voluntary periodical military exercise on the part of the citizens of the state, who thereby seem to secure themselves and their country against attack from without'.[65] However, this form of national defence required neither a conscripted standing army, nor professional mercenaries.

Such a position, with its emphasis upon the rule of law at all levels of social and political interaction, including the international, can be called 'anti-war internationalism'. It shares the pacifist objective of eliminating war as a feature of international relations, but not the pacifist insistence upon exclusively nonviolent or peaceful methods for dealing with conflict. Although it allows for the limited use of coercive physical violence or even military force, it differs from just war theory, because it does not accept the possibility of a 'just war' between states as an inevitable feature of international relations. Even though some just war principles have been incorporated into international humanitarian law, these are somewhat limited from an anti-war internationalist perspective, because such laws are aimed at governing the conduct of war, rather than its explicit abolition or elimination.

The UN Charter, with its general prohibition against the use of armed force by member states, can be seen as a recent embodiment of aspects of such anti-war internationalism. Article 2(4) of the Charter requires that: 'All Members shall refrain in their international relations from the threat or use of force against the territorial integrity or political independence of any state'. The only exceptions to this general prohibition against the use of armed force in international relations concern 'individual or collective self-defence if an armed attack occurs against a Member of the United Nations' (Article 51) and actions 'necessary to maintain or restore international peace and security' (Article 42).

Nonetheless, the UN is not a full realisation of the ideals or objectives of anti-war internationalism, because it does not foresee or require the end of national standing armies, but, rather, relies on such armed forces to carry out its tasks of peacekeeping or 'peace enforcement'[66] to protect peace agreements or implement international law. The difficulty with such standing armies, from an anti-war internationalist perspective, as Kant pointed out almost two centuries previously, is that they can also be used for aggression and armed conflict.

The link between the rule of law and enforcement has led some pacifists to a form of anarchism, however, through rejecting government as the embodiment of law, backed up by violence. The role of the state presents a problem, particularly for conscientious pacifists, who object to the use of violence under any circumstances and not merely in the context of war. This undermines a central function of the state, with its claim over a monopoly of the legitimate use of violence, both internally and externally:[67]

> As every human government is upheld by physical strength, and its laws are enforced virtually at the point of a bayonet . . . We therefore voluntarily exclude ourselves from every legislative and judicial body, and repudiate all human politics, worldly honors, and stations of authority.[68]

This anarchist strand, or opposition to the coercive state, runs deep in pacifist thought and practice.

A. J. Coates also notes this link between anarchism and conscientious pacifism, in particular:

> Some form of anarchism would appear to be the logical conclusion of so universal a form of pacifism, since from this radical perspective the state constitutes a form of institutionalised violence and a source of moral corruption.[69]

Such pacifism rejects the state as a form of political and social organisation, because it depends on the use of violence as its ultimate method of enforcement. Martin Wight similarly equates anarchism as a political theory with pacifism in international relations.[70]

Mayer identifies Tolstoy as 'the great exponent in our time of the Christian anarchist position',[71] which is derived, in turn, from his

Christian pacifism. According to Fahey: 'Tolstoy . . . renounced institutions that relied on violence: governments, courts, armies, police and private property'.[72] Tolstoy argued, for example, that if the defence of the state and the existing political order requires the use of armed force and the taking of human life, then we need to find alternative forms of social and political organisation:

> And so should every soldier say if the necessity of maintaining the existing order founded on his readiness to murder were put before him. 'Organize the general order in a way that will not require murder,' the soldier should say. 'And then I shall not destroy it. I only do not wish to and cannot be a murderer'.[73]

According to proponents of conscientious pacifism, such as Tolstoy, we require an alternative to the modern conventional state, with its monopoly over the legitimate use of violence, both domestically and internationally. For Tolstoy, the state 'must be dismantled entirely and replaced by a voluntarist society before nonviolence could be fully effective'.[74] Our moral obligation to refrain from murder and the taking of human life supersedes any requirement to preserve social and political order through enforcing the law and defending the state.

Brock and Young also connect pacifism to the search for alternative forms of political, social and economic organisation in their comprehensive history of pacifism in the twentieth century, including an explicit link between pacifism and the libertarian anarcho-syndicalist tradition in Europe.[75] Such approaches combined a rejection of the state with a commitment to cooperation, rather than competition, as the basis for an economy that served human needs, rather than private profit.[76]

This discussion of the political and economic conditions necessary to achieve international peace connects to the opening distinction between the two complementary aspects of pacifism. Duane L. Cady refers to this transition from a 'negative peace' to a 'positive peace' paradigm as being a second central characteristic of pacifism, in addition to moral opposition to war.[77] In other words, pacifism is not merely concerned with enunciating an anti-war position, it also outlines or suggests a positive vision of forms of social and political organisation that would eliminate armed conflict:

> Peace is not merely the absence of war; that is at best negative peace, a condition necessary but insufficient for a more genuine and complete positive peace. Pacifism goes well beyond moral opposition to war and involves commitment to order arising from within society by the cooperative participation of its members.[78]

This vision of a cooperative and peaceful social order is contrasted with a social order achieved ultimately through the threat or use of coercion, force and even violence. Furthermore, this transition to a positive peace paradigm applies both domestically and internationally.

There is a crucial difference here between conscientious pacifists, or those who object to the taking of human life under any circumstances for moral or theological reasons, and those who seek to abolish war as a feature of international relations. Conscientious pacifists often extend their position to include a rejection of the state as the epitome of institutionalised violence, while anti-war internationalists view the rule of law, enforced by the state, as a necessary mechanism for eliminating war. As Mayer points out, from this anti-war perspective: 'Absolute pacifists objected to the principle of international force which ultimately would guarantee the peace'.[79]

On the other hand, from a pacifist perspective, anti-war internationalists limit themselves to a 'negative peace' paradigm, because they insist that some form of organised, coercive state violence (in the form of policing or peacekeeping or peacemaking) is necessary to enforce the rule of law and to replace war and armed conflict as central features of international relations. The achievement of a peaceful international order still depends ultimately on the threat or availability of armed force and not on the construction of an alternative social and political order, based on cooperation and the satisfaction of fundamental human needs (or 'positive peace'). The refusal to participate in armed conflict associated with anti-war pacifism becomes a form of anti-war internationalism, in which the abolition of war is achieved through the sometimes coercive or even violent enforcement of international law.

It may be possible to arrive at some intermediate approach to eliminating war as a feature of international relations, in accordance with the pacifist ideal, that does not require the revolutionary or utopian anarchism of Tolstoy and others and yet goes beyond the acceptance of some level of coercive physical force or violence as an inevitable feature of a law-governed international system associated with anti-war internationalism. In other words, there may be forms of active nonviolence that can be used to defend more conventional political structures associated with the state and the rule of law, for example, such as civilian-based defence, unarmed peacekeeping or the 'peace brigades' (*shanti sena*) promoted by Gandhi, amongst others.

CIVILIAN-BASED DEFENCE

In his book, *The Strategy of Nonviolent Defense: A Gandhian Approach*, Robert Burrowes distinguishes between two types of nonviolent defence: 'civilian-based defence' and 'social defence'. Burrowes states that:

> Advocates of civilian-based defense are concerned with defense of the nation-state, its government and territory. According to its leading exponent, Gene Sharp, it is a form of national defense that is designed to deter and defeat foreign military invasions and occupations, as well as domestic coups.[80]

In other words, 'proponents of civilian-based defense regard it as a functional equivalent for military defense'[81] aimed at achieving conventional military objectives, such as the defence of a state or government against external aggression or internal enemies, by peaceful or nonviolent methods.

Adam Roberts is one of many who have offered more conventional proposals for civilian-based defence in the last half-century or so. He assumes that the primary purpose of 'civilian defence' is to protect a state or government and its territory as a replacement for or 'on its own rather than in combination with military defence'.[82] Roberts assesses both peacetime preparations and wartime strategy for civilian-based defence, against various forms of external aggression, in particular, but also against internal threats, such as *coup d'état*. Like many proponents of the pragmatic use of nonviolent political action, such as Gene Sharp, Roberts seems to emphasise various forms of non-cooperation, on the part of a civilian population with an invading or occupying army or enemy, from instances of 'micro-resistance' through 'legal resistance and polite non-cooperation'[83] to 'the general strike, and total non-cooperation with the occupier'.[84]

Roberts concedes, however, that:

A ruthless and determined opponent will not tolerate sustained resistance to his orders and the use by the defenders of massive non-cooperation and non-violent intervention. He is likely to attempt to repress the civilian population by force, and readiness to face his repression must be a central feature of a civilan defence policy.[85]

Furthermore: 'The problem of facing repression in all its various forms – murder, imprisonment, brain-washing, torture, and wanton destruction – is one to which there are no simple solutions which do not involve tragedy and suffering'.[86] The inevitability of repression and suffering exist, however, no matter what forms of resistance are selected, whether civilian-based and nonviolent or armed and militaristic. In any case, as Roberts points out, 'non-violent struggles, if they are to be successful, require quite as much overall direction and strategic planning as military struggles'.[87]

Even as a pragmatic proponent of civilian-based defence, Roberts acknowledges a theme, as part of his peacetime preparations, that points towards a different type of social order. Roberts suggests that 'the decentralization and diffusion of power, to encourage popular involvement in political and economic affairs and to make it harder for an enemy to seize control of the state machinery, could be promoted'.[88] In other words, even from a purely pragmatic point of view, it is much harder for an occupying power to seize control of the mechanisms of social and political organisation of a country or a society, and it is much easier for the civilian population to defend them or to maintain control over them, where such power is diffused as widely as possible among the members of that society. This is one of the key insights into the nature of political power, more generally, that helps to explain the political effectiveness of the various forms of nonviolent political action under a wide range of circumstances.

Burrowes outlines three criticisms of civilian-based defence, which lead him to an alternative theory or strategy of nonviolent defence, based instead on social defence. First, civilian-based defence is based explicitly upon a zero-sum, rather than a positive-sum, view of conflict. In other words, the purpose of civilian-based defence, as with conventional military strategy, is simply to defeat one's opponent. According to Burrowes, this contradicts a central insight of contemporary conflict resolution techniques, which approach conflict from a positive-sum perspective. Such conflict resolution techniques or methods view conflict as a shared problem between protagonists, involving frustrated human needs for recognition, identity and control (for example), for which shared or mutually beneficial (i.e. positive-sum) solutions must be found through the satisfaction of such needs, rather than through achieving victory over one's enemy.[89]

Secondly, Burrowes views civilian-based defence as self-contradictory if used to defend conventional, hierarchical political structures, such as the nation-state. In other words, the strength and effectiveness of civilian-based defence depends on its ability to mobilise mass popular resistance against either external aggression or internal threats, but such resistance is inimical to the survival of political structures aimed at preserving the privileges and power of an elite.

Burrowes' final criticism of 'civilian-based defence' is connected to his second and concerns its lack of structural analysis. This approach to nonviolent defence, for example, fails to identify and seek to change the sources of war and armed conflict in existing political, social and economic structures, involving the unjust or unequal distribution of political power or economic resources. Thus, according to Burrowes, effective nonviolent defence must not simply defend the economic and political status quo, but needs to be 'directed against the militarized state itself', for example.[90] 'If the gains won as a result of successful nonviolent defense are to be consolidated, then, among other things, new nonhierarchical structures are necessary'.[91]

This leads Burrowes to support a form of nonviolent defence based on a social defence model, rather than civilian-based defence. One of the distinguishing features of this approach to nonviolent defence is precisely that it allows and facilitates people to mobilise and organise themselves directly against immediate threats to the satisfaction of human needs, through defending their communities or whichever elements of their social fabric or social organisation they choose.[92] Furthermore, this approach to nonviolent defence can incorporate a commitment to the social changes necessary to achieving forms of social and political organisation more likely to result in the satisfaction of fundamental human needs. This 'strategy of nonviolent defense', according to Burrowes, 'is designed to assist activists and ordinary people in their struggle to create social cosmologies that satisfy human needs'.[93] In other words, Burrowes assessment of the requirements of 'nonviolent defence' also leads us towards the radical social vision associated with conscientious pacifists, such as Tolstoy, rather than towards the more constrained or limited objectives of anti-war internationalists.

CONCLUSION

This chapter has outlined three different, if overlapping, positions that share a common objective – the elimination of war as a feature of international relations. These positions are: conscientious pacifism, anti-war pacifism and anti-war internationalism. Conscientious pacifism and anti-war pacifism are both pacifist positions in that they object to war and the use of military force, although for different reasons. Conscientious pacifism is based upon deontological objections to killing or the taking of human life under any circumstances, whereas anti-war pacifism is derived from consequentialist considerations, associated with the destructiveness of modern or technological warfare, in particular.

Anti-war internationalism, on the other hand, allows for the limited use of coercive physical violence or even military force, in the form of policing or peacekeeping, as mechanisms for enforcing the rule of law. International law is seen as an essential alternative to, or substitute for, war or the unilateral use of armed force by states, in response to political and social conflict. Anti-war internationalism involves extending the social contract from the domestic to the international sphere, so that state behaviour in international relations is regulated by law in the same way that the behaviour of individual citizens is regulated within a civil society. Although they share an acceptance of the limited use of coercive physical violence, anti-war internationalism is more stringent than conventional just war theory, because it does not accept the notion of a 'just war' between states and (like the two pacifist positions) seeks the abolition or the elimination of war as a feature of international relations.

Nonetheless, although the two forms of pacifism and anti-war internationalism share the objective of abolishing war as a feature of international relations, they differ over the methods by which this is to be achieved. The pacifist position insists that the means must coincide, or be consistent with, the end of eliminating institutionalised violence. The anti-war internationalist, on the other hand, claims that the constrained or limited use of violence may be necessary to eliminate its wider and more unconstrained manifestations, in the form of war and armed conflict.

Thus, this chapter has also explored a tension between the two central elements of the pacifist position. These concern its opposition to war as a feature of international relations and its commitment to exclusively nonviolent methods for dealing with conflict. This tension is epitomised by the position of anti-war internationalism, which relies ultimately on the use, or availability of, armed force, in order to eliminate war as an aspect of international relations, through enforcing the rule of law. In other words, the pacifist objective of abolishing war can only be achieved through the threat or use of other forms of coercive political violence. One alternative for pacifism is the revolutionary utopian ideal of alternative forms of political and social organisation that are based ultimately upon cooperation, rather than coercion. Another alternative for pacifism, however, is to promote distinct and effective nonviolent mechanisms for dealing with international aggression against states and their citizens, in the same way that Gandhi and others pioneered nonviolent forms of resistance to domestic or internal injustice and oppression. Thus, the task for pacifism is to find an equivalent to *satyagraha*, as an effective political response to war and armed conflict. In other words, pacifism and anti-war internationalism can be fully reconciled, only to the extent that exclusively peaceful or nonviolent methods of international law enforcement can be developed and implemented.

Notes

1 See Ihara, 'In defense of a version of pacifism', pp. 370–1.
2 Roberts, 'Introduction', p. 7.
3 Ibid. p. 8.
4 Ibid. p. 8.
5 Gene Sharp refers to 'a relative moral preference for nonviolent means' when he states: 'In some cases, there appear to have been mixed motives, with practical motives predominating but with a relative moral preference for nonviolent means'. See Sharp, *Waging Nonviolent Struggle: 20th Century Practice and 21st Century Potential*, p. 20.
6 Adam Roberts explains the term 'progressive substitution' in Roberts, 'Introduction', pp. 8–10.
7 Gandhi, *Selected Writings of Mahatma Gandhi*, p. 58.

 8 Ibid. p. 90.
 9 Ibid. p. 91.
10 Ibid. p. 90.
11 Ibid. pp. 90–1.
12 Ibid. p. 48.
13 Ibid. p. 59.
14 Ibid. p. 48.
15 Ibid. p. 48.
16 Ibid. p. 52.
17 King, 'A Christmas sermon on peace', p. 253.
18 King, 'Pilgrimage to nonviolence', p. 39.
19 Tolstoy, 'The beginning of the end', p. 15.
20 Tolstoy, 'Carthago delenda est', p. 98.
21 Tolstoy, 'Letter on the peace conference', p. 113.
22 Tolstoy, 'Notes for soldiers', pp. 34–5.
23 Ibid. p. 37.
24 Gandhi, *Non-Violent Resistance (Satyagraha)*, p. 359.
25 Norman, 'The case for pacifism', p. 166.
26 Ceadel, *Thinking about Peace and War*, p. 5.
27 Norman, 'The case for pacifism', p.171.
28 See Richard Norman, 'The case for pacifism', p. 174. I also discuss this
    point in my book, *The Ethics of Peace and War*, p. 82.
29 Ballou, 'Christian non-resistance', p. 135.
30 Ibid. p. 131.
31 Ibid. p. 137.
32 Ibid. p. 137.
33 Garrison, 'Non-resistance society: Declaration of principles, 1838', p. 125.
34 Ibid. p. 126.
35 Ibid. p. 127.
36 Mayer, 'Introduction', p. 22.
37 Muste, 'The individual conscience', p. 351.
38 Tolstoy, 'The beginning of the end', p. 11.
39 Ibid. p. 15.
40 Brock, *Varieties of Pacifism: A Survey from Antiquity to the Outset of the
    Twentieth Century*, p. 85.
41 Ibid. p. 87.
42 Tolstoy, 'Two wars', p. 20.
43 Ceadel, *Thinking about Peace and War*, p. 147.
44 See Atack, *The Ethics of Peace and War*.
45 Fahey, *War and the Christian Conscience: Where Do You Stand?*, p. 65.
46 Russell, 'Inconsistency?', p. 323.
47 Ceadel, *Thinking about Peace and War*, p. 152.

48 Brock and Young, *Pacifism in the Twentieth Century*, p. 107.
49 Neibuhr, 'Why I leave the F.O.R.', p. 250.
50 Tolstoy, 'Letter to a non-commissioned officer', p. 161.
51 Einstein, 'Why war?', p. 237.
52 Fahey, *War and the Christian Conscience: Where Do You Stand?*, p. 46.
53 Ibid. p. 54.
54 Rawls, *A Theory of Justice*, p. 382.
55 Atack, *The Ethics of Peace and War*, pp. 82–3.
56 Atack, 'From pacifism to war resistance', p. 180.
57 Ceadel, *Thinking about Peace and War*, p. 136.
58 Brock and Young, *Pacifism in the Twentieth Century*, p. 113.
59 Neibuhr, 'Why I leave the F.O.R.', pp. 252–3.
60 Mayer, 'Introduction', p. 23.
61 Kant, 'Perpetual peace', p. 74.
62 Ibid. p. 73.
63 Ibid. p. 73.
64 Ibid. p. 73.
65 Ibid. p. 73.
66 George F. Oliver provides a useful critical (and historical) discussion of UN engagement with peace enforcement. See Oliver, 'The other side of peace-keeping: Peace enforcement and who should do it?', pp. 99–117.
67 Atack, *The Ethics of Peace and War*, p. 85.
68 Garrison, 'Non-resistance society: Declaration of principles, 1838', p. 125.
69 Coates, *The Ethics of War*, pp. 86–7.
70 Wight, *International Theory: The Three Traditions*, p. 108.
71 Mayer, *The Pacifist Conscience*, p. 160.
72 Fahey, *War and the Christian Conscience: Where Do You Stand?* pp. 54–5.
73 Tolstoy, 'Notes for officers', p. 29.
74 Brock and Young, *Pacifism in the Twentieth Century*, p. 6.
75 Ibid. pp. 113–14.
76 Atack, *The Ethics of Peace and War*, p. 86.
77 See Cady, 'Pacifist perspectives on humanitarian intervention', p. 45.
78 Cady, 'Pacifist perspectives on humanitarian intervention', p. 45.
79 Mayer, 'Introduction', p. 22.
80 Burrowes, *A Strategy of Nonviolent Defense: A Gandhian Approach*, p. 154.
81 Ibid. p. 155.
82 Roberts, 'Civilian defence strategy', p. 249.
83 Ibid. p. 291.
84 Ibid. p. 283.
85 Ibid. p. 289.
86 Ibid. pp. 290–1.
87 Ibid. p. 249.

88 Ibid. p. 254.
89 Burrowes, *A Strategy of Nonviolent Defense: A Gandhian Approach*, pp. 156–7.
90 Ibid. p. 164.
91 Ibid. p. 166.
92 Ibid. p. 165.
93 Ibid. p. 161.

CONCLUSION

One of the central concerns emerging from this analysis of the intersection between nonviolent political action and political theory concerns social contract theory and justifications of the state as a centralised form of political authority (and power), with a monopoly over the use of violence to enforce order, internally, and for self-defence, externally. This provided a basis for distinguishing between two distinct forms of nonviolent political action – civil resistance, which accepts conventional social contract justifications of the state; and transformative nonviolence, which challenges them.

Tolstoy emerges as a seminal figure, in this regard, from the perspective of a political theory of nonviolent political action, because of his direct and explicit rejection of social contract justifications of the state. His Christian pacifism requires an immediate rejection of all forms of organised violence, including (and especially) the state. Those who have chronicled specific examples of nonviolent political action more recently have often approached it from a strategic and pragmatic perspective, however, identifying its distinctive features as a form of political activity, without challenging the role of the state in maintaining social order, for example.[1] They have analysed the use of nonviolent political action by non-state actors, such as civil society groups and social movements, while accepting a legitimate state's monopoly over the use of violence.

Gandhi and Sharp perhaps provide a middle way between the radical pacifism of Tolstoy and the more restricted commitment to nonviolence associated with civil resistance. They both have a longer-term vision of a peaceful or nonviolent society, achievable by means of 'progressive substitution' or finding functional alternatives to violence, as the ultimate sanction for maintaining social order within political communities, as well as defending them from external threats. Gandhi, of course, combined this vision with a philosophical and ethical commitment to nonviolence as a regulative ideal, whereas Sharp has increasingly emphasised the pragmatic and strategic requirements of improving the techniques and methods of nonviolence as a form of political action.

One could argue that there are three reasons for using violence – in terms of social contract justifications of the state, in particular – that nonviolence must replace, as part of such a process of progressive substitution. These are enforcement of the rule of law, self-defence against external aggression and resistance against oppression or injustice. The first is a rule- or law-governed activity, occurring in accordance with the norms or regulations established by means of the social contract embodied by the state. The other two forms of political violence, it could be argued, occur outside the rule-governed political order established by the social contract. They occur, instead, in the state of nature and are aimed at more existential concerns, revolving around the immediate and basic survival of political communities, social groups and individuals.

One of the central tasks of those committed to a more peaceful and less violent world, then, is to bring these two forms of political violence – self-defence and resistance to oppression – into the realm of the rule of law, by solidifying international law (including the laws of war and armed conflict) and expanding the jurisdiction of human rights and political sovereignty. In other words, the scope of political violence becomes increasingly restricted to its use as the ultimate sanction for enforcing the law at multiple levels of political and social organisation (including the international). Those who study nonviolent political action as a method for expanding liberal democracy and human rights, through forms of civil resistance, might be sympathetic to this interpretation of the role and impact of nonviolence in human affairs.

Those with a commitment to a transformative vision of the role of nonviolent political action might wish to move beyond this more circumscribed set of objectives, however. This could be based on pacifist ethical or religious objections to the role of violence in human interaction, for instance, or a structural critique of the state as a form of political organisation that depends upon violence to reinforce and maintain hierarchy, control and inequality. The ultimate objective of nonviolence as a method of political action, then, is not merely to achieve a liberal democratic state and the rule of law as mechanisms for circumscribing or limiting violence, but to provide the basis for forms of political organisation that can move beyond a dependence or reliance upon violence for social order and control.

This book has attempted to explore two of the central themes of nonviolent political action, power and violence, in the context of Western political theory. The initial focus was on social contract theory and its arguments for the power of the sovereign state as a necessary mechanism for constraining and controlling violence. Different forms of nonviolence were identified in terms of some of its central proponents, particularly Tolstoy, Gandhi, King and Sharp, and their attitude towards social contract justifications of the state. This opened up deeper discussions of the relationship between power and consent, for example, and the often ambivalent relationship between nonviolence as a form of resistance and the role of violence in maintaining the social order. The book is an exploration of these themes and it is hoped that it will prompt further critical reflection on the place of nonviolence in political theory, to supplement arguments for its political significance and the important efforts to systematise and explain its strategic effectiveness.

Note

1 See, in particular, Peter Ackerman and Jack DuVall, *A Force More Powerful: A Century of Nonviolent Conflict* (New York: Palgrave, 2000); Adam Roberts and Timothy Garton Ash (eds) *Civil Resistance and Power Politics: The Experience of Non-violent Action from Gandhi to the Present* (Oxford: Oxford University Press, 2009).

BIBLIOGRAPHY

Almond, Brenda and Donald Hill (eds), *Applied Philosophy: Morals and Metaphysics in Contemporary Debate* (London: Routledge, 1991).

Amoore, Louise (ed.), *The Global Resistance Reader* (London: Routledge, 2005).

Arendt, Hannah, *On Revolution* (London: Penguin Books, [1963] 2006).

Ash, Timothy Garton, 'A century of civil resistance: Some lessons and questions', in Adam Roberts and Timothy Garton Ash (eds), *Civil Resistance and Power Politics: The Experience of Non-violent Action from Gandhi to the Present* (Oxford: Oxford University Press, 2009), pp. 370–90.

Atack, Iain, 'From pacifism to war resistance', *Peace & Change* 26: 2 (April 2001), 177–86.

Atack, Iain, *The Ethics of Peace and War* (Edinburgh: Edinburgh University Press, 2005).

Atack, Iain, 'Pacifism in international relations', in Patrick Hayden (ed.), *The Ashgate Research Companion to Ethics and International Relations* (Aldershot: Ashgate, 2009), pp. 183–98.

Ballou, Adin, 'Christian non-resistance', in Peter Mayer (ed.), *The Pacifist Conscience* (Harmondsworth: Penguin Books, 1966), pp. 130–9.

Beissinger, Mark R., 'The intersection of ethnic nationalism and people power tactics in the Baltic States, 1987–91', in Adam Roberts and Timothy Garton Ash (eds), *Civil Resistance and Power Politics: The Experience of Non-violent Action from Gandhi to the Present* (Oxford: Oxford University Press, 2009), pp. 231–46

Bevir, Mark, 'Foucault, power, and institutions', *Political Studies* 47: 2 (June 1999), 345–59.

Bharadwaj, L. K., 'Principled versus pragmatic nonviolence', *Peace Review* 10: 1 (1998), 79–81.

Bleiker, Roland, 'Writing human agency after the death of God', in Louise Amoore (ed.), *The Global Resistance Reader* (London: Routledge, 2005), pp. 92–8.

189

Boulding, Kenneth E., 'Nonviolence and power in the twentieth century', in Stephen Zunes, Lester B. Kurtz and Sarah Beth Asher (eds), *Nonviolent Social Movements: A Geographical Perspective* (Oxford: Blackwell Publishing, 1999), pp. 9–17.

Brock, Peter, *Varieties of Pacifism: A Survey from Antiquity to the Outset of the Twentieth Century* (Syracuse, NY: Syracuse University Press, 1998).

Brock, Peter and Nigel Young, *Pacifism in the Twentieth Century* (Syracuse, NY: Syracuse University Press, 1999).

Brown, Judith M., 'Gandhi and civil resistance in India, 1917–47: Key issues', in Adam Roberts and Timothy Garton Ash (eds), *Civil Resistance and Power Politics: The Experience of Non-violent Action from Gandhi to the Present* (Oxford: Oxford University Press, 2009), pp. 43–57.

Burrowes, Robert, *The Strategy of Nonviolent Defense: A Gandhian Approach* (Albany, NY: State University of New York Press, 1996).

Cady, Duane L., 'Pacifist perspectives on humanitarian intervention', in Robert Lester Phillips and Duane L. Cady (eds), *Humanitarian Intervention: Just War vs. Pacifism* (Lanham, MD: Rowman and Littlefield Publishers, 1996), pp. 31–75.

Ceadel, Martin, *Thinking about Peace and War* (Oxford: Oxford University Press, 1989).

Clark, Howard (ed.), *People Power: Unarmed Resistance and Global Solidarity* (London and New York, NY: Pluto Press, 2009).

Clark, Howard, 'The limits of prudence: Civil resistance in Kosovo, 1990–98', in Adam Roberts and Timothy Garton Ash (eds), *Civil Resistance and Power Politics: The Experience of Non-violent Action from Gandhi to the Present* (Oxford: Oxford University Press, 2009), pp. 277–94.

Coates, A. J., *The Ethics of War* (Manchester: Manchester University Press, 1997).

Cocks, Joan, *The Oppositional Imagination: Feminism, Critique, and Political Theory* (London: Routledge, 1989).

Cox, Robert W., 'Civil society at the turn of the millennium: Prospects for an alternative world order', in Louise Amoore (ed.), *The Global Resistance Reader* (London: Routledge, 2005), pp. 103–23.

Cox, Robert W., 'Gramsci, hegemony and international relations: An essay in method', in Louise Amoore (ed.), *The Global Resistance Reader* (London: Routledge, 2005), pp. 35–47.

Cranston, Maurice, 'Introduction', in Jean-Jacques Rousseau, *The Social Contract* (Harmondsworth: Penguin Books, [1762] 1968), pp. 9–43.

Dreyfus, Herbert and Paul Rabinow, *Michel Foucault: Beyond Structuralism and Hermeneutics* (New York and London: Harvester Wheatsheaf, 1982).

Durst, David C., 'Hegel's conception of the ethical and Gramsci's notion of hegemony', *Contemporary Political Theory* 4: 2 (May 2005), 175–91.

Einstein, Albert, 'Why war?', in Peter Mayer (ed.), *The Pacifist Conscience* (Harmondsworth: Penguin Books, 1966), pp. 236–8.

Fahey, Joseph, *War and the Christian Conscience: Where Do You Stand?* (Maryknoll, NY: Orbis Books, 2005).

Fanon, Frantz, *The Wretched of the Earth* (New York, NY: Grove Press, [1961] 1968).

Fink, Christina, 'The moment of the monks: Burma, 2007', in Adam Roberts and Timothy Garton Ash (eds), *Civil Resistance and Power Politics: The Experience of Non-violent Action from Gandhi to the Present* (Oxford: Oxford University Press, 2009), pp. 354–70.

Foucault, Michel, 'Afterword: The subject and power', in Herbert Dreyfus and Paul Rabinow, *Michel Foucault: Beyond Structuralism and Hermeneutics* (New York and London: Harvester Wheatsheaf, 1982), pp. 208–26.

Foucault, Michel, 'Space, knowledge and power', in Paul Rabinow (ed.), *The Foucault Reader: An Introduction to Foucault's Thought* (London: Penguin Books, 1991), pp. 239–56.

Foucault, Michel, 'The body of the condemned', in Paul Rabinow (ed.), *The Foucault Reader: An Introduction to Foucault's Thought* (London: Penguin Books, 1991), pp. 170–8.

Foucault, Michel, 'The means of correct training', in Paul Rabinow (ed.), *The Foucault Reader: An Introduction to Foucault's Thought* (London: Penguin Books, 1991), pp. 188–205.

Foucault, Michel, 'Truth and power', in Paul Rabinow (ed.), *The Foucault Reader: An Introduction to Foucault's Thought* (London: Penguin Books, 1991), pp. 51–75.

Foucault, Michel, 'Method', in Louise Amoore (ed.), *The Global Resistance Reader* (London: Routledge, 2005), pp. 86–91.

Gandhi, Mohandas K., *Non-Violent Resistance (Satyagraha)*, ed. Bharatan Kumarappa (New York, NY: Schocken Books, 1961).

Gandhi, Mohandas K., *Selected Writings of Mahatma Gandhi*, ed. Ronald Duncan (London and Glasgow: Fontana/Collins, 1971).

Garavan, Mark, *The Politics of Moral Force: Davitt and Saro-Wiwa* (Dublin: Afri Publication, 2008).

Garrison, William Lloyd., 'Non-resistance society: Declaration of principles, 1838', in Peter Mayer (ed.), *The Pacifist Conscience* (Harmondsworth: Penguin Books, 1966), pp. 124–8.

Gregg, Richard, *The Power of Nonviolence*, 2nd edn (London: James Clarke & Co., 1960).

Goldman, Merle, 'The 1989 demonstrations in Tiananmen Square and beyond: Echoes of Gandhi', in Adam Roberts and Timothy Garton Ash (eds), *Civil Resistance and Power Politics: The Experience of Non-violent Action from Gandhi to the Present* (Oxford: Oxford University Press, 2009), pp. 247–59.

Gramsci, Antonio, *Selections from the Prison Notebooks* (London: Lawrence and Wishart, 1971).

Havel, Václav, 'The power of the powerless', in Václav Havel, *Living in Truth*, Jan Vadislav (ed.) (London and Boston, MA: Faber and Faber, 1986), pp. 36–122.

Hindess, Barry, 'Terrortory', *Alternatives* 31: 3 (2006), 243–57.

Hobbes, Thomas, *Leviathan*, ed. C. B. Macpherson (Harmondsworth: Penguin Books, [1651] 1977).

Huneeus, Carlos, 'Political mass mobilization against authoritarian rule: Pinochet's Chile, 1983–88', in Adam Roberts and Timothy Garton Ash (eds), *Civil Resistance and Power Politics: The Experience of Non-violent Action from Gandhi to the Present* (Oxford: Oxford University Press, 2009), pp. 197–212.

Ihara, Craig K., 'In defense of a version of pacifism', *Ethics* 88: 4 (July 1978), 369–74.

Jones, Stephen, 'Georgia's "Rose Revolution" of 2003: Enforcing peaceful change', in Adam Roberts and Timothy Garton Ash (eds), *Civil Resistance and Power Politics: The Experience of Non-violent Action from Gandhi to the Present* (Oxford: Oxford University Press, 2009), pp. 317–34.

Kant, Immanuel, 'Perpetual peace' in Peter Mayer (ed.), *The Pacifist Conscience* (Harmondsworth: Penguin Books, 1966), pp. 71–83.

King, Jr, Martin Luther, 'Pilgrimage to nonviolence', in Peter Mayer (ed.), *The Pacifist Conscience* (Harmondsworth: Penguin Books, 1966), pp. 402–9.

King, Jr, Martin Luther, 'A Christmas sermon on peace', in James Melvin Washington (ed.), *A Testament of Hope: The Essential Writings of Martin Luther King, Jr.* (New York, NY: HarperCollins Publishers, 1991), pp. 253–8.

King, Jr, Martin Luther, 'An experiment in love', in James Melvin Washington (ed.), *A Testament of Hope: The Essential Writings of Martin Luther King, Jr.* (New York, NY: HarperCollins Publishers, 1991), pp. 16–20.

King, Jr, Martin Luther, 'Letter from Birmingham Jail', in James Melvin Washington (ed.), *A Testament of Hope: The Essential Writings of Martin Luther King, Jr.* (New York, NY: HarperCollins Publishers, 1991), pp. 289–302.

King, Jr, Martin Luther, 'Love, law, and civil disobedience', in James Melvin Washington (ed.), *A Testament of Hope: The Essential Writings of Martin Luther King, Jr.* (New York, NY: HarperCollins Publishers, 1991), pp. 43–53.

King, Jr, Martin Luther, 'Nonviolence and racial justice', in James Melvin Washington (ed.), *A Testament of Hope: The Essential Writings of Martin Luther King, Jr.* (New York, NY: HarperCollins Publishers, 1991), pp. 5–9.

King, Jr, Martin Luther, 'Pilgrimage to nonviolence', in James Melvin Washington (ed.), *A Testament of Hope: The Essential Writings of Martin Luther King, Jr.* (New York, NY: HarperCollins Publishers, 1991), pp. 35–40.

King, Jr, Martin Luther, 'Stride toward freedom', in James Melvin Washington (ed.), *A Testament of Hope: The Essential Writings of Martin Luther King, Jr.* (New York, NY: HarperCollins Publishers, 1991), pp. 417–90.

King, Jr, Martin Luther, 'The power of nonviolence', in James Melvin Washington (ed.), *A Testament of Hope: The Essential Writings of Martin Luther King, Jr.* (New York, NY: HarperCollins Publishers, 1991), pp. 12–15.

King, Mary E., 'Nonviolent struggle in Africa: Essentials of knowledge and teaching', *Africa Peace and Conflict Journal* 1: 1 (December 2008), 19–44.

Kumarappa, Bharatan, 'Editor's note', in Mohandas K. Gandhi, *Non-Violent Resistance (Satyagraha)* (New York, NY: Schocken Books, 1961), pp iii–vi.

Laffin, Arthur J. (ed.), *Swords into Plowshares: A Chronology of Plowshares Disarmament Actions 1980–2003* (Marion, SD: Rose Hill Books, 2003).

Laslett, Peter, 'Introduction', in John Locke, *Two Treatises of Government* (New York, NY: New American Library, [1690] 1965), pp. 15–135.

Lodge, Tom, 'The interplay of non-violent and violent action in the movement against apartheid in South Africa, 1983–94', in Adam Roberts and Timothy Garton Ash (eds), *Civil Resistance and Power Politics: The Experience of Non-violent Action from Gandhi to the Present* (Oxford: Oxford University Press, 2009), pp. 213–30.

Locke, John, 'The second treatise of government', in Peter Laslett (ed.), *Two Treatises of Government* (New York, NY: New American Library, [1690] 1965), pp. 305–477.

Lummis, C. Douglas, 'The smallest army imaginable', *Alternatives* 31: 3 (2006), 313–43.

Macpherson, C. B., 'Introduction', in Thomas Hobbes, *Leviathan* (Harmondsworth: Penguin Books, [1651] 1977), pp. 9–63.

Maier, Charles S., 'Civil resistance and civil society: Lessons from the collapse of the German Democratic Republic in 1989', in Adam Roberts and Timothy Garton Ash (eds), *Civil Resistance and Power Politics: The Experience of Non-violent Action from Gandhi to the Present* (Oxford: Oxford University Press, 2009), pp. 261–76.

Martin, Brian, 'Gene Sharp's theory of power', *Journal of Peace Research* 26: 2 (1989), 213–22.

Mayer, Peter, 'Introduction', in Peter Mayer (ed.), *The Pacifist Conscience* (Harmondsworth: Penguin Books, 1966), pp. 11–27.

Mayer, Peter (ed.), *The Pacifist Conscience* (Harmondsworth: Penguin Books, 1966).

McGuinness, Kate, 'Gene Sharp's theory of power: A feminist critique of consent', *Journal of Peace Research* 31: 1 (1993), 101–15.

McNay, Lois, *Foucault: A Critical Introduction* (Cambridge: Polity Press, 1996).

Moseley, Alexander, 'John Locke's morality of war', *Journal of Military Ethics* 4: 2 (2005), 119–28.

Muste, A. J., 'The individual conscience', in Peter Mayer (ed.), *The Pacifist Conscience* (Harmondsworth: Penguin Books, 1996), pp. 346–52.

Norman, Richard, 'The case for pacifism', in Brenda Almond and Donald Hill (eds), *Applied Philosophy: Morals and Metaphysics in Contemporary Debate* (London: Routledge, 1991), pp. 166–79.

Neibuhr, Reinhold, 'Why I leave the F.O.R.', in Peter Mayer (ed.), *The Pacifist Conscience* (Harmondsworth: Penguin Books, 1996), pp. 250–5.

Nenadić, Danijel and Nenad Belčević, 'Serbia – nonviolent struggle for democracy: The role of Otpor', in Howard Clark (ed.), *People Power: Unarmed Resistance and Global Solidarity* (London and New York, NY: Pluto Press, 2009), pp. 26–34.

Nygren, Anders, *Agape and Eros* (London: SPCK, 1953).

Phillips, Robert Lester and Duane L. Cady, *Humanitarian Intervention: Just War vs. Pacifism* (Lanham, MD: Rowman and Littlefield Publishers, 1996).

Rabinow, Paul (ed.), *The Foucault Reader: An Introduction to Foucault's Thought* (London: Penguin Books, 1991).

Randle, Michael, *Civil Resistance*, (London: Fontana Press, 1994).

Rawls, John, *A Theory of Justice* (Oxford: Oxford University Press, 1973).

Roberts, Adam, 'Civilian defence strategy', in Adam Roberts (ed.), *Civilian Resistance as a National Defence: Non-violent Action against Aggression* (Harmondsworth: Penguin Books, 1969), pp. 249–94.

Roberts, Adam (ed.), *Civilian Resistance as a National Defence: Non-violent Action against Aggression* (Harmondsworth: Penguin Books, 1969).

Roberts, Adam, 'Introduction', Adam Roberts and Timothy Garton Ash (eds), *Civil Resistance and Power Politics: The Experience of Non-violent Action from Gandhi to the Present* (Oxford: Oxford University Press, 2009), pp. 1–24.

Roberts, Adam and Timothy Garton Ash (eds), *Civil Resistance and Power Politics: The Experience of Non-violent Action from Gandhi to the Present* (Oxford: Oxford University Press, 2009).

Rousseau, Jean-Jacques, *The Social Contract* (Harmondsworth: Penguin Books, [1762] 1968).

Russell, Bertrand, 'Inconsistency?' in Peter Mayer (ed.), *The Pacifist Conscience* (Harmondsworth: Penguin Books, 1996), pp. 322–4.

Sartre, Jean-Paul, 'Preface', in Frantz Fanon, *The Wretched of the Earth* (New York, NY: Grove Press, [1961] 1968), pp. 7–31.

Sharp, Gene, *The Politics of Nonviolent Political Action, Part One: Power and Struggle* (Boston, MA: Porter Sargent Publishers, 1973).

Sharp, Gene, *Social Power and Political Freedom* (Boston, MA: Porter Sargent Publishers, 1980).

Sharp, Gene, *Waging Nonviolent Struggle: 20th Century Practice and 21st Century Potential* (Boston, MA: Porter Sargent Publishers, 2005).

Schell, Jonathan, *The Unconquerable World: Power, Nonviolence, and the Will of the People* (London: Penguin Books, 2005).

Schell, Jonathan, 'Introduction', Hannah Arendt, *On Revolution* (London: Penguin Books, [1963] 2006), pp. xxi–ii.

Schock, Kurt, 'Nonviolent action and its misconceptions: Insights for social scientists', *Political Science and Politics* 36: 4 (October 2003), 705–12.

Schock, Kurt, *Unarmed Insurrections: People Power Movements in Nondemocracies* (Minneapolis, MN: University of Minnesota Press, 2005).

Sorel, Georges, *Reflections on Violence* (Mineola, NY: Dover Publications, [1908] 2004).

Stephens, David, 'The non-violent anarchism of Leo Tolstoy', in Leo Tolstoy, *Government is Violence: Essays on Anarchism and Pacifism* (London: Phoenix Press, 1990), pp. 7–19.

Thoreau, Henry David, 'On civil disobedience', in Peter Mayer (ed.), *The Pacifist Conscience* (Harmondsworth: Penguin Books, 1966), pp. 140–59.

Tolstoy, Leo, 'Letter to a non-commissioned officer', in Peter Mayer (ed.), *The Pacifist Conscience* (Harmondsworth: Penguin Books, 1966), pp. 160–5.

Tolstoy, Leo, 'Carthago delenda est', in Leo Tolstoy, *Tolstoy's Writings on Civil Disobedience and Non-Violence* (New York, NY: The New American Library, 1968), pp. 95–103.

Tolstoy, Leo, 'From *The Kingdom of God*', in Leo Tolstoy, *Tolstoy's Writings on Civil Disobedience and Non-Violence* (New York, NY: The New American Library, 1968), pp. 213–59.

Tolstoy, Leo, 'Letter on the peace conference', in Leo Tolstoy, *Tolstoy's Writings on Civil Disobedience and Non-Violence* (New York, NY: The New American Library, 1968), pp. 113–19.

Tolstoy, Leo, 'Letter to a non-commissioned officer', in Leo Tolstoy, *Tolstoy's Writings on Civil Disobedience and Non-Violence* (New York, NY: The New American Library, 1968), pp. 120–6.

Tolstoy, Leo 'Notes for officers', in Leo Tolstoy, *Tolstoy's Writings on Civil Disobedience and Non-Violence* (New York, NY: The New American Library, 1968), pp. 24–31.

Tolstoy, Leo, 'Notes for soldiers', in Leo Tolstoy, *Tolstoy's Writings on Civil Disobedience and Non-Violence* (New York, NY: The New American Library, 1968), pp. 32–9.

Tolstoy, Leo, 'On patriotism', *Tolstoy's Writings on Civil Disobedience and Non-Violence* (New York, NY: The New American Library, 1968), pp. 40–94.

Tolstoy, Leo, 'Postscript to the "Life and Death of Drozhin"', in Leo Tolstoy, *Tolstoy's Writings on Civil Disobedience and Non-Violence* (New York, NY: The New American Library, 1968), pp. 260–80.

Tolstoy, Leo, 'The beginning of the end', in Leo Tolstoy, *Tolstoy's Writings on*

Civil Disobedience and Non-Violence (New York, NY: The New American Library, 1968), pp. 9–17.

Tolstoy, Leo, *Tolstoy's Writings on Civil Disobedience and Non-Violence* (New York, NY: The New American Library, 1968).

Tolstoy, Leo, 'Two wars', in Leo Tolstoy, *Tolstoy's Writings on Civil Disobedience and Non-Violence* (New York, NY: The New American Library, 1968), pp. 18–23.

Tolstoy, Leo, 'A letter from Tolstoy to Gandhi', in Mohandas K. Gandhi, *Selected Writings of Mahatma Gandhi* (London and Glasgow: Fontana/ Collins, 1971), pp. 61–4.

Tolstoy, Leo, *Government is Violence: Essays on Anarchism and Pacifism* (London: Phoenix Press, 1990).

Tolstoy, Leo, 'Patriotism and government', in Leo Tolstoy, *Government is Violence: Essays on Anarchism and Pacifism* (London: Phoenix Press, 1990), pp. 77–92.

Tolstoy, Leo, 'The end of an age: An essay on the approaching revolution', in Leo Tolstoy, *Government is Violence: Essays on Anarchism and Pacifism* (London: Phoenix Press, 1990), pp. 21–52.

Tolstoy, Leo, 'The kingdom of God is within you, or Christianity not as a mystical doctrine but as a new conception of life', in Leo Tolstoy, *Government is Violence: Essays on Anarchism and Pacifism* (London: Phoenix Press, 1990), pp. 93–109.

Tolstoy, Leo, 'The slavery of our times', in Leo Tolstoy, *Government is Violence: Essays on Anarchism and Pacifism* (London: Phoenix Press, 1990), pp. 111–54.

Vejvoda, Ivan, 'Civil society versus Slobodan Milošević: Serbia, 1991–2000', in Adam Roberts and Timothy Garton Ash (eds), *Civil Resistance and Power Politics: The Experience of Non-violent Action from Gandhi to the Present* (Oxford: Oxford University Press, 2009), pp. 295–316.

Washington, James Melvin (ed.), *A Testament of Hope: The Essential Writings of Martin Luther King, Jr.* (New York, NY: HarperCollins Publishers, 1991).

Wight, Martin, *International Theory: The Three Traditions* (London: Leicester University Press, 1994).

Zunes, Stephen, Lester R. Kurtz and Sarah Beth Asher (eds), *Nonviolent Social Movements: A Geographical Perspective* (Oxford: Blackwell Publishing, 1999).

INDEX